TRULY
CRIMINAL

First published 2015

The History Press
The Mill, Brimscombe Port
Stroud, Gloucestershire, GL5 2QG
www.thehistorypress.co.uk

All individual essays © the authors

British Library Cataloguing in Publication Data.
A catalogue record for this book is available from the British Library.

ISBN 978 0 7509 6110 3

Typesetting and origination by The History Press
Printed in Great Britain

TRULY
CRIMINAL

A CRIME WRITERS' ASSOCIATION
ANTHOLOGY OF TRUE CRIME

The
History
Press

CONTENTS

PETER JAMES

Peter's seven consecutive Sunday Times No. 1
bestselling Roy Grace crime novels are published
in thirty-six languages with sales of over
fifteen million copies. They have also been
No. 1 bestsellers in France, Germany, Spain,
Russia, and Canada. His latest novel is 'Want
You Dead' and he has recently published a
volume of short stories, 'A Twist of the Knife'.
He lives in Notting Hill, London and near
Brighton in Sussex. He is a past chair of the
Crime Writers' Association and is on the board
of International Thriller Writers in the US.

www.peterjames.com

FOREWORD

PETER JAMES

People often say to me, 'You must have a very warped mind to come up with some of the stuff you write. Where on earth does it all come from?'

'I don't think I have a particularly warped mind,' I reply. 'I just read a lot of newspapers!'

There are few occasions, I believe, when an author conjures something from his or her imagination that is more bizarre or horrific than a true-life occurrence. That old saw, *Truth is stranger than fiction*, is one we are all familiar with. It's an expression we use when we dismiss, with a smile, yet another headline news story, whether in a paper, or on television or on the Internet, that leaves us once more pondering – or reeling – at the discovery of yet another bizarre, hideous or utterly repugnant aspect of human nature. One such example for me – and I think for many of us – was, in recent times, the news story, and footage, about a British soldier savagely attacked and beheaded on a South London street. I'm not sure that anyone would have believed that possible if they'd first read it as fiction.

Whenever I go out with the police in the course of my research for my novels, either here in my native Sussex, or in London, or in the USA, or Germany or anywhere else, I'm constantly reminded just how true that saying is. I remember entering a flat on Brighton seafront where a woman had lain dead for two months, locked in with her cats. They had eaten her face and much of her upper torso. A Johannesburg police officer told me only a few weeks ago of a house burglary during which, for fun, the burglars had poured boiling water down an old lady's throat. And an LA cop told me of a victim he had attended, who had been involved in drug dealings that had gone wrong, and who had been skinned alive in punishment.

One of the US's most notorious serial killers had a penchant for disembowelling his victims while they were still alive, and then masturbating in front of them while he watched. Not necessarily the stuff we want to write in books, but sadly stuff that actually happened in true life.

Countless of our greatest crime novels, right back to *The Hound of the Baskervilles* and beyond that, owe their origins to true stories. Some of these books have been game-changers in the world of crime fiction. That's certainly true of Truman Capote's 1966 *In Cold Blood*, the non-fiction account of a quadruple homicide in Kansas, which became the biggest selling crime book of its time. Thomas Harris's *The Silence of the Lambs* in 1988 both changed the rules and raised the bar on crime fiction. The protagonist, Buffalo Bill, who liked to make suits out of human skin, was inspired by Ed Gein, an American bodysnatcher who liked to skin his victims and make artefacts out of it – and their bones.

When I go out with the police, I watch, I listen, I remember. And pretty often I have nightmares. For fiction is fiction, storytelling, mining the deep seams of our imagination and making our readers do the same. But true crime is different, true crime is truly the stuff of nightmares.

I've often heard it, from detectives, from lawyers and from forensic psychiatrists, that with few exceptions all murders are committed for one of two reasons: for money or love. I think you will find good examples of both in the pages that follow.

So will you be able to read this marvellously disturbing collection of accounts of very dark deeds, whilst safely tucked up in bed, late in the evening, without suffering nightmares from the contents yourselves? I have my share of nightmares both from what I read and from what I write. I think it is no bad thing that stories like these should shock us. I think it would be far more disturbing, in what they say about us, if they did not.

Peter James

INTRODUCTION

MARTIN EDWARDS

Members of the Crime Writers' Association (CWA) have always been fascinated by real-life criminal cases. A good many of our members specialise in writing 'true crime' (this is not a universally popular term, but at least it has the merit that it is generally understood) and the CWA has awarded a Gold Dagger for Non-Fiction since 1978. The Dagger has been won by many accomplished exponents of factual crime writing.

The CWA has, however, only once before published a collection of pieces by members about real life crimes. *Blood on My Mind*, edited by H.R.F. Keating, and including ten essays, appeared as long ago as 1972. Having edited the CWA's annual fiction anthology since the mid-1990s, I felt it was high time for us to put together another book of original essays on the theme of, to quote the sub-title of *Blood on My Mind*, 'real crimes, some notable and some obscure'.

I was delighted by the response from members, some of whom have not previously contributed to CWA anthologies. Our contributors include several specialists in true crime (although most of them write fiction as well), including Kate Clarke, who with Bernard Taylor was co-author of *Murder at the Priory*, shortlisted for the CWA Non-Fiction Dagger in 1988. Paul French, who won the Dagger in 2013 with *Midnight in Peking*, returns to China with his essay. In the spirit of originality that characterises the contributions, Linda Stratmann's impeccably researched essay includes a special bonus – a highly appropriate recipe for rice pottage, updated from the nineteenth-century original. As she says, arsenic should not be added …

Several leading novelists also made fascinating submissions. They included two CWA Diamond Dagger winners, Peter Lovesey and Andrew Taylor, as well as Catherine Aird and Kate Ellis. The CWA's membership is increasingly international, and I was pleased to receive contributions from Quentin Bates (a Brit who lives in Iceland), Jürgen Ehlers from Germany, and Jim Doherty from the US.

All but one of the contributions to this book are brand new. This exception is a real find. Thanks to the good offices of Barry Pike and Julia Jones of the Margery Allingham Society, to whom I'm extremely grateful, I have been lucky enough to include an essay by Allingham about the Wallace case that was unpublished during her lifetime, and has previously only appeared in the Society's journal for members. Margery Allingham was a member of the CWA, and a pleasing connection with her past involvement arose last year when the Society sponsored a national short story prize in tandem with the CWA.

The Wallace case has fascinated writers for over eighty years. Dorothy L. Sayers wrote an excellent study of it, and Raymond Chandler was fascinated by the puzzle. More recently, the late P.D. James published a thoughtful reassessment of the question about whether Wallace murdered his wife. Allingham's essay makes an interesting companion piece to the extensive literature about the case, though the only thing of which we can be sure is that the debate will continue.

Several other well-known murder cases are considered here. These include a highly original take on the 'Brides in the Bath' case, an account of the Maybrick murder (if it was murder), a study of the Moat Farm mystery by a novelist with a distant family connection to it, and an overview of the Rouse case, and its offshoots in fiction and fact. These explorations of famous crimes appear side by side with stories that I am sure will be unfamiliar even to true crime buffs, including a story from Shetland, and a Kentish mystery.

At the outset of this project, I decided that the book would work best if I avoided trying to impose any arbitrary rules or uniformity of approach upon the contributors. Far better that they tell their tales in their own way, sometimes with a personal touch, and at whatever length did justice to their subject matter. To say that I am delighted with the results is an understatement. I like to think that, as a result of the contributors' diligent research and storytelling expertise, *Truly Criminal* offers readers a mix of information and entertainment that is rarely matched in anthologies about real life cases.

The very first person to send me a contribution for this book was Brian Innes, once a chart-topping musician with the Temperance Seven, but more recently a stalwart of true crime writing and the CWA, and the long-serving chair of judges for the CWA's Non-Fiction Dagger. Brian's enthusiasm for this project prior to his death in July 2014 was typical of the man, and it is sad that he did not live to see it come to fruition. Brian is a real loss to the CWA, and it seems fitting to dedicate this book to his memory.

My thanks go first and foremost to the contributors, Barry Pike and Julia Jones, and to Peter James for his kind foreword. I must also express my thanks to my colleagues on the CWA committee who have given this project their enthusiastic backing, and to Matilda Richards, our editor at The Mystery Press, and everyone else who has worked on this book.

Martin Edwards
Editor, Truly Criminal

CATHERINE AIRD

Catherine is the author of some twenty-seven
detective novels and short story collections,
most of which feature Detective Inspector
C.D. Sloan and his rather less than dynamic
assistant, Constable Crosby. Taking an active
part in the life of the village in Kent in
which she lives, she has edited and published
a number of parish histories and several
autobiographies for private publication.
She was an early winner of the Hertfordshire
County Library's Golden Handcuffs Award
and the 2015 CWA Diamond Dagger Winner.

www.catherineaird.com

THE DEATH OF THE STURRY DOCTOR

CATHERINE AIRD

On the night of Friday, 4th September 1896, Edward Jameson, called doctor, of Sturry, a large agricultural village near Canterbury, left a house in King Street, Fordwich, an adjacent ancient port and the smallest township in England, where he had been having a late supper with his friend Captain Alfred Cotton, at 10.30 p.m. and was not seen alive again.

This case is particularly interesting because of the conspiracy of silence it occasioned. So much so that seventy years later when I was talking about it to an old man who remembered it well and I foolishly got out a pencil and paper, he said, 'Oh, you mustn't write anything down. It was all hushed up at the time.' Quite how right he was – and who it was who hushed it up I didn't discover until later.

Edward Jameson was one of three sons of Dr William Jameson – no connection with Jameson's Raid – who had been Sturry's doctor for the middle years of the nineteenth century. He had died in 1875 at the age of seventy-eight, and, very unusually for those times, left his widow as his sole executrix and legatee – something that I came to see as significant. His three sons were called Edward, John and Willy. John died of cirrhosis of the liver at the age of thirty-three, ten years after his father. Willy, too, died from this condition but much later.

Edward had attempted to follow in his father's footsteps as a doctor but unfortunately wasn't clever enough to pass the Conjoint Examination. In those days this did not prevent him from following the calling of doctor's assistant – one of whose earlier functions, you will remember, was to hold the patient down as a substitute for anaesthesia.

Brother Willy seems to have been much less bright and became a games coach at one of Canterbury's several public schools. He used to teach the boys to bowl by marking out the field into squares and calling out to them the number of the square to which they were to pitch the ball. He was known to be often short of money and to have rows with his surviving brother over this. There is some suggestion that he was even a sandwich short of a picnic.

Edward Jameson, called doctor, served Sturry as such for twenty years. When his father died, he became assistant first to a Dr Wheeler and then, when he moved away, to Dr T.M. Johnson of Canterbury. When anything beyond his medical capabilities arose, a telegraph message would be sent to Upper Chantry Lane where Dr Johnson lived in a house bombed in 1942. Dr Johnson would then saddle his horse and ride the three miles north out to Sturry. (He probably got there more quickly than by a car in today's traffic.) Incidentally – but not irrelevantly – Dr Johnson happened to be the Canterbury City Coroner.

Jameson himself had no horse, going everywhere on foot – to Stodmarsh in one direction and to Broad Oak in the other. It may be fairly presumed that he knew the roads of the village like the back of his hand and this is important and you should remember it.

He was a big man, a powerful man with a dimple on his chin and he left a reputation of joviality, cheerfulness and kindness behind him. While he always had a bottle of medicine in one pocket, he inevitably had a bag of sweets in the other and never dispensed the one without the other. He was extremely popular with children and generally of such a well-liked, amiable disposition that the question of suicide was never considered.

He was a strong swimmer and a keen cricketer. The Sturry Cricket Club, which celebrated its centenary in 1963, had him in its team in 1878 when playing Harbledown, which scored 130. Sturry knocked up 209, of which E. Jameson had scored 104 not out for Sturry – the first recorded century for the village team. Dr Jameson bowled between his legs and if it has been reported that I had been seen in Sturry High Street watching a lively demonstration of this by a notably sprightly octogenarian who remembered him well, then I assure you that it was done purely in the interests of research.

The next doctor to come to Sturry was Dr A.H.D. Salt. He was a Parsee and was graphically described to me as a gentleman but not a teetotaller. The year is 1896, the old Queen is on the throne and all's right with the world – or very nearly. The explorer, Dr Nansen, is on his way to Canterbury to lecture, Mr Weedon Grossmith was there already producing a play, football in the city was at a low ebb, and Kent County Council was bringing in a bye-law that all vehicles were to carry lights at night. Mr Daniel Brice is chair of the Bridge-Blean Rural District Council and is busy writing letters to Kent County Council imploring them not to let the matter of building a bridge at Grove Ferry drop.

They didn't, but it took them until 1962 to do it …

Dr Jameson is forty-six years old and unmarried. A smart, upright man, he always wore a hat called a 'Muller-Cut-Down'. (This was a hat half-way between a top hat and a bowler and named after Franz Muller, who was hanged for the killing of Thomas Briggs, the first man to be murdered on the railway in Britain. Muller had altered his black beaver hat by cutting the crown by half and sewing it to the brim.)

And now – as the writers of detective fiction say – we come to the night of … what? Shall we say the night of Dr Jameson's death?

Friday, 4th September 1896, during which he went about his work, was a fine day until the evening. At ten o'clock that night he walked from his house in Sturry High Street to his friend's house in Fordwich – about a third of a mile. His host, Captain Albert Cotton, said later that he had known the doctor for about ten years and he had arrived late and stayed to supper before.

At 10.30 p.m. Edward Jameson said he was in a hurry to get home and went away, Cotton letting him out but seeing no one about in the street.

He had on his head his hard felt Muller-Cut-Down hat but carried no umbrella or stick. It was then very dark and just beginning to rain. He was, deposed Cotton, perfectly sober and walked quite straight.

Early next morning a wood reeve called Farrier went fishing down-river in the Stour for eels. At 6.30 a.m. he was coming back upstream when he saw a body floating face downwards in the water some thirty yards below the bridge. He had set out before sunrise, which had been at 5.31 a.m. that morning, and had seen nothing then.

The body was removed from the river and was soon identified as that of Edward Jameson. Mark you, no search had been instituted for the doctor in spite of the fact that he had been in a hurry to get home the night before and no alarm of any sort raised until his body was found.

This may strike you as curious.

The body was fully clothed save that his Muller-Cut-Down hat was missing. He had on an overcoat. There were several things in his pockets including a purse containing £3 15s 4d – a considerable sum at the time. The wood reeve noticed that the doctor's watch had stopped at five o'clock. The clothing was in no way disarranged and according to the local newspaper report of the finding of the body (although not in the newspaper report of the inquest) there was a slight wound on the forehead.

The wood reeve went for the police and PC 'Ginger' Callaway took charge. He promptly and properly reported the body to the County Coroner, Mr R.M. Mercer. (It has only been since 1963 that the city of Canterbury and the county of Kent have shared a Coroner). You will remember that Dr Jameson had at one time been an assistant to the City Coroner, Dr T.M. Johnson.

The County Coroner decided to hold an inquest that very afternoon and a jury was summonsed to be at the Fordwich Arms public house at 5.30 p.m. The Coroner opened an inquest to determine how it was that the popular, amiable doctor, Edward Jameson, who knew the roads of the village like the back of his hand, who was a big and powerful man and a good swimmer, who had left Captain Cotton's house quite sober at 10.30 p.m. had come to be found dead in the river, with a bruise on his forehead, at 6.30 a.m. the next morning with his watch stopped at five o'clock.

There had been barely time for PC Callaway to search for the missing hat, which was presumed to have fallen off as the doctor fell over the low wall at the bridge opposite The George public house. (The Dragon came later.) The Coroner asked him about this at the inquest. Callaway said the river had been dragged but the hat had not been found.

The Coroner said, 'If it is assumed that the deceased fell over the wall at the bridge in the agile manner that has been suggested, surely his hat would have been found?'

The police constable (very rightly sticking to fact and refusing to be drawn into speculation) said, 'I have searched the river but cannot find it anywhere.'

The Coroner took evidence from a neighbour who knew the doctor, Farrier, the wood reeve, and the policeman and that was all – there was no mention of brother Willy.

He went on to observe that as far as he could see there was not a scrap of evidence from which the jury could come to any verdict as to how the deceased had got into the river. It had been suggested that he had stumbled over the low railing on the left of the bridge and toppled. He, the Coroner, had carefully looked at the spot and certainly thought that was possible. He did not think there was any suggestion of foul play but they could not say actually when the deceased entered the water and there was nothing to show even that he went in at the bridge.

Under all the circumstances he felt that their verdict ought to be 'found drowned between the hours of 10.30pm on 4th September and 5am on 5th September'. You've noticed that Freudian slip, haven't you? He said 5 a.m. – the time the watch stopped – even though the body wasn't found until 6.30 a.m.

So far, so good.

But not far enough and not good enough for the village jury.

They carefully considered their verdict and agreed that Dr Edward Jameson had been found drowned, adding firmly that, 'How or by what means the deceased so came into the river there was insufficient evidence to show, but in the opinion of the jury, owing to darkness the deceased accidentally fell into the river on his way home.'

Grounds for a legend there, do you think?

Perhaps not.

There the legal proceedings rested. At the inquest begun and finished on Saturday, 5th September, within twelve hours of the body being found.

Between then and the afternoon of Tuesday, 8th September, but at a time I was unable to establish, a post-mortem examination was held.

A report of the findings appeared rather shyly under the anonymity of some person calling him or herself 'A well-informed correspondent' who wrote to the local paper, the *Kentish Gazette*, as follows:

It will no doubt be interesting to your readers to learn a few further particulars concerning the so-called mysterious death of the late Mr Edward Jameson, of Sturry. To throw further light on the subject it was thought necessary to have a post-mortem examination. This was held by Messrs Frank Wacher – [a famous name in Canterbury's medical history; his house was also bombed in 1942] – and A.H.D. Salt, the former being appointed by the Scottish Accidental Employers' Liability Insurance Company of Moorgate Street, London, in which the deceased was insured. [They aren't there any longer.]

The results of the post-mortem examination showed that the deceased had received injuries on the left side of the head, left arm and both knees which were in themselves sufficient to render him insensible. The condition of the lungs was not that of drowning but suffocation; the stomach was full of undigested food, the state of the digestion proving that that he had come to his death very shortly after supper.

But it was proved that his watch had stopped at 5.00 a.m. This would seem to show that the deceased must have fallen into shallow water which only covered his head, but that owing to the heavy rain, the mill and other causes, the river rose by morning and it must have been about 5.00 a.m. that the body actually floated and the watch stopped.

Dynamite.

So the doctor wasn't drowned at all but suffocated. And suffocated, in all probability, while insensible from injuries to head, arm and both knees – injuries, you will remember, described earlier as a slight bruise or wound of the forehead. And dead, as proved by the state of the digestion, very soon after leaving Captain Cotton's house at 10.30 p.m.

What happened after that newspaper report?

First of all Edward Jameson's mother, Harriet, took to her bed with an attack of paralysis and nervous aphonia and spoke to no one.

Secondly, a man called Harry Enston took on – or was paid to take on – the role of keeper to Willy Jameson and from that day forward was his constant companion – so constant a companion that Willy was never questioned or left alone with anyone. In fact, when Willy died in 1898, then aged forty-six, it was Harry Enston who was present at death and who registered it.

And what happened after that?

Very little.

The miller might have been asked if he had indeed opened the floodgates upstream at 5 a.m. that fateful morning. I don't know. I do know that with the kind assistance of the Kent River Board (whom I am sure thought I was at least two sandwiches short of a picnic when I asked them) I calculated that high tide, such as it was, at the bridge at Fordwich would have been at 11.30 p.m. on the Friday evening and low tide therefore at 5.30 a.m. the next morning. Certainly any body – and I do mean 'any body' – would travel more than thirty yards in eight and a half hours in the River Stour, especially on an ebb tide flowing at three knots.

'an attack of paralysis and nervous aphonia'

On the Monday evening a parishioners meeting unanimously agreed that they would send a wreath. The Cricket Club settled on what was called as 'a characteristic floral token of a touching description'.

The funeral, taken by the Vicar, the Reverend George Billing, and attended by Willy as the only family mourner, was held on the Tuesday afternoon, the occasion being one of general mourning in all three local villages.

And then – I had a surprise.

Checking, some seventy years later, on the death certificate, I found that this had been received at the General Register Office, at Somerset House, on Thursday morning, September 10th from R.M. Mercer, Her Majesty's Coroner for Kent, who certified that the inquest had been held on the day before, that is Wednesday, 9th September. The place of death was given as the River Stour and the cause 'Found Drowned' and it stated that Edward Jameson's death had taken place on the previous Saturday, 5th September.

This may strike you as strange. It did me, too. I can't explain how it is that if the report in the *Kentish Gazette* is correct on the one hand, the inquest was held on the Saturday, and on the other hand if the death certificate is correct that it was held the following Wednesday.

I can only say that if it was held on the Saturday it was before the post-mortem, which may strike you as unusual, (the more especially so since it was in the days when the jury were expected to view the body – *super visum corporis*), and if it was held on the Wednesday then not only was it held after the post-mortem but it was after the funeral, too, which is even more unusual.

Then what happened?

The *Kentish Gazette*, having dropped the bombshell about the post-mortem, got itself into a high state of indignation about the Armenian Massacres. The Sturry Cricket Club went ahead with their averages and recorded the late E. Jameson as having 23 innings, 5 times not out, 117 runs … some things are quite immutable, aren't they? A public subscription was opened to pay for a gravestone. You can still see it by the north door of St Nicholas' Church, at Sturry.

What you couldn't see at the time is as good an example of professional solidarity as you'll ever find, and completely hidden from 1896 until

1963, when I first looked into this murder – when a Coroner of all people knowingly put his head into a noose and risked his professional reputation and his medical career by acting for what he considered for the best to save the widow of a former colleague from losing her third – and last – son to the gallows.

And which of us shall say he was wrong?

MARGERY ALLINGHAM

Margery came from a literary family, and rose to prominence in the 1930s as the author of a series of increasingly ambitious and unorthodox novels featuring Albert Campion. Her best-known book is probably 'The Tiger in the Smoke', which was filmed in 1956, while Peter Davison played Campion in a BBC Television series in 1979–80. She also wrote three books under the pseudonym Maxwell March. Allingham's husband, the artist Philip Youngman Carter, continued to write about Campion after her death, and the Margery Allingham Society flourishes to this day.

(20 May 1904–30 June 1966)

THE COMPASSIONATE MACHINE

MARGERY ALLINGHAM

When William Herbert Wallace, mild, elderly, poker-faced agent of the vast Prudential Assurance Company, was committed for trial for the indescribably brutal murder of his wife with whom he had lived happily for eighteen years, it seemed as if every man's hand was instantly turned against him.

Everybody, from the very children playing on the corner of the street to the public prosecutor himself, appeared prepared to declare him guilty almost without a second thought. Overnight, the warm human city of Liverpool, the great British shipping centre in which he had been such a respected resident for so many years, suddenly became hostile.

A machine came to his aid. In this strange, topsy-turvy story that made British legal history, the apparently cold and precise machine of his fellow insurance collectors' union took the unprecedented and even dangerous step of holding a secret mock trial of their fellow member. The machine found him innocent on the evidence and in the end the machine saved his life.

It is not popularly supposed that there is much spontaneous charity to be found in the insurance business. Accountants neither deal in nor are romantic figures. So when Mr Hector Munro, Wallace's solicitor – one of the few people in his home town who believed him not guilty – travelled to London one day in March 1931 to lay the story before the executive council of the Prudential Staff Union he must have wondered what hope he had of finding succour there.

The details had already been published in every newspaper in the Kingdom and the snap verdict from the 'man in the street' was 'Guilty'.

Yet there was nothing so very obvious in the history of the crime.

It began on the night of January 19th when Wallace, who was a keen player, was due at the City Chess Club some way from his home, to take part in a match. Everyone knew he was expected to be there and there was even a notice to that effect on the board just inside the warm, smoke-laden shop. At seven o'clock a phone call came through for him from a man who said his name was Qualtrough. As Wallace had not yet arrived the message was taken by the captain of the club, a certain Mr Sam Beattie, who knew Wallace well. It appeared to be an ordinary commercial communication. Qualtrough said it was his daughter's twenty-first birthday and he would like to see Mr Wallace the following evening at half after seven 'about a matter of considerable importance to do with his business.'

People often take out endowment policies for their children as twenty-first birthday presents and Sam Beattie, realising that it sounded like a bit of luck for Wallace, wrote down the unusual name and the address, which was '25 Menlove Gardens East'. Wallace had no phone in his own home and there seemed nothing strange in him being called at the club where there was one.

Wallace came in some few minutes later and settled down to his board. He was engrossed in his opening move when Sam Beattie caught sight of him and went over to pass on the message. Wallace, a tall, thin, precise looking man of fifty odd, seemed interested but not excited. He commented on the name and remarked that he did not know Menlove Gardens East but supposed it must be in the Menlove Avenue area, a district some miles from his home. He wrote down the particulars, thanked Beattie and went on with his game, which he won after a struggle lasting two hours.

The next day he spent as usual making his collections and paying out sick benefits with none of the dozens of people he met noticing anything at all peculiar in his manner. Just after six in the evening he went home, changed his clothes as was his custom, and went out to keep his appointment with the then utterly unmysterious Qualtrough. According to his own story he left home about a quarter before seven and it was certainly proved true that he was seen on a tramcar twenty-five minutes away from his house ten minutes after seven that evening.

Meanwhile, a small boy, delivering milk at a little after half past six, saw and talked to Mrs Julia Wallace on her own doorstep. Five minutes later still, a second boy laid a newspaper on the same doorstep and, later that night, when the police were summoned, that paper was found, presumably read, on the kitchen table. Yet after she spoke to the milk boy and told him to hurry home to take care of his cold, Mrs Wallace was never seen alive again.

Wallace came home at a quarter before eight in a state of irritation. His journey has been fruitless. After wandering for miles and asking everyone he met including a constable on duty, he had discovered that there was no Menlove Gardens East in the city and no Qualtrough in the area. To add to his troubles his front door, which had a faulty lock, appeared to have stuck. Mr and Mrs Johnston, his next door neighbours, found him at the back of the house as they were going out.

'Now the back door seems to be bolted,' he said. 'Have you heard anything unusual tonight?'

He tried it again and, as they watched, it moved.

'Well, it opens now,' Wallace muttered and went in. The Johnstons stood waiting, marking the flicker of his match as he passed through the house. They heard him call out twice as he reached the stairhead and then his light appeared in the back bedroom. Once more there was silence as he came down again and stepped into the tiny front parlour, which he and his wife never used unless they had visitors or wanted to have a little music, she at the old-fashioned piano and he at his new violin.

A moment later he came hurrying out to them and said in a nervous hurried voice, 'Come and see; she has been killed.'

At a later date these words sounded unemotional to the point of callousness. In court they appeared so inadequate that they almost hanged Wallace; but that night, outside the dark little house, they did not strike the Johnstons as anything but frightful and they pressed in after him to the door of the small front room.

There the scene was horrific. Poor little Mrs Wallace had been murdered by eleven maniac blows, which had covered her and half the room beside with so much blood that the very walls were splattered with it. A blood-soaked mackintosh, doubled up and thrust under one shoulder, turned out to be Wallace's own. He recognised it at once and volunteered the information that he has worn it that very afternoon and had left it hanging up in the lobby by the front door.

Mr Johnston rushed out to call the police and Mrs Johnston stayed with Wallace while he searched the house. From first to last this kindly neighbour was the only person who saw the prim, cold man show any sign of emotion at all at the appalling catastrophe. To her 'he almost broke down twice but controlled himself immediately on each occasion'. Not a great show of grief perhaps, but it was something. No one else saw anything of the kind. Professor MacFall who examined the body for the police was particularly shocked. 'Why,' he exclaimed at the trial, 'he was not so affected as I was myself!'

'There the scene was horrific'

The police formed the notion that Wallace was implicated very early on in the inquiry and in one way it was fortunate for him, for they searched him very carefully that night and at once one of the most extraordinary features of the whole story became apparent.

Neither Wallace himself – on his clothes, on his boots, in his nails – nor in any part of the house save in that one terrible room was there any trace of blood whatever, although it was estimated that something over a quart had been spilled. Any man who had ever cut himself whilst shaving must appreciate the full significance of that discovery!

Since any case against the insurance agent had to admit that he could have had less than twenty minutes to kill his wife, remove all traces of blood from himself, hide or destroy the weapon (which was never discovered) and get himself on a tramcar to Menlove Avenue, the point was of importance. There was no sign of recent washing in bathroom or sink, no wet towels.

The house was only slightly disturbed and no robbery had been committed but it was admitted that at that particular time in the month anyone who knew anything of an insurance collector's business might have supposed that there was a considerable sum of the Company's money in the house.

The cloud of suspicion hung over Wallace like a vulture for several days and then the police made an astonishing discovery. By one chance in ten thousand, the telephone message from the mythical Qualtrough was traced. There had been a fault at the exchange at the time and the superintendent had made a note of the call and was able to say definitely that it came from one particular box not four hundred yards from Wallace's own front door.

That was just enough. The police decided that he had telephoned the club himself on his way down there using a voice so disguised that it deceived an old friend like Beattie and had then, by some means unknown, reached the City Café in a much shorter time than the trip would normally have taken him. They saw his fussy enquiries round Menlove Avenue as an ingenious alibi and they arrested him.

He appeared before the preliminary court, where his unnatural calm and self-possession damned him, and he was committed for trial with all the big guns of the prosecution, advocates famous all over the country for their brilliance, ranged against him.

His entire life savings amounted to round about four hundred pounds and his defence, if it was to be at all adequate, must cost him something nearer fifteen hundred.

That was the story which Mr Munro had to lay before the Prudential Staff Union.

The thing he could not tell them, for it had not yet emerged from Wallace's own writings, was the strange man's peculiar belief in a stoic attitude towards misfortune. He belonged to that breed of Anglo-Saxon which has been somewhat flippantly described as the 'stiff upper lip boys'. He clung to his pathetic dignity as if it was a pole sticking up out of the torrent and his human feelings as if they were indecent.

There were twenty executive members in the small office in the Gray's Inn Road and at first the gathering was as cold towards Wallace as Wallace was thought to be towards the world. But gradually as the pure clear logic of the facts was retailed to them a new interest sprang up. It was not yet a conviction by any means but several facts of the truth, hitherto glossed over in the newspapers, had been given their real prominence. After he had stated his case Mr Munro was asked to leave.

What happened then is one of those rare romantic things which sometimes occur to prove that modern commercial companies and institutions, if machines, are not quite so soulless as they are so often supposed even by those who work for them.

Those twenty men shut themselves up in secret in the small office and produced not a resolution but a *verdict*.

On the authority of Thomas Scrafton, the president secretary, it can be said that both E.J. Palmer MP and W.T. Brown, who were in command at that time, always spoke of that remarkable meeting as 'The Mock Trial at which Wallace was found innocent'.

Of necessity the proceedings were utterly private. The penalties for contempt of court – and a trial of this kind before the real one could only have been considered gross contempt – are very great. But the mock trial was held and the verdict was given.

The machine, having declared him innocent, then set out to help their colleague by every means in its power and from all over the Islands other insurance agents contributed, not so much to save a brother as to preserve an innocent man.

After that the fight was on. The well-known advocate Mr Rowland Oliver KC was briefed for the defence, and experts engaged to fight these other expert witnesses called by the prosecution.

The trial lasted four days. To account for the absence of blood on the prisoner, the astounding suggestion was made that Wallace had stripped save for his mackintosh and had persuaded his wife into the little-used front room to kill her so that he might escape naked upstairs to wash! Even so there was no vestige of a motive. Witness after witness insisted that the two people were happily married. There was no 'other woman'. Wallace stood to gain nothing but loneliness from his wife's death.

As last the Judge, representative of another cold and perfect machine, the Law, summed up in Wallace's favour. As far as he was permitted to lead the jury he did so, pointing out to them every weakness in the long chain of circumstantial evidence. After he has spoken it seemed impossible that any twelve men could convict. But Wallace's happy gift for controlling himself too perfectly did its work once again. There was nothing of the machine about the jury. After only an hour's discussion they returned a verdict of guilty and the insurance agent was sentenced to hang.

Again the Prudential Staff Union stuck to the verdict of the Mock Trial. More funds were raised, an appeal was lodged and this time another and ever greater Machine of Justice behaved in a new way.

The Court of Criminal Appeal quashed the conviction on the grounds that the jury's verdict of guilty was unreasonable and could not be supported by the evidence. *No other conviction for murder has ever been quashed on these grounds in British legal history.*

William Herbert Wallace was free: saved by the two unprecedented and romantic actions of two apparently rigid machines. The Prudential Assurance Company gave him back his job. But the men and women of his home town would have nothing to do with him and he crept away to die eighteen months later in a house in Cheshire which, so he wrote, always made him think how much his wife would have loved it.

The murderer was never found. Many people today believe still that Wallace was guilty but it is significant that in the house in Cheshire he fitted up an ingenious arrangement so that on returning home at night he could light up the whole house at a touch and see at once if any dark figure was waiting there to attack him ...

MARTIN BAGGOLEY

Martin is a retired probation officer
who lives in Ramsbottom. He has
written a number of true crime books
and is especially interested in
murders committed in the eighteenth
and nineteenth centuries.

THE STANFIELD HALL MURDERS

MARTIN BAGGOLEY

On Tuesday, 5th December 1848, the lanes of Wymondham, nine miles to the south-west of Norwich, were lined with several hundred people, who were there to pay their respects at the funerals of fifty-nine-year-old Isaac Jermy and his twenty-seven-year-old son, also Isaac, both of whom were well known and much respected locally. The older man had been the Recorder of Norwich and a director of the city's life insurance and fire insurance societies. His son had helped with the management of the family estate and their brutal murders a few days earlier had caused great sadness throughout the district.

The Recorder was a widower and lived in Stanfield Hall, which stood close to Wymondham. On the evening of 28th November, he dined there with his fourteen-year-old daughter Isabella, and his son and daughter-in-law Sophia, who had their baby daughter with them. At a little after eight, dinner was finished and Isaac senior left the table, as he often went out alone to stroll in the garden after a meal. He had been gone for a few moments only when the silence was shattered by a gunshot.

Those inside were unaware that he was lying dead in the porch and his killer had entered the house by a side door. On hearing the shot, the butler, James Watson, who was in the pantry, stepped into the corridor and was immediately pushed aside by the killer. Young Isaac had also heard the shot and was by this time emerging from the dining room, intending to make for the front of the house. However, he did not make it and the butler watched helplessly as the intruder pointed a gun at the young man and fired, killing him instantly.

Sophia grabbed the baby and followed her husband into the corridor, where, on seeing his body, screamed and began to sob uncontrollably. She was heard by the housemaid Eliza Chestney and the cook Margaret Read, who were in the servants' quarters. Eliza was the first to reach her mistress and as she attempted to console her, the killer came out from behind a door and shot both women. Eliza was wounded in the leg and Sophia's elbow was very badly damaged. Margaret reached them as the killer was running out of the house and she was joined by the nursemaid, Maria Blanchflower, who had been in her bedroom. They comforted the badly wounded women until the police and medical assistance arrived.

Norwich surgeon William Nicholls treated the wounds of Sophia and Eliza, both of whom would survive, before examining the bodies of the two men. There was a large open wound to Isaac senior's left side, two inches above the nipple. Mr Nicholls removed a great number of slugs from the corpse, found three broken ribs and noted the heart had been almost totally destroyed. Many pieces of lead were also taken from Isaac junior's body and there was a massive wound at his right nipple, two of his ribs were in pieces and the fatal injury was to the heart.

The police found there was confusion surrounding the one or more weapons used in the shootings. James Watson insisted the killer had a pistol in each hand, but Margaret Read saw only one firearm. There was no trace of a weapon but the killer dropped a ramrod, and two handwritten notes were left behind, which read:

> There are seven of us here, three of us outside and four of us inside the hall, all armed as you see us two. If any of you servants offer to leave the premises or to follow us, you will be shot dead; therefore, all of you keep to the servants' hall and you nor anyone else will take any harm, for we are only come to take possession of the Stanfield Hall property.
>
> THOMAS JERMY, the Owner.

Mrs Jermy was too badly injured to be interviewed but the servants reported the killer wore a long cloak and was heavily disguised in a false wig and bushy beard. Nevertheless, the butler, cook and housemaid were adamant that he was local farmer James Blomfield Rush, a regular visitor to the house and well known to them. All had noticed the man was short, stout, had broad shoulders and they commented on his distinctive gait. Only Maria Blanchflower could not be positive, but she had not worked at the Hall for long and did not know Rush well. At five thirty the following morning, several police officers, led by Inspector George Pont, visited Rush at his home, Potash Farm, which was about a mile from the murder scene, where he was arrested on suspicion of committing the murders. A search of the farmhouse yielded a cloak similar to that which the killer was said to have worn, together with a wig and false whiskers.

The case against Rush was strengthened when police later interviewed Mrs Bailey, a servant of the Jermys, who recalled Rush approaching her in the grounds of the mansion at about five on the evening of the murders, asking who would be dining there that night. She told him and noticed him walking towards a young woman who was just leaving the Hall. This proved to be dressmaker Elizabeth Cooper, who reported Rush was keen to confirm that father and son were both at home.

To better understand the circumstances surrounding the murders and why Rush was regarded as a suspect, it is necessary to look at events which occurred a decade and more earlier. Stanfield Hall was a large moated country house, which was inherited by the Reverend George Preston towards the close of the eighteenth century. It stood in 800 acres of land and included several cottages and farms. George died in 1837, leaving the estate to his son, Isaac Preston. It was known that more than a century earlier, a forebear had left a will stating that the property should not be occupied by anyone who did not have the surname Jermy, but it was believed this had no legal standing and contact was no longer kept with that branch of the family.

However, in the summer of 1838, Isaac held an auction of his late father's possessions at the Hall and on that day was approached by two men, John Larner and Daniel Wingfield, who told him they were there to claim the estate for the Jermys, who were the rightful owners. Isaac was ordered to leave immediately with his family and servants. Of course, he refused to do so and called for the police, who ejected the two men. This did not prevent Larner and Wingfield persisting with the claim and on 24th September, with a number of other men, they occupied the Hall for much of the day, having forced Isaac and his family to leave. The militia arrived and following their arrests the occupiers were detained in the gaol at Norwich Castle.

At the assizes held the following March, Larner and Wingfield were convicted of simple riot and sentenced to three months' imprisonment. A more serious charge, which could have led to the pair being transported, was dropped, apparently on the understanding no more attempts to acquire the property would be made either through the courts or by direct action. As a further insurance, Isaac changed his family's surname from Preston to Jermy and believed the matter was closed.

Forty-eight-year-old Rush was born the illegitimate son of Mary Blomfield, who in 1802 married farmer John Rush, who accepted her son as his own and who, in 1811, rented a farm in Felmingham from Reverend Preston. In 1828, James, who had followed his stepfather into farming, married and he and his wife Susannah eventually had nine children. In 1835, James rented a farm neighbouring that of his stepfather, from Reverend Preston, who enjoyed good relationships with his two tenants.

Following his landlord's death, James Rush purchased Potash Farm from Isaac Preston. A mortgage of £5,000 was agreed, which was to be repaid in full ten years hence, on 30th November 1848, which, with interest, would require a one-off payment of £7,000. By the early 1840s, members of John Rush's family occupied the farm at Felmingham, another on the estate, known as Stanfield Hall Farm and Potash Farm. Unfortunately, James would prove to have little business acumen and he quickly fell into debt. However, he was able to survive after benefitting financially following the untimely deaths of his stepfather, wife and mother between 1844 and 1848.

In October 1844, John Rush died in suspicious circumstances following the supposed accidental discharge of a gun, when his stepson was the only other person in the room at the time. A few weeks later, Rush's wife died unexpectedly. In 1848, his mother died and she left her fortune of several thousand pounds to her grandchildren. It was believed that Rush forged his mother's signature on a document stating the youngest child must reach eighteen years of age before any of them could inherit a share of their inheritance, which led to him retaining control of the money for the foreseeable future.

By this time, Rush had been evicted from Stanfield Hall Farm because of unpaid rent but remained in Potash Farm and his son continued to manage the farm at Felmingham. He was now in serious debt and his creditors applied to have him declared bankrupt. However, having gained control of his late mother's fortune, he offered to repay the debts at the rate of twelve shillings in the pound. All agreed to accept the offer except for Isaac Jermy, as he suspected that shortly before his mother's death, Rush had sold her a great deal of valuable equipment and livestock at a price very much less than the true value. Isaac insisted the documentation relating to the transactions did not reflect the actual amount of cash he received from her. He had thus misled his creditors and kept a large amount of money hidden away and out of their reach. As a result of his landlord's stance, Rush was bankrupted in the autumn of 1848. It was claimed that Rush chose to murder the Jermys as a means of avoiding paying the £7,000 mortgage, due two days after the killings, and also as revenge on the men he blamed for his problems.

Rush had recently written a pamphlet entitled *A Case; Jermy v Jermy Showing the Rightful Heir and Owner of the Stanfield Hall Estate*, in which he made his antipathy towards the Recorder evident. One section read, 'But after all there is no reason why I should now be ruined in character by this villain, as well as my own property being sold up by him'; another states, 'This fellow has no right to the Stanfield property and he knows it well. His whole conduct in keeping possession and taking the name Jermy and his behaviour to these poor people who have the right to it, has been most villainous and disgraceful to any man who can have pretensions to respectability.'

The Crown knew its case would be greatly strengthened if the murder weapon could be discovered and linked to Rush and fifty labourers were employed to help the police in the search for it, which focused on the route between the Hall and Potash Farm. The moat was drained and ditches cleared, but nothing was found. The Coroner received a number of letters from concerned citizens, including one who suggested that £30 be spent to hire the French mesmerist Alexis Didier, who could put Rush into a 'somnambulist condition' so that the weapon's whereabouts would be revealed. His address in the Rue de Grange, Paris was given, but the suggestion was not taken up.

Another major drawback for the Crown was that he had an alibi. Following his wife's death, Rush advertised for a nursemaid to care for his younger children and employed Emily Sandford, who was at Potash Farm on the night of the killings. She told police she and the suspect had dined together and between six and nine thirty, when she went to bed, they had drunk tea and chatted. He had gone out but only for a few minutes, which would have left insufficient time for him to reach the Hall, commit the murders and return home.

It therefore came as no surprise when the governor of Norwich Gaol reported that shortly after his arrival on remand, Rush declared himself confident of being cleared. However, he would not remain so for very long, as within days Emily made another, far different statement to the police. She revealed that she and Rush were lovers and she was due to have his baby. On the night of the murders he persuaded her to provide a false alibi. He had in fact left the farmhouse at seven that evening in an agitated state. He did not return until after nine and told her, 'If any enquiries should be made, you must say that I was not out for more than ten minutes.'

Later that night they went to separate bedrooms, but at three in the morning, Rush came to her and said, 'Now you must be firm and remember that I was out only ten minutes last night.' She took his trembling hand and asked what had happened but he told her nothing. It was now apparent that Rush was absent long enough to have committed the murders. However, Emily did more than destroy his alibi, for she gave information which, the Crown was satisfied, demonstrated that Rush had been planning the crime for some time.

He had not forgotten the events of a decade earlier and several months before the murders, he traced John Larner, who had played a major role in attempting to take possession of Stanfield Hall. Larner introduced him to Thomas Jermy, an elderly labourer, and Rush persuaded them he had studied the case and would support a new attempt by Thomas to regain the estate. As an act of good faith Rush wrote and published the pamphlet in support of the claim. Emily was present at several of the meetings the three men had in London.

In late 1848, Rush persuaded them to travel to Norfolk and they stayed at Felmingham Farm for some time. However, they returned to the capital as little seemed to be happening. Rush, it was claimed, had no intention of helping Thomas and had simply wanted the men in the area so suspicion would fall on them. This explained the notes, supposedly written and signed by Thomas, which were dropped at the murder scene. It was concluded Rush decided to go ahead with the plan despite their decision to leave, as the mortgage repayment was imminent. However, extensive enquiries by the London police led to the pair being cleared of any involvement in the scheme.

A more thorough search was made of Potash Farm, which led to the discovery of several documents. One was a memorandum of agreement dated 10th October 1848, purporting to show that Isaac senior would rent Felmingham Farm to Rush and his son at an annual rent of £300, but the Jermys would retain the right to shoot on the property.

A second agreement, dated 21st November 1848, suggested that Rush would do all he could in support of the Recorder's right of ownership to the Stanfield Hall estate. In return, Isaac promised to destroy the mortgage papers relating to Potash Farm, which would remain in the ownership of Rush.

A colleague of the Recorder, who knew his signature, insisted those on the documents were forgeries and Emily acknowledged she wrote and later signed them as a witness, to appease her lover. Two copies of each document had been written and the police believed on the night of the killings, Rush had entered the house intending to place a copy of each of them among his victims' papers, but had been unable to do so. Had he succeeded, he would have been able to claim ownership of Potash Farm without any further financial outlay and retain the tenancy of Felmingham Farm for his son.

Another document was an agreement dated 24th October 1848, signed by Rush and bearing the marks of Thomas Jermy and John Larner, which was also witnessed by Emily. It stated that Rush would help Thomas with his claim to Stanfield Hall and in return he could rent Felmingham, Skeyton and North Walsham Farms, all of which were part of the estate, for twenty-one years at an annual rent of £230, less any expense incurred by Rush in helping with the claim. This was not a forgery as it was believed Rush had it drawn up to instil confidence in the claimant and Larner of his determination to help, and it would not have been used for any other purpose. As far as the Crown was concerned, these documents demonstrated the planning the accused had put into framing Thomas Jermy and Larner for the murders.

It was also proposed that the notes left at the Hall, supposedly signed by Thomas Jermy, provided incriminating evidence. They were shown to a man who knew Rush's handwriting and he was convinced it was that of the accused, despite his attempt to disguise it. Furthermore, it was argued that the paper on which they were written had been taken from the front of one of a set of three books on accountancy, two of which were found at Potash Farm. Rush was said to have torn the front sheets from the third book before destroying it, but without realising just how distinctive the paper was. Despite its strong case, the prosecution recognised that Emily's testimony would be crucial and, as an important Crown witness unable to provide a surety, she was held in custody to ensure her attendance at the trial, as was common practice at the time. As she waited in the local workhouse for the trial to begin, she gave birth to Rush's daughter.

The trial, at which Rush defended himself, opened on 29th March 1849 and lasted for six days. In response to the Crown's witnesses, who provided identification evidence, he countered by saying that Maria Blanchflower had seen the killer but did not identify him and the others could not therefore be relied on. He also drew the jury's attention to the discrepancies regarding the murder weapon, which had not been found. He acknowledged his poor relationship with the Jermys but claimed this was not something that would drive him to murder. He agreed he would have found it difficult to raise the mortgage payment, due two days later, but he had been hopeful of reaching an amicable agreement with them and rejected the claim that he had powerful motives to commit the murders.

'this was not something that would drive him to murder'

However, Emily's testimony was devastating and Rush realised its significance. The governor of the gaol arrived at court early on the morning after her appearance and described events of the previous evening. On returning to the gaol, Rush had become enraged and threatened violent revenge against his former lover, claiming she had done enough to send him to the gallows. The journalists covering the trial and others in the courtroom were asked to ensure any penknives or other items that might be used as a weapon were kept hidden and out of the prisoner's reach. It was also feared he might make a suicide attempt, which led to the iron spikes around the dock being covered with pieces of wood.

He was now forced to admit he was out for between two and three hours on the night in question. He insisted he was searching for a poacher he believed to be on the property and met two men he knew only as Dick and Joe. They had visited him a few days earlier, saying they intended to seize Stanfield Hall by force and asked if he would help. He had refused and saw them with a number of other men heading towards the Hall. As he made his way home, he heard three shots. He repeated that he was not involved in the murders and had not told Emily the truth about what had happened that night as he did not want to worry her.

The jury deliberated for five minutes before returning with a guilty verdict. As he sentenced him to death, the Judge described Rush as 'an object of unmitigated abhorrence to every well regulated mind.' He was hanged before a large crowd outside Norwich Castle on 21st April 1849 and the last thing he heard must have been the loud cheers of the spectators as he fell through the trap.

Four weeks after the execution, the murder weapon was found buried a few paces from the backdoor of Potash farmhouse. It was a double-barrelled carbine, which the ramrod discovered at the crime scene fitted perfectly. Its discovery led to more criticism of the police for their failure to find it before the trial.

Sophia Jermy recovered from her wounds and despite inheriting Stanfield Hall, refused to live in it. She later married Thomas, the eldest son of Sir Thomas Branthwayt Beevor, Baronet. Eliza Chestney also made a full recovery and her bravery on the night of the murders led to a public subscription on her behalf which raised almost £800. In April 1850, she married Wymondham builder George Harvey.

Stanfield Hall lay empty for fifteen years before being sold to another family. There had been several owners by 1924, the year bottle merchant Charles Jermy Larner made a final unsuccessful attempt through the courts to gain the estate for that branch of the family.

There were many who believed Emily Sandford should have been tried as an accomplice. However, during the trial, the Judge emphasised that once she had realised what her lover's plan was, she co-operated fully with the police. He described her as an unfortunate young woman Rush had used as a tool to commit his forgeries and that she had no prior knowledge of the murders. Nevertheless, her relatives believed she had brought shame on the family and abandoned her. Charitable donations raised sufficient funds enabling her to emigrate to Australia, where in the summer of 1857 she committed suicide. She was working as housekeeper in the home of a single gentleman and one evening, after failing to serve dinner, was discovered barely conscious in her room. She had taken a large quantity of arsenic and a doctor was called for. Following a brief examination he told her she was close to death, to which she replied, 'Thank God.'

QUENTIN BATES

Quentin escaped English suburbia as a
teenager, after which his gap year in
Iceland gradually became a gap decade,
during which he went native and acquired
a family, a new language and sea legs as a
trawlerman. These days he lives in England
and writes books set in Iceland, but the
north still calls and is never far away.

graskeggur.com

DISAPPEARING ICELANDERS

QUENTIN BATES

The ancestors of present-day Icelanders weren't keen on paying their taxes. More than a thousand years ago disgruntled Norse chieftains set sail to seek out new homes on a barely inhabited island a week's sailing west of Norway, assuming they had a decent wind behind them. These renegade noblemen had fallen out with the new king of Norway who was determined to bring them all to heel, and arriving on the new island, they set about establishing a brand-new society based on the rule of law and without a king to rule over them. These were undoubtedly noble aims, and downright radical back then when absolute monarchy was the accepted form of government.

It's the winners who write history and in this case the history was written down a couple of centuries later, undoubtedly based on a few generations' worth of oral storytelling and the inevitable embroidery that goes with it. The ancient sagas are spare, taut narratives that concentrate on the essential bits: the intrigue, the killings and the exploits of Icelanders who ventured abroad to trade or pillage. There are tantalising gaps in the tales, such as what happened to the original pre-Viking settlers who were there but who are never mentioned, and where did all the women come from? Research into the DNA of present-day Icelanders indicates plenty of male genes from western Norway, but a much lower level of female genes from the same areas. Presumably the wives of those early tax avoiders weren't so keen on leaving their homes to venture into the unknown, and the men, seeking a tax-free paradise to the west, had to stop off and help themselves to some womenfolk on the way.

Things didn't work out quite as comfortably as some people had hoped. They rubbed along fairly well without a king for several centuries until the vicious feuding of the Sturlunga era forced Icelanders to ask the king of Norway to resume his role. But the intervening centuries weren't all plain sailing. Although there was no monarchy, there was a definite hierarchy and it's all set out in the ancient sagas. Icelanders managed to come up with a society that was rife with intrigue, feuding, patronage, bribery, blackmail, nepotism, cliques, sorcery, vendettas – and bloody murder.

Today, Iceland's political turmoil leading up to and in the wake of the financial disaster a few years ago shows that most of these elements are all alive and kicking. The intrigue is still there but the sorcery has gone and Icelanders no longer resort to sorting out their grievances with swords. Murder is rare in Iceland, although becoming less rare as the murder rate is now roughly two per year. The list of killings in modern times is a depressing litany of relatively straightforward alcohol-related crime, plus a few with financial gain or some bitter jealousy at the core.

There are virtually no serial killers after the end of the bloodthirsty saga age. Iceland's most prolific murderer was Axlar-Björn, a farmer by the name of Björn Pétursson. The Axlar-Björn name comes from the farm at Öxl in the far west of Iceland, where he robbed and murdered passing travellers towards the end of the sixteenth century. The few known facts and the folktales about Axlar-Björn don't tie up particularly well. Records state that he committed nine murders, while the folklore puts the tally as high as eighteen, with the bodies disposed of in a deep pool. There's also disagreement on his execution in 1596. The tales say that his limbs were broken with clubs before he was decapitated and his body dismembered, but it seems brutal torture on this scale would have been against the law of Iceland at the time and the facts are lost in the historical haze. On the other hand, Axlar-Björn's son Sveinn, known as Skotti and born after his father's execution, also came to a bad end: hanged in 1648 after attempting to rape a farmer's wife. In turn, Sveinn's son Gísli is also believed to have met his death on the end of rope in much the same way as his father.

In modern times there have been two instances in particular of people who have killed more than once. One was a man who committed a second murder after being released from prison for a first killing, and the other was a disturbing case of two seven-year-old boys who drowned a year apart in the same river. Both were originally thought to be accidents, but when the matter was investigated it appeared that the same twelve year old had been present on both occasions and had been responsible for both deaths. That case never came to court.

There are only a handful of cases that have never been resolved, one of which took place on the US air base, with no locals involved, and was investigated by the US military. The killing of a Reykjavík taxi driver almost fifty years ago has likewise also never been solved, but more on that later.

Unlike the imaginative murders that take place in Icelandic crime fiction and which require all of the investigator's intuition and ingenuity, real murders in Iceland tend to be tragic, mundane affairs that the police rarely fail to solve. Sometimes the murderer is so drunk or stoned that he or she isn't even aware of what has happened until afterwards, and while booze has long been a frequent factor, narcotics of various kinds are increasingly prominent in Iceland's still rare murder cases.

There's no great mystery to genuine Icelandic murders, but what is intriguing is that Icelanders seem to disappear all the time. Since the end of the Second World War more than a hundred Icelanders have vanished and become missing persons. It's a lot for a country with a population that's roughly equivalent to that of a modest-sized European city.

Iceland is also a maritime nation with a sizeable fishing industry and although ships no longer vanish as they could in the days before satellite monitoring and reliable communications, a large proportion of those disappearances are men lost at sea. We know where they are – more or less.

But then there are the others. Iceland is an easy enough place to disappear. The interior is empty of people but strewn with ravines, glaciers and caves where the hapless traveller can get lost. The climate doesn't help and even locals can get caught out by a spell of bad weather. Driving snow reduces visibility to a few yards and this can be a recipe for disaster if you're unlucky enough to be in a mobile phone black spot and running low on fuel.

It seems that almost every year there's an incident with an over-optimistic traveller who gambles against the Icelandic winter and comes off worst. Often they're found, cold, shaken and grateful for the efforts of the volunteer rescue teams. Sometimes they're not so fortunate and are found too late – or not found at all.

In January 1994, a pair of fourteen-year-old boys, Júlíus Karlsson and Óskar Halldórsson, came home from school one afternoon and then went out together. They were last seen running along a street in Keflavík and laughing as if they were running away from some prank. The police were called that evening when they had failed to return home. At the coldest, darkest time of the year more than four hundred people took part in the search while divers fought the cold to scour the harbour.

The boys were declared legally dead three years later and to this day nobody has the slightest idea how they could vanish so completely in the middle of a busy town, leaving not a single trace or clue as to what might have happened to them.

These boys are among the mysteries, the people who just drop off the radar, and these are comparatively few, roughly one a year over the last forty years, all of them men. According to official sources, a handful of these are linked to criminal investigations, but who knows? Some of these people may have vanished by accident; it's possible to vanish in among the razor crags and ravines of a lava field while doing nothing more sinister than taking the dog for a walk. Some may have vanished deliberately and preferred to make sure they were never found. The odds are certainly that some of them may have been done away with.

There's one case, or maybe two, in particular that refuses to go away. It's a combination of two disappearances and what appears to be a grand scale miscarriage of justice that has never been resolved, and more than forty years after the event, it probably isn't likely to be.

In January 1974, eighteen-year-old Guðmundur Einarsson vanished after going to a dance in the coastal town of Hafnarfjörður, a port town a few miles south of Reykjavík. The assumption was that he simply got lost late on a snowy night. A search in the area where he was last seen walking home in the early hours was hampered by snow a foot deep and was called off after a while. His remains have never been found.

Forty kilometres further west lies the township of Keflavík, which back then was also home to the US military that until a few years ago maintained a presence in Iceland that began during the Second World War, a dusty, busy regional town that bears little resemblance to its modern self. Keflavík in the 1970s lived on fish and provided much of the workforce that served the US base, which also back then hosted the international airport. Anyone catching a flight overseas had to pass a military checkpoint on their way to the modest sheds that were the passenger terminal beside runways that were also home to the US Air Force bombers and spy aircraft that ranged over the North Atlantic throughout the Cold War.

On the 19th November of the same year that Guðmundur Einarsson disappeared in Hafnarfjörður, a middle-aged digger driver called Geirfinnur Einarsson took a phone call at his home in Keflavík and went out to meet someone at a local kiosk, without telling his wife who had called. He made it to the kiosk, leaving his car outside. That's the last anyone ever saw of him and Geirfinnur's disappearance has become one of the abiding mysteries of the last forty years.

Incidentally, the two men weren't related. Icelanders don't generally have surnames, instead using an ancient system of patronymics. Both men had fathers called Einar, hence both of them being Einarsson.

The local police force in Keflavík were baffled by Geirfinnur Einarsson's disappearance and were far from equipped to deal with this kind of case, and the same can be said of the Reykjavík police when they took over the now rapidly cooling trail.

By the following spring the case had ground to a halt. There was no body to be found in spite of an extensive search of both his background and a physical search for a body. There was no evidence to indicate that Geirfinnur Einarsson had been murdered. The last sighting of him had been in the kiosk in Keflavík the night he vanished, leaving the keys in the ignition of his car outside, and an exhaustive search for the mysterious man who had phoned him from the kiosk came to nothing.

It was only when a young woman called Erla Bolladóttir and her boyfriend Sævar Ciesielski were arrested the following year that something happened. The pair had been living in Hafnarfjörður at the fringes of what could be termed Iceland's underworld of petty crime of running small scams, dealing in illicit booze and a little dope, and had been brought in as part of an investigation into just such a minor scam. With her questioning almost over and anxious to get home to her young child, Erla was shown a photograph of Guðmundur Einarsson and asked if she knew him.

It seems she had met him and remembered meeting him briefly. After all, Hafnarfjörður is a smallish town today and was a lot smaller forty years ago, so everyone tends to encounter everyone else at some time or another. Her questioners pounced on the information and the seriousness of her interrogation was ratcheted up dramatically.

Various friends and people linked to them were also implicated and hauled in for questioning, held for long periods, released, re-arrested and held again in a convoluted process of interrogations, wildly conflicting statements that were later withdrawn and contradictory testimony from confused suspects – plus that small-town staple, gossip.

After many hours of questioning, Erla admitted that she had seen Sævar and others with a body wrapped in a sheet. Sævar admitted that he might know something about Guðmundur Einarsson's disappearance, and his friends who moved in similar circles with a background in labouring jobs and petty crime were also implicated. Kristján Viðarsson, Tryggvi Rúnar Leifsson and Albert Skaftason were all brought in for questioning. They finally admitted after weeks of questioning, in confusing and constantly changing versions of events, that they had murdered Guðmundur Einarsson in a disagreement over a bottle of booze before disposing of his body outside the town, where ancient gas bubbles from the rocks below had left deep fissures in the lava rocks.

The hole in the theory is that the weather on the night Guðmundur Einarsson disappeared was so bad that it is hard to believe they were able to wrap a corpse in a sheet, drive it out to a lava field in a battered VW Beetle, in the middle of a dark night, and dispose of it so effectively that it could never be found, accomplishing all this in spite of knee-deep snow.

But it was at this point that the investigators began to suggest that the disappearance of Geirfinnur Einarsson could be linked to the case they felt they had made a breakthrough with. The two disappearances had not even been linked to begin with, and even now there is no evidence that the eighteen year old from Hafnarfjörður or the thirty-two-year-old man from Keflavík knew each other. But one of the suspects had apparently been rumoured to have known what had happened to Geirfinnur Einarsson, which was enough for him to be implicated and for the two disappearances to be linked.

> 'Sævar admitted that he might know something about Guðmundur Einarsson's disappearance'

With attention from the newspapers, there was growing pressure to conclude two cases that had somehow become linked.

A retired detective from Germany, Karl Schütz, was brought in to manage the case. The German detective's role is also open to question, as he wasn't an officer with a long career in a homicide squad behind him, but had specialised in national security issues including tracking down the Red Army Faction terrorist group.

By the middle of 1976, Sævar and Kristján had been in solitary confinement for more than a year at the old Síðumúli lockup, known as Múlinn and eventually closed and demolished in 1996. Finally they admitted having murdered Geirfinnur, and managed to implicate another acquaintance, former teacher Guðjón Skarphéðinsson, who had also been on the edges of Iceland's fledgling drug scene. He was also arrested and questioned over a long period, and also asked to identify the place where Geirfinnur's body had been buried. Several of the suspects were taken repeatedly out into the countryside to locations that seemed likely, but the case remains an obstinate one. Forty years on there are still no bodies, no evidence, no murder weapons, and the confessions that the six accused signed were all retracted at various points, including during the trial itself.

There's no compelling evidence other than hearsay that either Guðmundur Einarsson or Geirfinnur Einarsson were genuinely victims of violence. People can disappear without trace in Iceland, as when Júlíus Karlsson and Óskar Halldórsson vanished from Keflavík twenty years, almost to the day, after Guðmundur Einarsson's disappearance, not far from the site of the kiosk where Geirfinnur Einarsson was last seen and the slipway where one theory had it that he could have been murdered in a disagreement over illicit liquor.

Back in 1977 the spotlight on the six accused in the Guðmundur and Geirfinnur case was such that Justice Minister Ólafur Jóhannesson was able to announce in Parliament that 'the burden of a nightmare has been lifted from the nation' when the six were found guilty. Verdicts were handed down at a criminal court and finally confirmed by the Supreme Court in 1980. Sævar Ciesielski was given seventeen years and Kristján Viðarsson sixteen years. Tryggvi Rúnar Leifsson was sentenced to thirteen years, Guðjón Skarphéðinsson to ten years and Erla Bolladóttir to three years. Albert Skaftason was sentenced to a year's detention for his role in disposing of a corpse.

Serious crime is a rarity in Iceland, and the police in 1974 were clearly ill-equipped to deal with such a challenging case, which is still deeply controversial, not least due to the methods used by the police to extract confessions. This is the aspect of the investigation that has repeatedly come under scrutiny. Even Karl Schütz is believed to have commented after the verdicts were handed down that the police methods were reminiscent of those of the Third Reich – and also that his handling of the case had kept the government of the day afloat.

The police and the Ministry of Justice were undoubtedly under enormous pressure from both above and from the media to come up with a result and to restore public confidence in the justice system. The Guðmundur and Geirfinnur case took place only a few years after the murder of taxi driver Gunnar Sigurður Tryggvason in a residential district of Reykjavík. He had been shot in the back of the head one January night. That night it had also rained hard, making it practically impossible to establish any clues other than a .32 calibre cartridge case, presumably from a pistol. A wallet containing his night's takings was missing and the murder was assumed to have been a robbery. The murderer was never found and the case remains one of Iceland's very few unsolved murders. The failure to identify Gunnar Sigurður Tryggvason's murderer was doubtless a frustration for Iceland's police force, providing added pressure to solve the cases of Guðmundur Einarsson and Geirfinnur Einarsson.

As soon as he was released, Sævar Ciesielski began fighting for his name to be cleared. In 1997 and again two years later, the Supreme Court rejected his requests for the case to be heard again, and in 2000 a request from Erla Bolladóttir was also turned down, even though the Prime Minister at the time, Davið Oddsson, had described the case as being 'judicial murder.'

Sævar Ciesielski died in 2011 at the age of fifty-six. He had fled Iceland and died of complications following an accident in Copenhagen where he had lived for some years after a lifetime of difficulty that saw him become one of the city's street people; and the Supreme Court's double refusal to re-open the case was certainly a huge blow to a deeply troubled man. Guðjón Skarphéðinsson became a Lutheran priest following his release. Kristján Viðarsson has never spoken about his experiences.

Following Tryggvi Rúnar Leifsson's death in 2009, some of the diaries he had kept during his detention came to the attention of a leading specialist in forensic psychology. Professor Gísli Gudjónsson had been a police officer in Iceland at the time of the original investigation, leaving the police force to continue his studies. He now lives and works in Britain, where he was a key witness in overturning the wrongful convictions of the Birmingham Six and the Guildford Four, and has said that Tryggvi Rúnar Leifsson's diaries indicate that he had been, as he had always protested, an innocent man. His comments on the methods used, not least the exceptionally long periods of solitary confinement – almost two years in Kristján Viðarsson's case – have been damning, even accepting that forty years ago things were done very differently.

Following Gísli Guðjónsson's verdict, things did start to move. During his relatively brief stint as Interior Minister during the 2009-2013 government, Ögmundur Jónasson commissioned a working group to examine the case. Almost two years later it produced a 500-page report, stating among other findings that according to psychological profiling and beyond any reasonable doubt, the confessions of five of the accused are unreliable and Guðjón Skarphéðinsson's confession is false.

Now the ball is in the government's court. It's understandable that there's little stomach within the establishment for re-opening a forty-year-old case with very little to work on other than a swathe of 10,000 pages of documents and six unreliable confessions. The strength of Iceland's establishment must also not be underestimated, plus the present government is closer to the establishment than the one that commissioned the working group's investigation. While many of those who were involved with the original investigation are either long retired or no longer among us, others are still about in senior positions or with influence that runs deep.

The authorities' attitude has been that the case shouldn't be re-opened without new evidence coming to light – not that there was any evidence to start with. Throughout the six-year process between Guðmundur

Einarsson's disappearance in January 1974 and the Supreme Court confirming sentences in 1980, there were no convincing motives, no forensic evidence, no murder weapons, no reliable witnesses, and no bodies – and that situation hasn't changed.

The case remains a deeply sore point in the history of modern Iceland's justice system, a reminder of what can go wrong when the rumour mill is running at full tilt, there's a case of completely new dimensions to deal with and pressure from all sides to get the loose ends neatly tied up.

Looking in from the outside, the cracks in the system and what went wrong look pretty clear. But the real mystery is what really did happen to Guðmundur Einarsson and Geirfinnur Einarsson in 1974, more than likely in unrelated incidents? Somewhere there have to be two sets of old bones that deserve to be laid to rest and two mysteries that are no closer to being unravelled than they were forty years ago.

KATE CLARKE

Kate is a crime writer and diarist: ex-London schoolteacher now living in Hay-on-Wye. Her books include 'Murder At The Priory: The Mysterious Poisoning of Charles Bravo' (with Bernard Taylor), shortlisted for the CWA's Gold Dagger Award; 'The Pimlico Murder', revised; 'Who Killed Simon Dale?'; 'Deadly Service'; 'Bad Companions'; 'Lethal Alliance' and 'Fatal Affairs'. She was involved in research for two other true crime books, one of which, 'Dead, Not Buried', won the CWA's Gold Dagger. Kate is currently collaborating on an A-Z of Victorian crime. All volumes of her Journal (as Kate Paul), are held in the Mass Observation Archive, Special Collections, at Sussex University Library.

CATHERINE FOSTER: A DEADLY DUMPLING AND A CLUTCH OF DEAD HENS

KATE CLARKE

It is often the case that when a young woman murders her husband she has already set her heart on his replacement. It is more unusual for a woman to murder her husband when there seems to be no such incentive, no promise of a passionate liaison waiting in the wings.

One such case was that of seventeen-year-old Catherine Foster, who, on 17th November 1846, poisoned her husband, John, by lacing his dumpling with arsenic. Their marriage, on 28th October, only three weeks before, had not been a spur of the moment, whirlwind romance; they had known each other since childhood, growing up in the village of Acton, near Sudbury, in Suffolk. John, who, at twenty-four, was seven years older than Catherine, had already set his heart on marrying her even when she was still at the small Charity School in the village. John was described in an article in the *Morning Post*, dated 5th April 1847, as a 'well-disposed and intelligent young man, exceedingly attentive to his home, and devotedly attached to his guilty partner, who, by her prepossessing appearance and engaging manners, had obtained for herself the somewhat flattering title of the "belle" of the village'. He worked as a labourer for a local farmer and was described in the *Yorkshire Gazette* as 'happy as the day was long; he worked with zeal, alacrity, and joyousness, in the daily discharge of his "lot in life".'

Both John and Catherine came from poor working families living in isolated communities where conditions were basic and every member of the family was expected to work. Catherine went into service as soon as she left school at fourteen. There were few diversions and transport was rudimentary – either on foot, on horseback or in a cart. More importantly to this story there was only a limited choice of marriageable young men in the area and, all in all, precious little to keep a teenaged girl content with her lot.

Problems within the marriage came to a head only four days after the wedding when Catherine reminded John that he'd promised to let her visit her aunt once they were married. It was arranged that the aunt would meet her at Bury St Edmunds and she would stay for a month. In fact, she returned to the family home ten days later. Having had time to assess her situation did she plan the murder of her husband during those few days of freedom? It was said that John was keener than Catherine to settle down yet marriage offered nothing new for Catherine; she was already accustomed to cooking and cleaning so it offered no real change in her circumstances. It is possible, therefore, that Catherine already had murder on her mind on the journey back to Acton.

*

On the day of the murder, 17th November 1846, Catherine's widowed mother, Maria Morley, had gone to work and her young son, Thomas, was at the village school. Catherine visited her mother-in-law but left at four o'clock, saying it was 'dumpling night'. At midday Thomas had come home for some bread and tea before returning to school, but he was back at the house at three o'clock and watched as Catherine prepared the evening meal. When John came home from work about six o'clock that evening, Catherine and Thomas were already eating their dumplings. She fetched another dumpling left warming on the stove, removed the cloth wrapping and gave it to her husband with a few potatoes and tea. After eating a portion of the dumpling John complained of heartburn before becoming violently ill, running into the yard to be sick. Taking the dumpling from her husband's plate Catherine scattered the pieces around the backyard for the chickens to eat.

At seven o'clock, when her mother, Maria, returned home from work, John was already in the bed downstairs, suffering from severe heartburn, stomach pains and bouts of vomiting. She sent Catherine for sixpenny worth of brandy, which she mixed with some gruel, but John couldn't keep it down and was sick once more.

In the morning, as her husband was no better, Catherine walked the two miles to the village of Melford to fetch the surgeon, Mr Robert Jones. Although she told him that John was suffering from painful stomach cramps she didn't mention that he was also vomiting badly. The surgeon assumed that John was suffering from a bout of 'English cholera' as, throughout that summer, the area had been in the grip of an outbreak; he gave her two powders, promising to call on the patient later in the day.

When Maria returned at about three o'clock John was still very sick and he died at about four o'clock that afternoon. Expecting to find his patient a lot better, Mr Jones arrived at five o'clock and was surprised to find him dead. He concluded that he had died from the rupture of a main artery due to violent vomiting. However, there was some disagreement over this diagnosis and suspicions soon spread – especially when it became common knowledge that a neighbour's chickens had also died after eating the remains of the dumpling that Catherine had given to her husband.

Informed of the sudden, unexplained death of a hitherto healthy young man – and the hapless hens – the Coroner, Mr Harry Wayman, opened an inquest on Saturday, 21st November, at the Crown Inn, Acton, during which Catherine, her mother and young Thomas gave evidence. Told what to say by Catherine on the night John became ill, the boy stated that he, Catherine and John had shared the *same* dumpling on the night he was taken ill. The Coroner, however, was not convinced and ordered a post-mortem which was carried out by Mr Robert Jones and another surgeon, on 24th November; the stomach and part of the intestine were sealed in jars and sent to Mr William Image at Bury for further examination. Having subjected the samples and the crops of the dead hens to the Marsh and Reinsch tests he was able to confirm the presence of arsenic.[1]

However, by the time the inquest was resumed Thomas had changed his story, saying that he'd seen his sister adding some powder to the dumpling mix for her husband and throwing the paper wrapping on the fire. Suspecting that the boy might have been coerced by the prosecution into changing his statement or might come under pressure to revert to his original statement the Coroner ordered the removal of him from his family for two weeks. He then ordered an exhumation and, on Friday, 27th November, Mr Jones performed a second post-mortem, assisted by Mr Image and Mr Samuel Newham, a surgeon at the West Suffolk Hospital. They took samples of organs and body tissue for tests and these confirmed the presence of arsenic. It was clear that the arsenic must have been in the meal served to the victim by Catherine as, had it been in his previous meal eaten about three o'clock whilst working on the farm, he would not have been in a fit state to continue with his labours and, moreover, return home, as usual, singing a cheerful song. It was also revealed that, during a police search of Maria Morley's cottage, samples of flour and some muslin cloths used to wrap the dumplings were sent to Mr Image for analysis and, whilst the flour was found to be free of any poisonous substance, one of the muslin cloths was contaminated with arsenic. As a result of this evidence, coupled with the analysis of the body parts and young Thomas's damning statement, the jury's verdict was that Catherine had administered the arsenic that poisoned her husband. She was arrested, charged with the murder of John Foster and incarcerated in the County Gaol at Bury St Edmunds.

---

1   The Marsh test, devised in 1836, would detect arsenic but a more accurate analysis could be obtained using the Reinsch test, of 1841, which could detect even small traces of antimony, strychnine, arsenic, mercury and other poisons.

The Trial

Catherine's trial for the murder of John Foster was held at the Shire Hall, Bury St Edmunds, on Saturday, 27th March 1847, before the Lord Chief Baron Pollock. According to a report in the *Bury and Norwich Post*, Catherine 'on being placed in the dock, presented a most calm and collected demeanour. She was rather an interesting looking person, and was dressed in mourning. She pleaded Not Guilty in a firm voice.'

The Times described her as 'somewhat good looking, but very simple'. The prosecution was led by Mr Gurdon who called several witnesses to give evidence, informing the jurors of the damning results of the post-mortem and the tests on the muslin cloths and the dead hens. He also reminded them that Catherine had told her brother to say that she only made one dumpling that evening and it was shared by him, Catherine and her husband.

At the start of the trial, Mr Power, for the defence, began by declaring that, as numerous pamphlets and broadsides had been circulating around the county of Suffolk, he feared that public opinion was already set against his client and therefore a fair trial would not be possible.[2]

Elizabeth, John Foster's mother, was the first to enter the witness box. She confirmed that Catherine had been at her house on the day of the murder from midday until four o'clock when she left, saying it was 'dumpling night' and she must go and prepare her husband's supper. When she hurried to the house the following day after hearing that her son was ill she found him already dead. Catherine was sitting by the fire, crying, and Mrs Foster upbraided her for not sending for her sooner.

Two of John Foster's workmates also gave evidence. James Pleasance said that on the fateful day they finished work about six and walked home together. John had been in good spirits, singing a song, seemingly happy to be married to his childhood sweetheart and looking forward

---

2   The same objection was made by Mary Blandy's defence advocate, Mr Ford, at the start of her trial for the murder of her father by arsenic in 1752.

to his supper after a hard day's labour. About two weeks before his death, John had an accident whilst loading hay onto a wagon, but soon recovered. He always seemed in good health and 'was as strong and blooming a young man as I ever saw'.

Catherine's mother, Maria, was questioned next. On the day of her son-in-law's death she had been out washing at the home of Mrs Upson, at Acton Green, from six-thirty that morning. When she got home that evening John was already in the bed downstairs, vomiting and purging. She sent Catherine to fetch six pennyworth of brandy to add to some gruel but John was immediately sick into a basin. The vomit was a dark colour, like coffee. Maria emptied the basin onto the dunghill in the back yard, which was shared by the row of three cottages.

That night, she and Catherine went upstairs to bed as John was too ill to have his wife in the downstairs bed with him. When Catherine checked on him during the night he seemed a little better but at four in the morning they heard him moving about. They both went downstairs and found that he had fallen to the floor – he said he felt dizzy and couldn't stand. Catherine gave him three cups of peppermint tea but he was sick again. Maria decided to stay with her son-in-law but told Catherine to go back to bed. At about six o'clock the next morning Catherine came back downstairs. The two women had breakfast and then, at eight o'clock Catherine walked over to Mr Jones's surgery in Melford and, a little later, Maria left to go to Sudbury. When she got back at about two o'clock John asked her to remake the bed but as she lifted him up he fell to his knees in a faint. She managed to hoist him onto a chair where he remained until he died a couple of hours later, leaning against her shoulder.

Regarding the courtship of her daughter and John Foster, Maria Morley said that even when Catherine was still at school John was always 'hanging about after her'. For two years, between the age of fourteen and sixteen, Catherine was in service to Mr H. Wade, of Waldingfield, which was two and half miles from John's house and he used to walk her back from the church to her master's house. He clearly had strong feelings for her and her mother testified that she had never heard 'a short word betwixt them'. As her daughter was so young, Maria had urged her to delay the wedding but she seemed keen and John was anxious to move into Maria Morley's cottage as he found his sisters' young children tiresome.

Catherine's brother, eight-year-old Thomas, was called next to give evidence. However, at one stage appearing a little confused and fearful, he was placed next to the Judge whilst being questioned. His confusion seemed to amuse Catherine as she was seen to be smiling as he gave evidence. Recalling the day of the murder, he said:

> I went to school which is against our house. Mrs Ward keeps it. She is a young lady. She teaches reading out of the Bible, and spelling…I generally have bread and butter for dinner. Sometimes I have cheese. I had a dumpling for supper. I ate my supper sitting by the side of my sister, near the fire. I had some potatoes also for supper and tea to drink. John had a dumpling for his supper. My sister gave it to him. She got it out of a large boiler on the fire. There was a bag tied round the dumpling.

In an earlier statement before the Coroner's inquest he'd said that he and Catherine had shared a dumpling and John Foster was given a *different* one. Questioned in court, however, he said that Catherine had told him to say that there was only *one* dumpling prepared for supper and that he, Catherine and John had eaten the same food. He now confirmed that his original statement was the correct one – that John was given a *separate* dumpling.

Catherine's next-door neighbour, Mary Ann Chinery, explained that there were three cottages in a row, the one in the middle belonging to Maria Morley – it was here that the first post-mortem on the body of John Foster was held. Catherine had come into her cottage, too upset to stay in her own during the operation. It was while she was sitting in Mary's house that she said, 'If I had went to Bury before I married, I would not have married him at all.'

Mr Robert Jones recalled Catherine coming to his surgery on the morning of Wednesday, 18th November. As she only mentioned her husband's stomach cramps he was sure the young man was suffering from 'English cholera' and prescribed two powders, which he mixed himself. When he called at the house at five that afternoon he was surprised to learn that his patient had just died – the body was still warm. He had been convinced that death was caused by a ruptured artery. He admitted that the findings at the second post-mortem had confirmed the presence of arsenic.

At five o'clock the case for the prosecution closed and it was left to Mr Power, for the defence, to plead his case. He addressed the jury at length but failed to call any witnesses on Catherine's behalf.

The Judge then summed up all the evidence given before the court in meticulous detail before instructing the jurors to retire to consider their verdict. In less than fifteen minutes they returned a verdict of 'Guilty'. As it was by then seven o'clock in the evening the Judge decided that the court should adjourn until the following Monday morning at nine o'clock, when he would pass sentence. Until that time, Catherine would be returned to Bury St Edmunds gaol to await her fate.

On the morning of Monday, 29th March, Catherine was brought back into the courtroom for sentencing. His Lordship, after having put on the black cap, proceeded to pass sentence, which was recorded in the *Chelmsford Chronicle* on Friday, 2nd April 1847:

Catherine Foster, you have been found guilty of the crime of murder, under circumstances that require no aggravation from me. It is sufficient to state that you were married on Wednesday, the 25th of October. On the following Wednesday fortnight your husband died, and died in consequence of the administration of poison. It is impossible to doubt that you prepared the food, that you administered it to your husband, and that your's was the hand that put the poison in that food. These are the facts which it is impossible to doubt. It seems to me clearly impossible to escape the conclusion, not only that your hand did the deed, but that your heart and mind had meditated that act, and it was wilfully done for the purpose of producing the death of the individual whom you so lately married, and towards whom, at the altar of God, you had so lately formed a connection the most sacred and divine that any human being can enter upon.

I have no desire to enter into the facts of the case, or to say anything of the circumstances beyond what I have done, but I may add that I entirely concur in the verdict which the jury pronounced. And it is my melancholy duty to pronounce the sentence of the law upon you, which in conformity and in obedience to the law of God, requires that your life should be forfeited for the crime you have committed. I would advise you to make the utmost use of the short time that may remain to you in this world. Seek peace and mercy where now alone you will be able to find them.

It remains for me but to pass the judgement of the law, that you be taken to the place from which you came, and then to the place of execution, and there be hanged by the neck till you are dead, and that your body be buried in the precincts of the prison in which you shall last be confined. And may God of his infinite mercy have compassion on your soul.

'The prisoner bore the sentence almost unmoved,' continued the *Chelmsford Chronicle*, 'merely applying a handkerchief to her eyes at the conclusion. She has since been somewhat more affected, but not in any great degree.'

The wording of the Judge's speech in an article on the same scene in the *London Standard*, on 31st March, differed slightly:

The learned judge, whose voice was at times almost inaudible from emotion, concluded his solemn address to the prisoner by passing the last sentence of the law upon her in the usual form, and the prisoner was removed, as on Saturday, without any apparent appreciation of the position in which she stood. Not a single tear glistened in her eye, which was unobservant and inattentive – not a single contraction of the facial muscles betoken the inward workings of suppressed feelings; but calm and composed she received the sentence as she had listened to the overwhelming evidence adduced against her, and she descended from the dock to the dark cell beneath with as light a step as if she had been convicted of an ordinary larceny.

The scene was also described in the *Bury and Norwich Post*, informing its readers that, although Catherine prayed, she didn't seem particularly contrite or aware of the enormity of her crime, adding that 'in the minds of this class, however, it is extremely difficult to judge of inward feeling by outward appearances, even in the last crisis of human trial. She parted with her mother on Thursday without much emotion.'

The version of the same event as recorded in the *Morning Post*, dated 5th April, also differed slightly from the previous two quotes and readers were kept informed of Catherine's demeanour whilst in Bury gaol:

The convict's conduct since her condemnation has been more becoming her awful situation than that which she evinced before trial. Every attention is paid to the spiritual condition of the wretched creature, and daily she is visited by the Rev. Mr. West, the chaplain of the gaol, the Rev. C.J.P. Eyre, minister of St. Mary's parish, and the Rev. Mr. Otley, of Acton, the clergyman who married her. The order of execution was received yesterday by the High Sheriff but the day has not been fixed on which it is to be carried into effect. She has not as yet made any confession.

The *London Daily News* on 7th April reported that:

The Condemned Murderess at Ipswich – Catherine Foster, sentenced to death last week for poisoning her husband and who, up to the time of her conviction, seemed utterly unmoved by the nature of her position, or the heinous character of her crime, appears now to realise her actual position. She is very penitent, and attends strictly to her religious duties, the chaplain attending her frequently. We understand a petition in her behalf is about to be got up in Bury, to be presented to the Secretary of State, it being hoped that the extreme youth of the prisoner (18), and some other circumstances attending the case, may operate in her favour. We fear, however, from the forcible manner in which the Judge expressed his concurrence in the verdict, and the abominable nature of the crime, that there must be some strong fact urged in her behalf to lead to the mitigation of her sentence. It is a singular fact connected with the prisoner that her grandfather was executed for the crime of murder, having, after committing the deed, hanged the man up by a rope to a finger-post, to induce the supposition that he had committed suicide.[1]

The prisoner sent on Friday for Rev. Mr. Ottley, of Sudbury, whom she had previously known, to whom she made a confession of guilt, and of her having bought the poison at Sudbury. In this interview she fully acknowledged the justice of her sentence. Her execution is fixed for Saturday, April 17.

On 12th April the *Morning Post* informed its readers that:

Three memorials in her behalf are in course of signature in the county, one recognising the general principle of capital punishment as un-Christianlike; the second praying for mercy in consequence of her age and sex; and the third addressed to Her Majesty by the females of Suffolk, earnestly soliciting the royal clemency to the wretched convict. The three have been forwarded to Sir George Grey, the Secretary of State, but it is generally thought that they will fail in inducing the Government to recommend the respite of the awful fate which awaits her. This presumption is considerably strengthened by the language of the Chief Baron on sentencing her to death, and who held out not the least hope of mercy to her.

Catherine's confession was reported in full in a number of newspapers. This version was printed in the *Bury and Norwich Post* on 7th April:

Since the condemnation of this unhappy young woman, for the murder of her husband, she has been unremittingly visited by the Chaplain of the Gaol (the Rev. T. West), and the Rev. C.J. P. Eyre…whose administrations have, it is believed, been of great service to her. She has also been visited several

---

1 Although it was rumoured that Catherine's father, Robert, who died in 1842, had been implicated in the robbery and death of William Kirkpatrick, in 1833, an inquest found that Kirkpatrick had 'hanged himself whilst in a state of temporary derangement'.

times by the Rev. L. Ottley, the Vicar of Acton, to whom the fall of a member of his pastoral charge, and formerly of his school, must be a matter of deep concern. The exhortations of these reverend gentlemen, and the Governor of the Gaol, Mr. Macintyre, have had the desired effect of drawing from the culprit a full acknowledgement of her guilt. At first she endeavoured to palliate the offence, by stating that she had been tempted by an offer from some person, who had given her a powder the nature of which she did not know; but, on being admonished of the folly and wickedness of persisting in falsehood, she declared her readiness to write the whole truth; and we understand that a confession has been made or taken in writing, which she begged might not be published until after her decease; but the purport of which we consider it only due to the public to make known at the earliest possible opportunity, as far as we have been able to collect it.

She stated that she alone had committed the deed; that the statement that she had previously made, of a person having tempted her to go away with him, was utterly unfounded; and the rumours of her having been provoked by her husband giving her any cause of jealousy were equally so; on the contrary, he had been uniformly kind to her; but that she never had any love for him, and had only married him at the wish of her mother, whom Foster was constantly urging to persuade her; and that after their marriage the feeling of dislike was stronger than ever. She declared, however, that the idea of destroying him did not enter her head until the day on which she committed the deed, when she purchased the poison at a shop in Sudbury, without any difficulty. It was 'white arsenic' and not a dark powder as stated by the boy before the Magistrates; and it was not true that the boy ate any of that dumpling.

The wretched woman appears to be anxious to be read to, thankful for the religious instruction afforded her, and apparently sincerely penitent; hoping for mercy in another world, but acknowledging that her punishment is justly deserved, and having no expectation or desire that her life should be spared. Her apparent apathy on the occasion of her sentence was in fact a complete prostration or stupor of her faculties; before she was taken to the Court to receive sentence she had declared her resolution to go down on her knees and beg for mercy, but she afterwards declared that she was unable either to open her mouth or to move. Her health has suffered considerably since her conviction, and evinces signs of great mental suffering although she sheds no tears.

Catherine Foster was always considered a girl of morose and obstinate disposition, and phlegmatic temperament, but apt in learning at school, and gave satisfaction during the greater part of the time she was in service. John Foster, the victim of her crime, was a man of exemplary character, and remarkable piety. Since their marriage he had kept up the practice of family prayer, and in his dying hour he invited his murderer to join him in devotion, which she did – with what sort of feelings it is not easy to imagine.

The execution will probably take place on Saturday, the 17th inst., as we understand the High Sheriff humanely desires to give her the utmost time that the law will allow to make her peace with God. She was prayed for by name in the Bury churches on Good Friday and Sunday last; and it is needless to say that the deepest interest in her awful condition is taken by the reverend gentlemen who have the daily task of visiting her, and whose duty it is, without extenuating in the smallest degree the enormity of her guilt, to set before her the inexhaustible mercy of God to those who seek it aright.

The London Standard, on 7th April, also printed Catherine's confession but added the following comment:

The loose and most reprehensible manner in which deadly poisons are permitted to be sold by apothecaries to persons applying singly, and frequently too young or too ignorant to know its fatal properties, demands immediate remedy. It is not to one case of poisoning only to which the public attention is now directed, but to a dozen; and these will not be the last unless the law step in and make provision for the careful dispensing of such dangerous articles.

Execution

On Sunday, 18th April, *The Era* provided its readers with a graphic description of the execution of Catherine Foster:

The wretched convict, Catherine Foster, condemned to death by the Chief Baron Pollock, at the late Suffolk Assizes, for the murder of her husband three weeks after marriage, by means of poisoning a dumpling with arsenic, expiated her dreadful crime this morning on the public scaffold, adjacent to the county gaol in this town. At daybreak this morning hundreds were seen flocking into the town from all parts, and at the hour appointed for the execution the ground fronting the drop was densely crowded. There could not be less than 10,000 congregated, most of them were correctly clad women, and many had children in their arms.[1]

The unhappy female walked with a firm step, and unsupported. On reaching the steps at the foot of the gallows, one of the turnkeys made an attempt to assist her in ascending. She passed him, however, unheeded, and walked up to the drop with the most extraordinary deliberation. Her youthful appearance created the most awful sensation amongst the assembled multitude, and, in a moment, the multitude seemed to be struck with the greatest awe.

The sun shone brilliantly during this horrible period, and the wretched creature stood unmoved. She scanned the mass of human beings with a firmness most astounding. The governor inquired of her if she had anything to say, she appearing, from her manner, to be desirous of speaking, and, in a charming tone, she replied, 'No; I can't speak.'

The executioner having completed the preliminary arrangements, the signal was given, and the drop fell.[2] Her struggles were painful in the extreme, and a thrill of horror ran through the crowd, voices being heard in many places, 'Shame, shame; murder, murder.' It must have been a couple of minutes ere life had ceased. The last execution of a female in this town was forty-seven years ago, for setting fire to her master's house.

---

1   A broadside printed by James Broadhurst described Catherine as a 'good-looking country girl' who was first taken, trembling violently, to the Press Room where her leg-irons were struck off. The barbarity of Catherine's execution was raised in the Houses of Parliament.

2   William Calcraft: 1829-1874. A prolific hangman, notorious for employing a short drop in his botched-up hangings, resulting in strangulation rather than a quick break of the neck and, playing to the huge crowds gathered to witness the gruesome spectacle, would sometimes pull on the culprit's legs to complete the job. The crowd that day was estimated as 10,000 – the population of Bury was 12,538 in 1841.

The newspaper also printed a copy of Catherine Foster's confession, contained in the following letter:

Bury Gaol, April 12, 1847
To the Governor,

First of all I must confess that I am guilty, and very guilty of this awful crime, and well deserve the death that I am condemned to die; and as I am soon to stand before my heavenly Judge, I wish to speak the truth. I am sorry to say I bought the poison at the shop of Mr. Eley, chemist, Sudbury, three days before I mixed it in the dumpling, which I gave to my husband. It was served to me by a young man in the shop; Mr. Eley was not present. Had he been present he would have known me, as I had been frequently in his shop on errands, when I was at service. The act was entirely my own. No person persuaded me to it, and my mother had no knowledge or suspicion of it. I had no cause of complaint against my husband; he was always good and kind to me, but I never had any affection for him, and wished to go back to service. I do not wish to live, for I never could be happy in this world, and I hope, through the merits and blood of my Saviour, and a sincere repentance of this and all my sins, to obtain forgiveness of God, and to be received into heaven. I die at peace with all living. No complaint to make of any witness that appeared against me on my trial, and full of remorse for the crime which brings me to this premature death. I wish to express my grateful thanks to the Rev. Mr. West, the chaplain of the jail, the Rev. Mr. Ottley, my parish minister, and the Rev. W. Eyre, for their great attention to my eternal interest, and for the spiritual hope and consolation I have received from their instructions and admonitions. I should wish Mr. Eyre to attend me in my last moments, and earnestly request that he will do so.

CATHERINE FOSTER [3]

---

3 In 1815, young Eliza Fenning was hanged for attempting to poison her employers with arsenic in dumplings – but unlike Catherine Foster, even on the gallows, she protested her innocence.

The *London Daily News* on Monday, 19th April, added the following detail:

> The drop was not erected, as in other county gaols, on the summits, but in a large meadow on the London side of the prison, access being obtained by a door in the boundary-wall of the gaol which was made on the execution for murder at that gaol – that of the notorious Corder for the murder of Maria Martin. [1]

The *Norwich Post*, on 28th April, published Catherine's last letters – the following was to Revd Ottley:

> *I am, Sir, heartily sorry and sincerely confess that I am guilty of this awful crime, and deserve the punishment that I am condemned for to die. I, Sir, do not wish to have forgiveness from man; all I want is pardon from God Almighty, and, Sir, what I did it for I cannot tell anyone. I did do the deed, and I am, Sir, heartily sorry for it. Oh! Sir, I remember the advice you gave me when I left Acton School; and also the advice you gave me on the day of my marriage; but, Sir, I forgot all that, and now I am sorry for it.*

In his lengthy sermon after Catherine's death, Revd Ottley urged young men to choose a wife with great care, one that shared their religious convictions.

Broadsheets, ballads and pamphlets were quickly printed for sale on the streets, both before and after an execution. The ballads were extremely popular, full of hand-wringing regret for wrongdoing, laced with saccharine pleas for divine forgiveness and expressing the hope of entry into heaven. They were also intended to act as a warning to others engaged in criminal behaviour. One such publication, entitled *A Voice From The Gaol*,[2] published several verses, the first as follows:

---

1   In 1828, William Corder was hanged for the murder of Maria Marten, a mole-catcher's daughter, a case often referred to as *The Red Barn Murder*.
2   *A Voice From The Gaol or The Horrors of the Condemned Cell*. C. Paul, Printer, 18 Great St Andrew Street, Broad-street, Bloomsbury, and sold by J. Morgan, Brick Lane, Spitalfields.

The solemn knell I think I hear,
Which fills my heart with woe,
For slaying of my husband dear,
I to the grave must go!
Oh! What thousands will approach,
My wretched end to see,
A female eighteen years of age,
Upon the gallows tree …

The last verse reads:

My fate is nigh approaching,
The thought does me amaze,
At eighteen years of age,
As I John Foster could not love,
I took away his life,
Oh! That I never had agreed,
For to become his wife.

A letter to her mother was found on Catherine's body when it was removed from the gallows in which she said, '*I have a great hope that I am going to Heaven, and there to see my Saviour face to face, and also that dear creature I have injured; and the years that I might have spent in pleasure with him on earth, I hope I shall rest with him in Heaven.*'

*

By the mid-nineteenth century, the Industrial Revolution was well under way and, with the decline in cottage industries, many rural folk sought alternative employment in city factories and shops. Catherine must have discussed with her aunt the exciting prospect of the rail link between Bury and London that was due to be completed in December 1846. This would offer the thrilling possibility of travelling to the Metropolis in four hours as opposed to a gruelling day's journey by stagecoach. The new railway link would have opened up the chance to find employment in London with its grand houses, entertainments and enticingly fashionable Emporia; offering slightly better terms of employment, wages and living conditions than those in rural Suffolk.

Catherine's glimpse of Bury during her ten days from home may have opened her eyes to an alternative lifestyle far removed from that of her sparsely populated village. In addition to the opening of the railway link, Bury St Edmunds had recently acquired street lighting and pavements and had all the bustle of a thriving market town; more importantly, a wider choice of attractive young men that were not covered in sweat and grime after a long day's toil on a farm.

It was rumoured at the time that Catherine had a preferred suitor referred to as 'young Spraggons' and may have met him in Bury, but there was no evidence of this. Had she moved to London or even a large town like Bury she might have caught the eye of a local landowner's son or a young man set up in a family business or, at the very least, had the chance to embrace an alternative way of life, one that she might have found more congenial. Did all this turn her head and, when she went home and saw the gloomy interior of the cottage and her mother still going out washing for other people from dawn to dusk – did she take out all her resentment on her young husband? What did she think she would gain from such a cruel act? Clearly, she didn't consider the consequences but just focused on removing the shackles of a life she couldn't tolerate. It is generally accepted that the undeveloped brain of an adolescent can affect the understanding of risk and inhibit the concept of the consequence of reckless behaviour.

'What did she think she would gain from such a cruel act?'

It seems that the killing of her husband was the desperate action of a young girl facing a lifetime of drudgery that was unlikely to change. A seventeen year old faced with such a dilemma would not necessarily realise the enormity of what she had decided to do and the terrible suffering she would inflict – or even contemplate the consequences of an action that she believed would bring about her release, not a hideous death on the gallows before a braying crowd of 10,000 – an outcome that probably didn't enter her mind or, if it did, presented a scenario too remote for her to imagine. Discussing the functions of the adolescent brain in his book, *We Are Our Brains*, Dr Swaab has this to say:

> The craving for new experiences, the readiness to take great risks, and the impulsive behaviour are all part of preparations to leave the nest. Because their prefrontal cortex hasn't yet matured, adolescents can think only in the short term and are unable to take in the negative consequences of risky choices.

It is disturbing to imagine the spectacle of a human being hanging from the gallows – even more tragic, perhaps, if the person, male or female, was too young to resist the impulse to annihilate the cause of their frustration as Catherine did that fateful day by simply sprinkling a few deadly grains of arsenic into a mixing bowl.

CAROL ANNE DAVIS

Carol is the author of seven true crime books, the latest of which is an update of her landmark 'Parents Who Kill'. All of her non-fiction books offer themed profiles and include interviews with top psychologists and criminologists. She has also published seven crime novels including 'Near Death Experience', which draws on her understanding of Munchausen's syndrome by proxy and 'angels of death'. She was born in Scotland but has lived in England for the past sixteen years and now spends most of her royalties on importing white puddings and black bun.

www.carolannedavis.co.uk

SINS OF THE FATHER

CAROL ANNE DAVIS

Lynn Siddons hadn't a care in the world on Easter Monday 1978. The sixteen year old had recently left school and was looking forward to starting her first job in a local supermarket. She was meeting her new boyfriend that night so that they could spend the evening at the fair.

Lynn lived on the outskirts of Derby, as did one of her friends, Roy Brookes. Though the boy was fifteen he was barely five foot tall and only weighed six and a half stone. Lynn, who was much taller and bigger, was able to take hold of his arms and whirl him around. Roy had the mental age of a twelve year old, couldn't read or write, and had been bullied by local yobs for being mixed race. He lived with his housewife mother, his unemployed stepfather and his seven-year-old half-sister and the house was often visited by the neighbourhood teenagers as his mother liked to chat. He was a sweet-natured boy and seemed pleased when Lynn brought him a small gift from her recent holiday in Milan, a pack of cards.

Roy told her that he was looking for part-time work and that his stepfather Michael had bumped into a farmer who had said he was hiring labourers. This would turn out to be a lie as the ground was still frozen that day, 3rd April, so there was no work to be done in the fields.

The teenagers wrapped up warmly and left the house at the same time as Roy's stepfather, though Michael soon went in the opposite direction. Lynn was glad as the older man made her uneasy and was always ogling her and her friends.

That night, Lynn didn't come home for her evening meal and her worried grandmother Flo, who had brought her up, went to Roy Brookes' home and asked if he'd seen her. The fifteen-year-old said that they'd walked past Red Wood and he'd gone behind a tree to urinate. When he came back, Lynn had gone. Flo pointed out that there was nothing but open fields in that area so he should have been able to see her if she was walking away in any direction but Roy insisted that she had simply disappeared.

Lynn's family searched the fields to no avail and contacted the police but they said she'd probably just run away and would be back in a few days. They maintained this casual stance until the family went to see their local MP and he galvanised the local press.

Determined to remain proactive, the Siddons family went to the Brookes house to question Roy further but his stepfather Michael kept butting in. Michael said that Lynn had run away with her boyfriend and that the teens had been having sex in an empty house nearby, but Flo knew that wasn't the case as her granddaughter had been sleeping with her since her grandfather died. Moreover, there were no vacant properties in the street which Michael Brookes mentioned so they knew they'd caught him out in a double lie.

Almost a week after the sixteen-year-old's disappearance, a police cadet cycling along the local canal bank spotted a Guy Fawkes dummy in the undergrowth but when he crouched down he realised that he was staring at a dead girl. Police quickly identified her as Lynn Siddons and a cursory look at the body showed that she had been savagely stabbed to death. Within an hour they had arrested Roy, the last known person to see her alive.

At the police station, Roy wept copiously but stuck to his story so the police left him alone with his stepfather for a few minutes. When they came back, the teenager brokenly confessed to killing her. He said that she had put her hand on his crotch then taunted him when he failed to become erect, calling him a nigger. She had also lifted up her top and bra.

It was an unlikely scenario – as Lynn regarded Roy as a child and moreover she was menstruating at the time – but police charged the young boy with murder. He was remanded in custody and refused to talk further, withdrawing completely into his shell.

Afterwards an autopsy was performed and it was found out that Lynn had been both stabbed and strangled and that earth had been forced into her mouth and her face had been held down forcefully in a puddle. Most of the knife wounds were deep, penetrating at least four inches, but there was also a series of marks where the tip of the knife had just nicked the skin.

After six months in prison, Roy Brookes' behaviour had deteriorated so badly that a psychiatrist was brought in to examine him. The psychiatrist was friendly and, after three sessions, the teenager opened up. He admitted that his stepfather had a history of stalking women and that the older man liked to tear pages out of clothing catalogues, featuring models in their underwear, and repeatedly stab a knife into them. He had allegedly told Roy to lure Lynn to the canal so that they could stab her to death. His stepfather, he continued, had said that he would hurt his beloved mother if Roy didn't participate.

He added that Michael Brookes had come up behind Lynn and held her and that he, Roy, had stuck a carving knife in lightly, putting it in sideways so that it would break away from the handle. Michael then told him to use a second knife that he, Roy, also had on his person and he stabbed her lightly with that too. She had fallen to the ground and he too had sunk to the ground and watched as his stepfather repeatedly hacked at the girl.

Michael Brookes was arrested and interrogated for forty-eight hours but stuck to his story that he had left the teenagers shortly after they left the house and had walked in the opposite direction. He was released without charge.

Eight months after Lynn's body was discovered, Roy Brookes went on trial. Though he had previously admitted to lightly stabbing her, he pleaded not guilty to murder. The eleven tiny perforations on the victim's skin tallied with his account of using the knife at his stepfather's insistence, something he said he hadn't wanted to do. The other wounds were ferocious, particularly aimed at her lower abdomen, loins and buttocks and some of the wounds had been inflicted after death. She had been strangled by pressure from hands and perhaps a forearm, pressure beyond which a puny boy like Roy Brookes could have applied. The body had also been dragged from the path into the undergrowth and again the fifteen year old simply did not possess that kind of strength.

During cross-examination, thirty-three-year-old Michael Brookes denied that he had a knife fetish. His alibi was that he had gone to visit his mother as he wanted to borrow money from her to pay his electricity bill and get it reconnected but he had walked there and left without ringing her bell in case her partner, who disliked him, was at home.

The police said that Roy had asked them at the station, 'Can dad tell you what happened?' and had refused to answer any questions until his father was left alone with him, after which he'd suddenly confessed.

The Judge said that there was evidence that Michael Brookes had been an accomplice but that he was not on trial. The trial lasted four days, after which the jury took less than twenty minutes to find the teenager not guilty and he was released into a place of safety as the authorities felt he would be at risk if he returned home.

Lynn Siddons' family were convinced that Michael Brookes was the real mastermind behind the teenager's death and they set about finding out more about him. He'd married Dot when her illegitimate son, Roy, was two, and they had been targeted by racists and had to flee a former home, at one stage sleeping rough. He was known to be obsessed with the Jack the Ripper story and had talked to various acquaintances about wanting to 'get' women, a theme he had also pursued when talking to Roy.

A deeply troubled man, he suffered from anxiety and had made two suicide attempts, once by taking tablets and once by putting his head in a gas oven. After the second attempt he had been admitted to a mental hospital on a voluntary basis for a short time. His two brothers said that he was mad, a compulsive liar and that they wanted nothing to do with him. His stepfather felt the same way and wouldn't allow him into the house.

Psychiatrists wanted to give the teenage Roy a truth drug so that they could find out the full story of what happened on that April day but both Michael and Dot Brookes refused to give permission.

Now, the Siddons family – particularly Lynn's grandmother Flo – began to haunt Michael Brookes. Flo would stand across the road from his house every morning before going on to her job in a shoe factory and would call him a murderer when she met him in the street. The family smashed his windows late at night and other neighbours sent a card saying, 'We're coming to get you'. His unfortunate daughter was taunted at school with the other children telling her that her father was a killer.

The Brookes moved house and the new tenant found partially burned pornographic magazines in the garden. (The police had previously taken away posters of women, mutilated by stab wounds, from the walls of Michael Brookes' bedroom.) The tenant also found a knife, potentially the murder weapon, and took it to the police but they somehow lost it. The Siddons clan were incensed. The tenant continued to dig (he was making a vegetable plot) and soon found charred clothing and a man's shoe hidden in the soil. This time the Siddons took the items, in a sealed bag, to their solicitor and he handed them over to the police. Incredibly, the police lost those too.

Michael Brookes now left his wife for a teenage girl (who he would later threaten) and they moved into a caravan together, hoping to find work at the fairground. Incensed, his wife phoned Flo and said, 'Mick did it – he killed Lynn.'

Lynn's mother, grandmother and aunt raced to the house, where Dot Brookes told them that she had found Michael burning his trousers and a sheath knife after Lynn's disappearance. She kept questioning him and he had eventually said, 'If you must know I did kill Lynn and I fucking enjoyed it.' He added that she was a slut like all women and that he kept stabbing her but she would not die. He also said that Roy had stood there trembling in a cowardly fashion and had not wanted to join in.

Dot repeated this statement to the researcher of the local MP who was helping the Siddons in their fight for justice. She promised that she would lure Michael Brookes back to the marital bed and put a tape recorder in the room because he liked to fantasise about stabbing her whenever they were having sex. It would be easy for her to turn the conversation to Lynn's murder and his confession would then be on record for the police.

Unfortunately for the Siddons, Dot Brookes reunited with her husband at this stage and she refused to repeat her story, knowing that a wife cannot be made to give evidence against her husband in court. His estranged girlfriend would later claim that he admitted to killing Lynn but police neglected to interview her, even when he was briefly arrested him for the murder. There was deemed to be insufficient evidence and he wasn't charged.

Four months later, in an act of enraged abandonment, Lynn's aunt, Cynthia, saw the Brookes walking along the street. She aimed her car at them and they had to jump over a wall to escape and take refuge in a nearby nunnery. She was initially charged with attempted murder but this was later reduced to a charge of reckless driving and she was fined £100.

The terrified Brookes family moved house again and would do so a total of fourteen times over the ensuing years: they even changed their surname but Flo still found them. Crime writers would later believe that this stopped Michael Brookes from stalking other women as he was always in the public eye, though one Internet justice site believes that he was unfairly targeted by Lynn's relatives. He was questioned by police over the Yorkshire Ripper murders, crimes for which lorry driver Peter Sutcliffe was later sent down. Both men had held driving jobs, Sutcliffe spending much of his life behind the wheel of a lorry whilst Michael Brookes had at one stage run a taxi cab.

Meanwhile, Cynthia's reckless driving and the reasons for it were reported in the local paper and this was seen by a prisoner who had known Michael Brookes and had been on trial at around the same time as his stepson, Roy. He had bumped into Michael subsequently and the latter had given the impression that they both had a hand in Lynn Siddons' death. The prisoner added that Michael Brookes liked to throw darts at pictures of nude women and would be especially jubilant if he managed to stab them in the breast.

The plot thickened when Dot Brookes told a neighbour that her diary, which included entries on the days after Lynn's death, was her insurance policy that Michael would never leave her again.

Dot also told her brother-in-law's girlfriend that Michael slept with a knife under his pillow and liked to have sex whilst holding the blade to her neck and that he also liked to prod her in the stomach using his thumb in a stabbing gesture. The girlfriend repeated this in a signed statement to the Siddons' solicitor.

The late Paul Foot, who had just been nominated for Campaigning Journalist of the Year, now got involved – in early 1981 – and wrote a dramatic feature entitled 'Who Killed Lynn Siddons?' for the *Daily Mirror*. Foot believed that the police had erred by arresting Roy Brookes before the autopsy had been performed, as the autopsy report showed a stronger man than Roy had had a hand in Lynn's murder. (Michael Brookes was six foot one and powerfully built.) They had also moved the body before conducting forensic tests and had accepted a vague confession from the teenager because they didn't know at this stage exactly what had caused Lynn's demise. After Roy had been found not guilty it was difficult for detectives to arrest Michael Brookes as he had been the chief witness for the prosecution.

'no one was serving time for the death of their teenage relative'

The years passed and the Siddons mourned that justice had not been done, that no one was serving time for the death of their teenage relative. In October 1984, Flo made an official complaint against Derbyshire Police for their mishandling of the case. After six months they produced a report but refused to make it public and even Flo wasn't allowed to see the results. The report was passed on to the Director of Public Prosecutions but he decided that there wasn't enough evidence against Michael Brookes to warrant a new trial. Still the Siddons refused to admit defeat.

By now they had spent more than £14,000 on legal costs but the compensation cheque they received from the Criminal Injuries Board for Lynn's death was a mere £27.

Fortunately they still had Paul Foot in their corner and he found them a new solicitor, who they were able to pay by arranging raffles, bring and buy sales and other sponsored events. In 1991, thirteen years after Lynn's death, they travelled to the High Court in London and were told that their civil action for damages against Michael and Roy Brookes could go ahead. The case had made legal history, being the first civil case in which damages were being claimed for a murder for which no one had yet been convicted, and for many years it would be taught to law students at university.

The nine-day hearing took place in July 1991 at the Royal Courts of Justice in London. On the third day, Roy – now a married man aged twenty-eight – told of how he had taken a minimal part in the murder that fateful day, how his stepfather had stabbed Lynn ferociously. He said he had sat down on the ground feeling sick as his stepfather shoved soil into Lynn's mouth and used his foot to push her face into the ground.

Two witnesses spoke of Michael Brookes' obsession with knives and one of them remembered that he would stab photographs of women when he was only eight or nine years old and become eerily excited. Another said that Brookes had dated his daughter but acted so strangely that he tried not to leave the two of them alone together. He said that the man was a knife freak who demonstrated a hatred of women and often seemed to be in a world of his own. Brookes elected not to give evidence on his own behalf.

In September, the court found for the plaintiffs, ruling that Roy Brookes was twenty per cent liable and Michael Brookes eighty per cent liable for the trauma inflicted on Lynn before she died and that they must pay the Siddons compensation. The Brookes replied that they were penniless. This was true as Michael Brookes had often been unemployed and would help feed his family by catching rabbits for the pot. The widespread awareness of the Siddons murder and his potential part in it had also made it impossible for him to find work and he had spent the last few years at home watching television, a virtual recluse. Brookes' solicitor now stated that this did not amount to a criminal finding of guilty and begged the media to leave his client alone.

Two months later the Siddons were awarded £10,641 as compensation based on Lynn's potential earnings. Fortunately their case hadn't been motivated by money but by their determination to keep the murder in the media's gaze.

By now there was a new Director of Public Prosecutions who decided there was enough evidence to try Michael Brookes. In July 1992 he was arrested at his home and looked deeply shocked. He remained mute but his wife shouted, 'He didn't do it. Fuck off and leave us alone.' He was later bailed and moved to another part of the country with her, where they were allocated a council house.

His trial, at the Old Bailey in the summer of 1996, lasted for six weeks, though he did not give evidence as a psychiatrist deemed that he was suffering from depression and unfit to do so. A second psychiatrist said that he was fit to take the stand but his defence team elected not to call him. Roy Brookes, however, took the stand and described the murder exactly as he had described it at his own trial eighteen years before.

A pathologist testified that, though it was possible that one person had killed her, it was more likely to be two people and the major wounds suggested that the killer was left handed. The jury passed a note to the judiciary enquiring if Michael Brookes was left handed and the answer was in the affirmative. Still protesting his innocence, Brookes was sent to jail – beginning his sentence in HMP Lincoln – for a minimum of twenty-six years.

In 1998 he appealed, stating that the media publicity surrounding the case had made it impossible for him to have a fair trial but the appeal was turned down, with the Judges declaring that they had no lurking doubt about the safety of the conviction. He is scheduled for release in 2022.

In 2003, Flo Siddons unveiled a plaque in memory of Lynn at the place where she was murdered. She spent her later years in a nursing home and died there, age ninety-two, in 2007.

JIM DOHERTY

Jim is a sergeant in the police force of a railroad serving forty-six states (the American equivalent of a British Transport policeman), he has served US law enforcement at the federal, state, and local levels, policing everything from inner city streets to suburban parks, university campuses to military bases. His true crime collection, Just the Facts, included 'Blood for Oil', which won a Spur Award from WWA. His first (still unpublished) novel, An Obscure Grave, was a finalist for the CWA's Debut Dagger. He's police consultant for the Dick Tracy comic strip. He lives in Chicago with his lovely wife, Katy.

www.facebook.com/ProSeProductions
www.dicktracy.wikia.com/wiki/Sgt._Jim_Doherty

THE COP KILLER WHO CREATED COP FICTION

JIM DOHERTY

As a policeman who writes mysteries, I'm naturally drawn to that particular sub-genre that purports to portray the profession of law enforcement with a high level of authenticity and verisimilitude, the so-called police procedural.

So I find it interesting to speculate that the sub-genre might not have existed at all, had not a decorated US Army veteran, and former honor student at the California Institute of Technology, turned to violent crime.

Well, that's an exaggeration. There had already been stories, in a variety of fictional mediums, that had attempted to show police work realistically and accurately. Novels like Henry Wade's *Lonely Magdalen* and Maurice Procter's *No Proud Chivalry* in Britain, or Lawrence Treat's *V as in Victim* and Leslie T. White's *Harness Bull* in the US; stage plays like Sidney Kingsley's *Detective Story* and Bartlett Cormack's *The Racket*; or such post-war 'semi-documentary' crime films as *The Naked City* and *The Blue Lamp*, all made an effort to depict police work with accuracy, or at least the appearance of accuracy. One could make a case that the comic strip *Dick Tracy*, for which creator Chester Gould spent hours researching law enforcement, even to the point of taking criminology courses at Northwestern University, was one of the first authentic depictions of police work in any medium.

And undoubtedly, had the young soldier never turned to crime, there would have been more examples, in many different mediums, in the future.

Yet if that ex-G.I. had not turned outlaw, it's very possible that CWA founder John Creasey might never have created his most critically acclaimed character, Scotland Yard Commander George Gideon. Bestselling novelist Evan Hunter might not have created his classic series about the cops who police a thinly fictionalized New York City's 87th Precinct. And the very term 'police procedural' might never have been coined.

The soldier's name was William Erwin Walker, and nothing in his early life suggested a predilection for violent crime.

Born in California in 1918, Walker was raised in the Los Angeles suburb of Glendale. His father worked for LA County as a flood engineer. His uncle was a prominent Los Angeles lawyer, who'd once been the chief deputy for the Los Angeles County District Attorney, and who would later be appointed a Superior Court judge. After graduating from Glendale's Herbert Hoover High School, Walker matriculated at the California Institute of Technology, where he excelled at radio engineering and electronics.

There was a depression on, however, and CIT was a private institution. Private and expensive. Walker left after completing only a year, forced to seek employment. He was eventually hired as a civilian employee of the Glendale Police Department, where he worked as a radio technician and dispatcher.

The cliché so often heard about violent offenders, when their criminality is finally uncovered, is that they seemed like such quiet, unassuming guys. People who knew Walker went farther than that, describing him as unusually kind and considerate, seeming to be sincerely concerned for others.

What seems to have changed him was military duty.

He was drafted into the Army shortly after America's entry into the Second World War. Very near-sighted, his vision was bad enough that it would have ordinarily rendered him '4F', physically unfit for the armed services, but Walker's skill at radio technology and electronics made him a valuable enough military asset that the eyesight requirement was waived. After boot camp, he was first posted to Australia, where he was selected for Officer Candidate School in Brisbane. Commissioned as a Second Lieutenant upon his graduation, he was, in November 1944, placed in charge of a Signal Corps radar outpost, and its eighty-five soldiers, on Leyte Island. It was on Leyte that he got his only battle experience, but it was, by every account, an experience that was particularly searing.

US Forces had landed on Leyte the previous month, after winning the Battle of Leyte Gulf. Nevertheless, there were still Japanese units active on the island, and American control was far from absolute. In late November, Lt Walker's group was attacked by Japanese paratroopers, and subjected to three days and nights of almost continuous combat. Walker and his men were technicians, not front-line soldiers, and, pitted against the well-trained airborne infantry of Imperial Japan, suffered heavy losses before the attack was finally fought off. Walker was lauded for his leadership during the battle, and promoted to First Lieutenant, but privately told his commanding officer that he no longer felt fit to lead other men. He was transferred stateside for the rest of the war, and posted near his hometown.

Prior to his separation from the Army following VJ-Day, Walker committed his first crime, burglarizing an auto repair facility, and stealing various tools, including some radio equipment. A few months later, he broke into an Army ordnance warehouse, and stole a large quantity of weapons and ammunition, including, but not limited to, seven Tommy guns, eight .45 Colt semi-automatic pistols, six .38 caliber revolvers, along with magazines, holsters, and other related equipment.

Discharged from military service in November of 1945, almost exactly a year after leading his soldiers into battle against the Japanese, Walker, scorning a return to his low-paid job with the Glendale Police, immediately started his criminal career in earnest, renting a garage that he used as a base of operations, and stealing a car that he used for transportation to his various crimes. He began a series of burglaries, stealing electronic and film equipment from recording studios and film companies, which he then sold to legitimate dealers.

One such dealer, Willard Starr, who bought and sold movie and radio equipment out of his home, had done several deals with Walker (who called himself 'Paul Norris' during these transactions), but gradually became suspicious and reported his suspicions to the police. Two detectives from LAPD's Hollywood Division, Lt Colin Forbes and Sgt Stewart Johnson, checked out the equipment Starr had bought from Walker, and, finding that it was stolen, arranged to stake out Starr's home on 25th April 1946, hoping to apprehend 'Norris', who had an appointment to make another sale that evening.

When confronted by the two cops as he approached the house, Walker pulled a pistol and opened fire. Forbes was badly wounded when a slug entered his abdomen and lodged near his spine. Johnson, also hit, was still able to effectively return fire, wounding Walker twice, in the stomach and left leg. Despite his injuries, Walker managed to get away, fleeing the house and using the massive network of underground storm sewers beneath the city streets, a system with which he was intimately familiar thanks to his dad's county job, as an escape route.

Experienced at treating combat injuries, Walker successfully tended his wounds himself, and, by June, was ready to resume his new career. He was about to take a step up in class, going from mere burglary to safecracking and, to that end, had acquired priming cord and detonating fuses, and had made his own nitroglycerin. With the new equipment, he was, on 5th June 1946, in the process of breaking into a huge meat market at the corner of Los Feliz Boulevard and Brunswick Avenue in Glendale. It was here that he'd have his fatal encounter with California Highway Patrol Officer Loren Roosevelt.

Roosevelt, forty-three, married, one daughter, had only been a member of the state's highway police force for about three years, but he'd been a cop of one kind or another for a lot longer than that, including prior state service as a guard at California's 'Big Max' prison, Folsom, as well as many years as a local officer in various jurisdictions. In 1938, he'd been hired by the City of Arcadia, California, a suburb about thirteen miles northeast of downtown LA, as the chief of police. He was fired a year later during some ugly political infighting involving a recall election and allegations of bookie joints operating near Arcadia's most famous landmark, the Santa Anita Racetrack. Out of work, but still only in his thirties, Roosevelt still had plenty of cop left in him. Available sources do not make it clear where he went immediately following his dismissal from the Arcadia Police, but, with the Second World War already raging in Europe and Asia, and conscription already underway, it's possible he entered one of the armed services, perhaps as a military policeman. In any event, by 1943, he was able to resume his civilian career in law enforcement, and, willing to start again at the bottom, was accepted into the CHP.

That night he'd finished his shift a short time earlier, and was driving to his home in Glendale, when, passing the meat market, he saw some suspicious activity, and, despite being off-duty, decided to check it out.

The night suddenly erupted in gunfire, awakening residents in the neighborhood, who rushed out to find Officer Roosevelt, bleeding from multiple gunshot wounds, lying next to his car. They immediately called the local police.

Roosevelt stayed conscious long enough to give responding officers an account of what happened. He'd spotted a vehicle speeding on Los Feliz, and decided to pull it over. The vehicle slowed down abruptly as Roosevelt began to catch up, and suddenly the driver opened fire without warning. Roosevelt was later found to have sustained nine hits from .45 caliber rounds. Since the Colt .45 pistol holds a maximum of eight rounds, the number of Roosevelt's wounds suggests that Walker had opened up on him with one of those Thompsons he'd stolen from the military warehouse months earlier.

The shooter exited his car. Roosevelt managed to get out of his, draw his revolver, and crank off a few shots, but apparently none that were effective. When the local cops arrived, he was able to give them a fairly detailed description of the shooter. He was then taken to a nearby hospital, where he died a few hours later.

There was no trace of the gunman. Walker had managed to disappear by again using the county's sewer system to escape, just as he had after the encounter with Forbes and Johnson.

When the abandoned car was searched, police found various tools, a container of nitroglycerin, a length of detonating cord, some blasting caps, and other explosives equipment, along with a loaded Tommy gun.

The description given by Roosevelt, which matched that given by Starr, Forbes and Johnson, and the similarity of the attacks, led investigators to theorize that the same offender was responsible. The hunt was now being pressed hard for the man who'd wounded two cops in one encounter, and killed a third in another.

The problem was that they had no idea who they were looking for. They weren't even sure, despite the generally matching descriptions and methods of attack, that it was the same man. It was a reasonable theory, but it was far from a proven fact.

Walker, for his part, was changing his M.O. again. Deciding that the possibilities for either straight burglary or safecracking were exhausted, he'd transitioned to armed robbery. Still possessing most of the arsenal he'd stolen from the Army, he started on a series of liquor store hold-ups. He also started stealing and reselling cars, using fake license plates and driver licenses he'd made himself.

In the meantime, the cops were bumping into nothing but dead ends. Six months after Roosevelt's murder, they were no closer to finding his killer than when they started looking for him.

What finally tripped Walker up was his mouth. He'd started dating a young lady who was a devout Catholic. Why he thought a religious girl would be favorably impressed by a career in banditry and murder is not clear, but apparently he thought she would be, since, one night, after swearing her to secrecy, he bragged about his life of crime.

She did what a devout Catholic might be expected to do, and consulted her priest, possibly within the context of a sacramental confession.

According to at least one source, the priest then passed along her information to the police. If the girlfriend did, in fact, reveal Walker's identity during confession, this is extremely unlikely because the sanctity of confessional confidentiality is so deeply ingrained a part of Catholicism. Priests have died keeping the Seal of Confession. What is far more likely is either that the priest persuaded the girl to go to the police, probably accompanying her to provide moral support, or that he obtained her permission to pass along the information himself.

Acting on the information received, LAPD Central Homicide detectives located Walker's residence, an apartment on Argyle Avenue in Hollywood. At 2 a.m., on 20th December 1946, Captain Jack Donahoe, the commander of Homicide, and Sergeants Marty Wynn and Earle Rombeau, using a key they'd obtained from the landlord, burst into the studio apartment.

Walker had been asleep. A .45 pistol was on his nightstand. A loaded Thompson was cradled beside him on the bed. He awakened instantly when he heard the key inserted into the lock, and grabbed the submachine gun. The detectives jumped on him before he could bring the Tommy to bear, wresting it from his grip and throwing it to the floor.

Captain Donahoe covered the gun with his body while Wynn and Rombeau continued to struggle with Walker. Despite sustaining several blows to the head, Walker shook off the two sergeants, reached underneath Donahoe, and managed to pull the Thompson free. He stood up and started to swing the weapon toward the three cops. Wynn drew his revolver and fired twice, hitting Walker in the shoulder both times. Walker dropped the gun, but, amazingly, still had enough fight left that a fair amount of effort was required to get cuffs on him.

Once cuffed, Walker calmed down and started to cooperate.

While they were waiting for an ambulance, the three cops questioned Walker, who admitted both to killing Roosevelt and to wounding the two Hollywood Station detectives.

Walker's trial commenced on 2nd June 1947. Relying on a family history that included a paternal grandfather who'd spent over three decades in a mental institution, Walker pled not guilty by reason of insanity.

Walker testified himself during his trial. His grasp of scientific facts and his general intelligence were obvious. The Judge later commented that, 'I seldom recall a more intelligent witness, a witness who gave clearer answers to the questions than Mr. Walker.' Ironically, the very intelligence Walker displayed doomed his insanity plea. He was found guilty and sentenced to death.

And it was at this point that fact was about to impinge on fiction.

Clearly the notion of a scientific genius who was also a master criminal, a real-life Moriarty figure whose skill with firearms gave him a touch of 'Old West desperado', a daring bandit already dubbed 'Machine-Gun' Walker by the media, was too tempting for filmmakers to ignore, and one small studio intended to cash in on the Walker story.

Eagle-Lion Films was an American subsidiary of the Rank Organization, founded in 1946 to serve as a US distributor for British films. But it also produced its own line of high-quality, low-budget movies. Bryan Foy, famous on vaudeville as the oldest of the 'Seven Little Foys', and one-time chief of the 'B' Movie Division of Warner Brothers, was Eagle-Lion's production head.

One genre with which Eagle-Lion had a great deal of success, both critical and financial, was the burgeoning 'semi-documentary' crime film. In response to 20th Century Fox's two films about the FBI, *The House on 92nd Street* and *The Street With No Name*, Eagle-Lion had released *T-Men*, a film based on files from a lesser-known federal police agency, the US Secret Service. A high-budget, fact-based film from Columbia about US agents working to stem the global narcotics trade, *To the Ends of the Earth*, was followed by a lower-budget Eagle-Lion offering about federal narcotics officers called *The Port of New York* (which introduced future Oscar-winner Yul Brynner).

And the success of Universal's *The Naked City*, which dramatized a murder investigation carried out by the New York City Police, suggested that the time was ripe for a film about local cops. And they didn't have to go all the way to New York, because 'Machine-Gun' Walker was right in their own back yard.

Screenwriter and director Crane Wilbur, who had already written or directed four Eagle-Lion movies, wrote a screen treatment based on the case that he titled *The L.A. Investigator*. Foy liked it and, because Wilbur was already slated to direct another semi-documentary crime film for E/L, *Cañon City*, based on the massive 1947 prison break from the Colorado State Penitentiary located in the titular town, assigned another journeyman screenwriter, John C. Higgins, to help Wilbur flesh the treatment out to a full script. The credited director was to be Alfred Werker (though it's generally acknowledged that much, perhaps most, of the film was actually directed by Anthony Mann, who probably should have at least gotten co-credit, if not sole credit). Camera work would be handled by John Alton, the legendary Oscar-winning cinematographer who put the *noir* in film *noir*.

Ultimately released in 1948 under the title *He Walked by Night*, the film followed the facts fairly closely. Some details were changed (e.g. the doomed Roosevelt figure is changed from a CHP officer to an LAPD traffic cop), some events were rearranged (e.g. the murder of the Roosevelt figure precedes the stakeout gunfight between Walker and the two detectives from Hollywood Division), and, because Production Code censors insisted that the villain suffer an immediate righteous comeuppance, the film ends, not with Walker (fictionalized into Roy Martin for the film) arrested in his apartment after a struggle, but with Walker escaping from the apartment, and leading the cops on a long chase-cum-shootout in those storm sewers he'd used as an escape route on earlier occasions, culminating in his death. Given that *He Walked by Night* preceded *The Third Man* by a full year, one wonders whether Carol Reed might have seen this sequence and been inspired to end his classic Vienna-set crime film with a similar climax.

In any case, despite the changes, it was clear to anyone familiar with recent events in Los Angeles that the Walker case had been the source material for the film.

Eagle-Lion was able to get full cooperation from the LAPD. Scenes were filmed at Police Headquarters in City Hall. Officers involved in the case were made available to the screenwriters for interviews. And Detective Sergeant Marty Wynn, the man who'd actually fired the shots that finally brought Walker down, was assigned to be the film's technical advisor.

While on the set Wynn formed a friendship with one of the actors, a young guy named Jack Webb, who was making his first credited screen appearance. Webb was playing a character named 'Lee', a lab cop apparently modeled on Lt Lee Jones, the commander of LAPD's Scientific Investigation Division. To that point, Webb was better known as a radio actor, and had made a name for himself as the titular hero on three different series featuring hard-boiled private eye characters, *Pat Novak for Hire*, *Johnny Modero: Pier 23*, and *Jeff Regan: Investigator*. All three protagonists routinely made official law enforcement figures look ridiculous in virtually every episode.

Upon finding that Webb was the voice behind a trio of characters who habitually humiliated cops, Wynn wasted no time telling him what policemen thought about characters like Pat Novak.

'It rankles every damn cop in the country when they hear those far-fetched stories about crime'

'It rankles every damn cop in the country when they hear those far-fetched stories about crime,' Wynn told Webb. 'They're all jazzed up, and the detectives are supermen, and they do it with mirrors. *Real* cops don't work like that.'

Suddenly inspired, Wynn continued. 'I can arrange for you to have access to cases in the police files. Maybe you could do something with them.'

Later Wynn would claim that he'd forgotten the conversation an hour later, but he'd planted a seed that would grow into a multi-media sensation.

The 'something' that Webb did with Wynn's suggestion was a radio show called *Dragnet*, fictionalizing cases from the files of the

Los Angeles Police in the style of *He Walked by Night*. Though it started small, it soon grew from a tiny ripple to a full-scale, internationally successful tsunami.

By 1951, with television overtaking radio as the most popular entertainment medium, the show moved to TV, where it achieved its greatest popularity. In 1954, a full-length, theatrical motion picture version was released to theatres, becoming one of the top-grossing films of the year.

It's hard to realise, particularly if you're familiar with *Dragnet* primarily from the 1967 revival series Webb did some eight years after the original show left the air, how influential that original program was. But so great was its impact that, in the 1950s, there were literally dozens of shows on radio and TV slavishly following the *Dragnet* formula.

Within a few years of *Dragnet*'s debut, there were *The Lineup* (*Dragnet* with the Golden Gate Bridge), *21st Precinct* ('Big Apple' *Dragnet*), *Decoy* (distaff *Dragnet*), *Tales of the Texas Rangers* (Lone Star *Dragnet*), *N.O.P.D.* (Big Easy *Dragnet*), and *Harbor Command* (maritime *Dragnet*), all using scripts based on actual cases, and all claiming cooperation from the law enforcement agencies depicted.

One of the most slavish *Dragnet* clones, following closely on *Dragnet*'s debut in Britain, was *Fabian of the Yard*, which dramatized cases from the career of Superintendent Robert Fabian, one the most famous detectives in the London Metropolitan Police. Like *Dragnet*, it featured voice-over first-person narration by the lead character. Like *Dragnet* (the first dramatic show produced for network television on film, rather than being broadcast live), *Fabian* was the first BBC show on film. And, like *Dragnet*, it became an international hit.

Novelists were also struck by the popularity of *Dragnet*. New Englander Ben Benson created two different series that used the Massachusetts State Police as background, one featuring Chief of Detectives Wade Paris, the other about rookie uniformed Trooper Ralph Lindsey. Jonathan Craig began a series of carefully researched novels featuring the investigations of two detectives (one of them the narrator) assigned to NYPD's Sixth Precinct. Former FBI Agent Gordon Gordon (that was really his name), in collaboration with his wife Mildred, started a series featuring a young agent in the Bureau's Chicago Office (where Gordon had worked) named John Ripley.

Two authors who took particular note of the trend were John Creasey, the prolific creator of such characters as the Toff, the Baron, and Dr Palfrey, and Evan Hunter, the bestselling writer of such acclaimed novels as *The Blackboard Jungle* and *Strangers When We Meet*.

Creasey had already been writing cop novels, featuring a Scotland Yard detective named Roger West, since 1942. This series was the result of a challenge by his next-door neighbor, a retired Met detective, who dared Creasey to 'write about us as we are. You can leave out the dull stuff.'

Creasey certainly left out the dull stuff. The West series, at least the early entries, may have described police work with a modicum of accuracy, thanks to the neighbor he was able to use as a technical advisor, but they were also packed with the kind of red-blooded melodrama one would expect in a Sax Rohmer yarn rather than a realistic police novel.

But, as Creasey later wrote, the success of *Dragnet*, and its British counterpart *Fabian*, suggested to Creasey that perhaps the 'dull stuff' wasn't really that dull after all, that police work, even without the crutch of melodrama, was an interesting thing in itself. Inspired, he wrote a convincingly authentic novel about one day in the career of George Gideon, a high-ranking detective at Scotland Yard (apparently based on real-life Yard legend George Hatherill, with whom Creasey had formed a friendship), supervising several different, unrelated investigations in the course of a single shift. That novel *Gideon's Day*, first published in 1955 under the pseudonym 'J.J. Marric', garnered Creasey the best reviews he'd ever received. Later entries in the series would earn him a Gold Dagger nomination from the CWA and an Edgar for Best Novel from the Mystery

Writers of America. His other series characters made him successful. Gideon made him respected.

Evan Hunter, a one-time actor and playwright, as well as a novelist, would later say that he was particularly impressed by *Dragnet* in its radio incarnation. The quick-moving, rat-a-tat dialog, and the casual use of police argot, without explanation, trusting that the audience would be intelligent enough to pick up the meaning from the context, impressed him greatly. He started experimenting with *Dragnet*-like short stories, all set in New York City, for crime fiction digests like *Manhunt* and *Verdict*, and slicks like *Argosy*. When he was invited by editor Herb Alexander to develop a mystery series for Pocket Books, he decided to try the form at novel-length. Adopting the pseudonym 'Ed McBain', he conceived a series featuring a 'collective hero', a group of cops who worked out of a busy police precinct in Manhattan (though a Manhattan that was thinly fictionalized), with no single character standing out (though ultimately, one of the cops, Detective Steve Carella, would emerge as 'first among equals'). The series debuted in 1956 with *Cop Hater*.

1956 was also the year that *Dragnet* made the jump to prose fiction with a novel titled *Case No. 561* by top-selling private-eye writer Richard S. Prather, writing under the pseudonym of 'David Knight'. The case Prather chose to fictionalize for the first *Dragnet* novel? The pursuit of a decorated soldier turned cop-killer named Erwin Walker.

Finally, 1956 was also the year that the term 'police procedural' got coined, when, in his end-of-the-year retrospective column, *New York Times* mystery critic Anthony Boucher (the same Anthony Boucher for whom the World Mystery Convention, Bouchercon, is named) devoted his article to the growing number of crime novels built around the authentic depiction of law enforcement, singling out Marric and McBain for particular praise. Crediting the phenomenal success of the radio-TV series *Dragnet* for starting the trend, he referred to such stories as 'police procedurals', stories in which the *raison d'etre* was the accurate depiction of proper law enforcement procedure. Stories in which the point was not so much the crime, nor even the solution of the crime, as it was the authentic depiction of how cops work on the job, and maybe, at its best, (as cop-turned-novelist Joseph Wambaugh would later put it) of how the job works on cops.

And none of it would have happened had not Lt Erwin Walker burglarized a garage, and broken into a military armory to make off with some guns and ammo, thus setting in motion the chain of events that led to the creation of *Dragnet*.

As for Walker himself, he managed to cheat the gallows (gallows in a figurative sense only, since California had long since transitioned to the gas chamber). Though found sane at his trial, he went bonkers a few hours before his scheduled death sentence, and was declared too unbalanced to be executed, since, by law, persons being executed have to understand why. He was transferred to a state hospital for the criminally insane (from which he escaped at one point, though he was recaptured soon afterwards). When, more than ten years later, he was found sane enough to be executed, California Governor Pat Brown, a notorious foe of the death penalty, commuted his sentence to life without the possibility of parole, on the theory that Walker would go nuts again as his execution neared, so it made no sense to try to carry out the original sentence. In 1970, Walker appealed his conviction on the grounds that his confession had been coerced. The California State Supreme Court denied that appeal, but did instruct the trial court to vacate the 'no parole' portion of his sentence. In 1974, Walker applied for, and received, a parole from the Adult Authority of the California Department of Corrections. After viciously killing one cop, crippling

'viciously killing one cop, crippling a second, wounding a third, and trying his level best to murder three more'

a second, wounding a third, and trying his level best to murder three more, he was, within the fairly mild limits of that parole, a free man, and he stayed free until his death in 1982.

Kind of makes me wish that Marty Wynn had been more accurate when he capped him.

MARTIN EDWARDS

Martin is an award-winning crime writer
whose latest Lake District Mystery is
'The Frozen Shroud'. The series includes
'The Coffin Trail' (shortlisted for the
Theakston's prize for best British crime
novel. He has written eight novels about
Harry Devlin, now available again as
e-books, and two stand-alone novels,
including 'Dancing for the Hangman'. He won
the CWA Short Story Dagger in 2008, and the
CWA Margery Allingham Prize in 2014. He has
edited twenty-two anthologies and published
eight non-fiction books, most recently
'The Golden Age of Murder'. He is archivist
of the Crime Writers' Association.

www.martinedwardsbooks.com
www.doyouwriteunderyourownname.blogspot.com

BAD LUCK AND A BLAZING CAR

MARTIN EDWARDS

If Alfred Arthur Rouse had not mistaken a meadow for a ploughed field one moonlit night, he might never have been arrested for murder. Even then, had he not, when talking to the police, chosen to describe his flock of female admirers as his 'harem', he might have dodged the gallows. These fatal errors are a potent reminder of the part luck can play in even the most cleverly contrived criminal schemes. The Rouse case is a multi-faceted classic involving controversial forensic pathology and deadly cross-examination. It has supplied plot material for novelists, and may even have been inspired by an ingenious work of fiction. To this day, the case remains newsworthy. For despite all the ink that has been spilt over Rouse and his antics, one extraordinary mystery endures.

Who was Rouse's victim?

*

Rouse was born in Herne Hill on 6th April 1894. His father was a hosier, but family difficulties led to his being raised mostly by his aunt. Educated at a local board school, he took a job in an estate agent's, and then spent five years working for a soft-furnishings firm. When war broke out, he enlisted, but before setting off for the Front, he married, as so many young soldiers facing an uncertain future did. He was twenty, his wife Lily three years older. Weeks after arriving in France, he was caught in a shell-burst, and severely wounded in the head, leg and thigh. A piece of shrapnel had lodged in his brain. After a slow and painful convalescence, he was no longer fit for active service.

Did the head injury cause Rouse to suffer from a personality disorder? He seemed to have made a good recovery, and became a commercial traveller, but he took advantage of long absences from home to embark on a career as a charming philanderer who reinvented himself as a product of Eton and Cambridge, and promoted himself to the rank of major. His interests included motor cars and women; even during his brief time in France, he had fathered a son. In 1920, a fourteen-year-old girl called Helen Campbell gave birth to his child, though the baby died in infancy. A young woman called Nellie Tucker, to whom he also promised marriage, bore him two more children, and by the autumn of 1930, he had made another teenage girl, Ivy Jenkins, pregnant. Helen too had become pregnant again, and Rouse went through a bigamous marriage ceremony with her on 1st November. The long-suffering Lily was, at this point, still standing by him, but even if he was hard-faced enough to cope with the emotional complications of all these entanglements, Rouse risked financial ruin. He earned about £500 a year, and could not afford to provide for all the women and children in his life.

He simply had to do something about it.

*

Two cousins, William Bailey and Alfred Thomas Brown, were walking home from a Guy Fawkes Night dance to their homes in Hardingstone, a village on the outskirts of Northampton, when two strange things happened at the same time. They saw a bright red glow in the distance, and spotted a man climbing out of a nearby ditch.

'What's the blaze?' Bailey asked his cousin.

The stranger volunteered an answer: 'It looks like someone is having a bonfire.'

With that, he walked away. The cousins noticed that he was out of breath, and not wearing a hat, although otherwise he was smartly dressed. They approached the blaze, and realised that a Morris Minor motor car was on fire. Running into Hardingstone, they spoke to Bailey's father, who happened to be the village constable, and soon the police were at the scene of the fire. The blaze was extinguished – but a charred body was seen inside the vehicle. Three officers who were present gave conflicting accounts of their first observations of the state of the corpse, and there was some confusion about its precise position inside the Morris Minor. They assumed the car's driver – apparently a man in his early thirties – had met his death in an accidental fire, and soon traced ownership of the vehicle to Rouse.

The newspapers made a good deal of the sensational story, and printed a description of Rouse. The police visited Lily Rouse at her home in Finchley to break the news. She was not allowed to see the burnt human remains, but was shown brace buckles and pieces of clothing that had been found in the car, and thought that they might belong to her husband.

But was Rouse really dead? The police soon received a tip-off that Rouse had been seen, setting off in a motor coach travelling from Cardiff to London. Two officers met him on arrival, and took him to the police station at Hammersmith.

Rouse admitted straight away that he owned the Morris Minor. He claimed that he had picked up a respectable-looking male hitchhiker on the Great North Road, but stopped at Hardingstone when the engine started to spit. He asked the hitchhiker to pour some petrol from a can into the tank, and as he walked away to relieve himself, the man said that he wanted a smoke. According to Rouse, the next thing he saw was the car going up in flames. He was the hatless man whom Bailey and Brown had seen.

> 'Three officers who were present gave conflicting accounts of their first observations of the state of the corpse'

His story was that he 'lost his head' when he spoke to them, and had been in a state of shock ever since. In fact, after the blaze he had been given a lift to London in a lorry and then headed by charabanc to Gellygaer, the isolated village in Monmouthshire where the ailing Ivy Jenkins was staying with her parents. Any hope he had of lying low for a while was dashed by the publicity in the press. The Jenkins family were bound to see reference to him – and to the fact that he was married to Lily – hence his hasty decision to return to London. An unconvincing story that he told a man who took him to Cardiff was passed on to a journalist, and resulted in the tip-off.

Rouse asked the police if he could see his wife, and in his next statement once again said too much, 'She is already too good for me … I am friendly with several women, but it is an expensive game … My harem takes me several places…but my wife doesn't ask questions now.' That memorable word *harem* found its way on to newspaper placards within twenty-four hours. Rouse's chances of securing a fair trial untainted by the prejudices of a disapproving jury were seriously damaged by the leak.

The police found it impossible to identify the dead man, but this did not save Rouse from being charged with murder. The legal process gave rise to extensive arguments about the admissibility of evidence, including testimony about Rouse's track record as a womaniser, but the prosecution rested on three central arguments. First, the fact that the car was burned deliberately, not by accident. Second, that the position of the corpse in the car was more consistent with murder than accidental death. Third, that Rouse's behaviour following the blaze was highly suspicious. In short, there was no single 'killer fact' that established his guilt, although the weight of circumstantial evidence suggested that he was a murderer. But could his guilt be proved beyond reasonable doubt?

The answer lay in a ruthless combination of cross-examination and forensic analysis.

*

Most of Rouse's misfortunes were self-inflicted, but he had no control over the choice of prosecution's leading counsel and principal forensic expert. Sir Norman Birkett KC faced the challenge of dismantling the defence claim that the death occurred by accident so effectively that the jury would be convinced that murder had been committed, and by the man in the dock. The way he rose to that challenge cemented his reputation as a brilliant advocate.

The highlight of the trial from a legal perspective is so striking that it remains to this day a textbook example of deadly questioning. The defence called as an expert witness an engineer and fire assessor who said he had 'very vast experience of fires in motor cars'. He contended, with some confidence, that a junction in the car's fuel line had become loose. Birkett opened his cross-examination with quiet ferocity:

Birkett: 'What is the coefficient of the expansion of brass?'

Rouse: 'I beg your pardon?'

Birkett: 'Did you not catch the question?'

Rouse: 'I did not quite hear you.'

Birkett: 'What is the coefficient of expansion of brass?'

Rouse: 'I am afraid I cannot answer that question off-hand.'

Birkett: 'If you do not know, say so. What is the coefficient of expansion of brass? What do I mean by the term?'

Rouse: 'You want to know what is the expansion of the metal under heat?'

Birkett: 'I asked you: what is the coefficient of the expansion of brass? Do you know what it means?'

Rouse: 'Put it that way, probably I do not.'

Birkett: 'You are an engineer?'

Rouse: 'I dare say I am.'

Birkett: 'Let me understand what you are. You are a doctor?'

Rouse: 'No.'

Birkett: 'You are a crime investigator?'

Rouse: 'No.'

Birkett: 'You are an amateur detective?'

Rouse: 'No.'

Birkett: 'But an engineer?'

Rouse: 'Yes.'

Birkett: 'What is the coefficient of the expansion of brass? You do not know?'

Rouse: 'No, not put that way.'

Discrediting the defence's expert was only half the battle for the prosecution. They had to produce forensic evidence strong enough to secure a conviction. The legendary pathologist Bernard Spilsbury was just the man for the job. He had examined the charred remains (although not *in situ*) and noted that fine particles of soot were present in the lungs, while a scrap of cloth trapped by the body smelled of petrol. The prosecution's expert on motor cars and fire suggested that the petrol union joint of the carburettor had been loosened deliberately, rather than by accident, and that someone had splashed petrol from a can which had then been ignited. Taken together, this evidence pointed to murder by the man on the spot – Rouse. The jury was suitably impressed, whereas Rouse performed poorly when giving evidence in his own defence. As ever, he was over-confident, and the bad taste left by his reference to his 'harem' lingered. His conviction marks, arguably, career highpoints for both Birkett and Spilsbury.

For present-day tastes, Birkett's dazzling cross-examination may be perceived as too close to bullying for comfort. Spilsbury's methods have come in for much more severe criticism, notably from the lawyer and author Andrew Rose:

> Spilsbury ... postulated firmly ... that the victim had either 'pitched or was thrown' across the front seats of the car, the obvious conclusion being that he had been first struck on the head by Rouse with murderous intent and then thrown into the car. Although his original report had not mentioned this possibility, and he had not referred to it in committal proceedings,

he added to his report before the trial started the statement that 'the door on the passenger side was open' when the fire started, an entirely new and deadly element, which now must be seen as an unwarranted embellishment, crushing Rouse's story that the car had caught fire while he was some distance away. Here is a typical Spilsbury answer in the trial, so very definite: 'both legs extended, but the right leg was not able to get the consequences of heat rigor because of the seats. The left was free to contract'.

Was the trial fair? Judged by modern standards, this is highly debatable. Yet despite the difficulty of proving Rouse's guilt, it is impossible to believe that he was not a murderer. Shortly before his execution at Bedford Jail on 10th March 1931, he confessed to the crime in a statement published by the *Daily Sketch*. Nor did his final letter to Helen Campbell and his young son contain any protestations of innocence. With masterly understatement, he admitted, 'I expect I have been the most to blame.'

*

Two German murders committed at roughly the same time bear a striking resemblance to the Rouse case. Twelve months before Rouse's crime, police were called to a blazing green Opel near Regensburg. The car seemed to have crashed and burst into flames, killing the occupant. The deceased appeared to be a businessman from Leipzig called Kurt Erich Tetzner, and his wife promptly claimed on his insurance.

> 'The car seemed to have crashed and burst into flames'

However, forensic analysis revealed that the dead man appeared to be older than Tetzner, and also that he could not have been alive at the time the fire broke out. Police surveillance caught Tetzner's wife making contact with him in Strasbourg, where he was living under the name of Stranelli. He was arrested, confessed to murdering an unidentified hitchhiker, and was hanged a few weeks after Rouse, whom the public prosecutor described as Tetzner's 'pupil'.

In the same year, a similar conspiracy unravelled, implicating a young manager of a furniture dealing business, Fritz Saffran, Ella Augustin, his secretary, and his clerk, whose name was Kipnick. It is not clear whether Rouse deliberately imitated Tetzner's scheme, or thought up his plan independently, but Saffran did take criminal inspiration from Tetzner. Having insured his own life, Saffran and Kipnick drove around the countryside hunting for a suitable victim. After one abortive kidnap, they shot a milkman and took his body to a warehouse. The body was incinerated, and Saffran fled to Berlin while his secretary identified the corpse as his before claiming on the insurance. But when he reached Hamburg, on his way to South America and freedom, he was recognised. Like Tetzner and Rouse, he told a string of lies to the police, but to no avail. He and Kipnick were sentenced to death.

*

Is it conceivable that Rouse (and even Tetzner and Saffran) drew upon a work of fiction when planning their murders? The possibility was mooted by Helena Normanton, in her introduction to the transcript of the Rouse case in the *Famous Trials* series. She pointed out that in January 1929, the *Evening Standard* published a spy story called *The W Plan* by Graham Seton (the pen-name of Lieutenant-Colonel Graham Seton-Hutchinson, a former soldier and prolific author) which shared some elements with the real life crimes. *The W Plan* was also published as a novel, with proofs read by D.H. Lawrence, of all people. Lawrence was not impressed, but Arthur Conan Doyle enjoyed the book, and so did *The Spectator*: a review in November 1929 said, 'The murder is so well described that we have an uncomfortable feeling that it really happened.' And a year later, it did.

Whatever the truth, there is no doubt that the real life 'blazing car' mysteries influenced several writers of fiction, including – improbably – Vladmir Nabokov, who seems to have borrowed elements from the Tetzner, Rouse and Saffran cases when writing *Despair*. *Voice of the Fire* (1996) by the comic book writer Alan Moore also draws on the Rouse murder.

Naturally, most of the fiction inspired by Rouse falls within the mystery genre and was written by practitioners of the traditional or 'Golden Age' mystery puzzle, before DNA analysis complicated life for murderers who wanted to cause confusion about the identities of their victims' corpses. The most famous example is Dorothy L. Sayers' short story, 'In the Teeth of the Evidence', in which Lord Peter Wimsey solves the case with the assistance of forensic dentistry. Milward Kennedy's 'The Case of the Index Finger' offers a pleasing post-war variation on the Rouse ploy, as does Agatha Christie's *The Body in the Library*, published in 1942. Among other novels, Francis Everton's *The Young Vanish*, Alan Brock's *Earth to Ashes* and J.J. Connington's *The Four Defences* are nowadays little-known, but their ingenuity justifies the difficulty (if not perhaps, when it comes to first editions, the cost) of seeking them out.

*

Finally, what of the victim? At the time of writing, we still do not know who he was, but the search continues. In the 1950s, the family of William Briggs, a factory worker who had left his home in London to attend a doctor's appointment and was never seen again, became convinced that his path might have crossed with Rouse's, and asked the Northamptonshire Police to investigate. Nothing came of this, but with the advent of DNA technology, forensic scientists from the University of Leicester were given access to a tissue sample taken by Spilsbury from the remains of the charred body, and preserved – in uncontaminated form – on a microscope slide.

The scientific investigation was accompanied by a fanfare of publicity in the press and on television. To the natural disappointment of Briggs' descendants, however, the unequivocal conclusion reached was that Briggs was not Rouse's victim. However, the news of this forensic detective work led to more families coming forward to see if the dead man was a relative of theirs. In October 2014, scientists announced that they had whittled fifteen approaches down to 'nine strong leads', leading to fresh hope of a solution to the puzzle. At the time of writing, however, the identity of the dead man in the car remains a mystery.

*

Rouse was an unlucky murderer. If he had remained in the ditch a little longer, or had headed in a different direction, across an adjoining field, he would not have been spotted by the two cousins, and might have made good his escape. But he mistook the meadow for a ploughed field, and was afraid of leaving footprints.

He was unlucky, too, in finding his incautious use of the word 'harem' splashed across the press. But to a large extent, Rouse made his own bad luck; he was too vain and careless to be able to keep his mouth shut when in a tight corner. The gift of the gab that helped him to seduce vulnerable women was a calamitous weakness when he tried to answer questions from unsympathetic detectives, or from Birkett.

'he was too vain and careless to be able to keep his mouth shut when in a tight corner'

In any event, his misfortunes are nothing in comparison to those of his innocent victim. The dead man, perhaps one of those 'passing tramps' who often feature as suspects in Golden Age detective novels, but never turn out to be guilty, lost his life simply because he happened to meet someone who was desperate, selfish, and cruel enough to kill in order to make a new life for himself.

And in death, he has for more than eight decades suffered the enduring indignity of not even being known by his own name.

JÜRGEN EHLERS

Jürgen was born in 1948, and has
written numerous short stories. For his
'Weltspartag in Hamminkeln' ('World Savings
Day in Hamminkeln') he was awarded the
prestigious Friedrich Glauser Prize in 2005.
More recently he has specialised in writing
historical crime novels, the latest of
which, 'Ein ganz gewöhnlicher Mord' (2014),
is set in Germany and Poland of 1939. Jürgen
Ehlers is a member of the 'Syndikat' and
the Crime Writers' Association. He lives
with his family in Witzeeze, near Hamburg.

www.juergen-ehlers.com/en

THE GIRL FROM THE DÜSSEL

JÜRGEN EHLERS

Translated by Ann-Kathrin Ehlers

A murderer is haunting Düsseldorf. On 21st August 1929, he stabs three people at the fair in Lierenfeld. On 24th August, he kills two children in Flehe. On 25th August, he assaults the twenty-six-year-old Gertrud Schulte in the Rhine Meadows and leaves her critically injured. The Mordkommission is working flat out, but so far they have no leads to potential suspects.

Was that a scream? Anton Mattes wakes with a start. Yes, that was definitely a scream. He fumbles for the matches on the chair next to his bed that serves him as a bedside table. He strikes a match and lights the candle. The room is bathed in the dim glow of the single flame. There is no electricity out here in the allotment gardens. A woman screamed. He is quite sure.

'I'm coming!' a man close by shouts. That's Schischek, his neighbour. 'Does anybody need help? I'm coming!'

Mattes dives into yesterday's clothes and scrambles out of his hut. Schischek is standing by the fence. Torch in hand, his German Shepherd by his side. 'Did you hear that, too?' he asks.

'That was a cry for help,' Mattes confirms.

'Does anybody need help?' Schischek cries again. Then he beckons to Mattes. 'Come, let's check.'

The area belonging to the allotment society 'Am Ostpark' lies directly on the River Düssel. As the two men exit the gardens, they see a figure running.

'Stop!' Schischek bellows. 'Stay where you are!'

The stranger keeps on running. Mattes wonders whether Schischek should set the dog on him. But Schischek is afraid his dog could bite a harmless night-time wanderer.

And where is the woman who screamed? The two men listen into the dark. But all they can hear is the dog panting.

'Where are you?' Schischek calls. Nobody answers. And all of a sudden, Mattes senses that whoever just screamed is now dead. He thinks of the assaults that happened over the last couple of weeks. The dog is tugging on the lead. Any minute, we'll find a dead woman, thinks Mattes. Any minute now.

The dog drags them to a stretch of lawn along the Düssel. Schischek shines his torch all over the area, but they can't see anything unusual. The dog takes them down to the stream and then turns back. Schischek directs the beam of his torch into the Düssel. Nothing. A stream with slow-flowing water.

'Go on!' Schischek urges.

But his dog refuses. Instead, the dog pulls on the lead, taking them back to the area they have already searched. Once again the old man shines his torch everywhere. He even looks under the adjacent bushes. But there is nothing.

'I think,' says Mattes, 'we should call the police.'

*

The police arrive at ten past four in the morning. The *Überfallkommando Nord* combs the entire area, all the way down to the Ostpark sports ground. They have brought powerful searchlights. But they, too, are unsuccessful. The operation is called off at 5.20 a.m. without result.

As it turns light, Mattes and his neighbour set out once again to look for clues. On the bank of the Düssel, they meet a young man, who also seems to be searching the area. His name is Paul Grunwald. As it turns out, the woman whom Mattes and Schischek had heard scream in the night had fled into Grunwald's house on Dreherstraße. According to her, a man had assaulted her, strangled her and finally thrown her into the Düssel. She is now on her way to report the incident to the police.

'The mass murderer of Düsseldorf,' Mattes muses.

Grunwald nods.

'Why didn't she go to the police immediately?'

'She couldn't,' says Grunwald. 'She had fallen into the stream. Her clothes were soaked. I had to hang everything up to dry first.'

Mattes shows Grunwald the place where the woman probably fell into the Düssel. There is no trace of the incident. If the grass was trampled, it has righted itself again since.

'You haven't found a small suitcase, have you?' Grunwald asks.

Mattes shakes his head.

'She told me she lost her suitcase in the tussle. It's probably somewhere in the Düssel then.'

Together, the men search the bank of the stream. They continue all the way down to Grafenberger Allee, but the suitcase remains lost.

*

The *Kriminalpolizei* have finished questioning the young woman. 'You should go home now and rest, Fräulein Heerstrass,' says Wilhelm Berger. 'We will do everything in our power to track down that fellow.' Berger is the youngest of the three policemen.

'More questions may, of course, come up,' Kosinski adds. 'We'll call on you then.'

'Yes, yes certainly.' She gives a shy smile, then leaves.

The three investigators look at each other. 'Another survivor. And another detailed description of the offender,' Berger finally says. 'If our murderer continues like this, we'll catch him pretty quickly.'

'You think so?' Kosinski asks.

'You don't?' Berger is surprised.

'I'm dubious about everything,' Kosinski declares. 'First of all, I doubt this is the same offender. The assaults at the fair in Lierenfeld were committed with a knife. He slaughtered the two children in Lehe, again with a knife. And Gertrud Schulte, our best witness to date, was also attacked with a knife. So brutally, as you know, that the blade broke off and remained stuck between two vertebrae. But this Karoline Heerstrass was just strangled a little and then pushed into the stream before the offender ran away. This behaviour doesn't match the other assaults at all!'

'He heard the men calling from the allotment gardens,' Berger points out.

'The description of the offender is wrong. She said the man was much older. Forty-five instead of thirty! I doubt this woman has told the truth about anything.'

Wilhelm Berger shakes his head. 'You think she lied to us? This – this naive, harmless child?'

'Child? Karoline Heerstrass is twenty-eight years old! Old enough, I should think, to have learned how to lie.'

*

Three days later. Berger and Kosinski are about to leave, when Fuhrmann enters with a piece of paper. He places it on the table for his colleagues to see. 'Here. This is what Fräulein Heerstrass' boyfriend writes about her.'

I met Fräulein Heerstrass last winter. We have met up from time to time since – our most recent meeting was two days ago. On this occasion, Fräulein Heerstrass told me that she was assaulted and strangled. I had to smile. Upon which she accused me of not believing anything she says anyway.

Fräulein Heerstrass is not entirely wrong there. Over the course of our acquaintance, she has indeed told me a number of things that were not true. Most of these tales were about her. For example, she once told me that she worked as an assistant in a pharmacy. When I called the place, no one there had ever heard of Fräulein Heerstrass. On another occasion, Fräulein Heerstrass told me that she had come into an inheritance. She claimed that she was inheriting from her deceased groom.

Anyway, I had the feeling that her stories were not always true. I attribute Fräulein Heerstrass' tendency to a hysterical character trait that might have been caused by the fact that she has remained unmarried – probably due to her physical appearance (crooked legs). Since I know Fräulein Heerstrass well, I would advise you to be prudent when evaluating her statements.

'Arsehole!' Berger is outraged.

Kosinski chuckles.

*

Three days later, Fräulein Heerstrass has been summoned to another police interview. Berger had to leave for a hearing in Neuss. Kosinski and Fuhrmann are alone with her.

'Pharmacist's assistant! Why this fib?' asks Fuhrmann.

Karoline Heerstrass blushes. 'What does that have to do with the assault?'

Fuhrmann notes that she is nervous. Good. 'Please just answer my question,' he tells her calmly.

'I don't know,' says Karoline. 'I don't know why I said that.' They had fooled around. That was when Adolf Lange and she had only just met. He had claimed to be the manager at a large business in Neuss. Upon which she had claimed to be a pharmacist's assistant. How should she have known that he really was a manager? But she was deeply offended that he had told the *Kriminalpolizei* about this incident.

'Your statement regarding the assault on the bank of the Düssel – could it be that you again did not entirely stick to the truth?'

Karoline Heerstrass shakes her head indignantly.

'Nobody is reproaching you,' Fuhrmann assures her. 'We simply want to get to the bottom of that night's events.'

And Kosinski adds, 'Perhaps it would be easiest if you told us again in detail what happened that day.'

His request sounds innocent enough, but Karoline Heerstrass does not trust this man. She does not trust either of them. Kosinski is a mean, sinister character and Fuhrmann a perfidious sycophant. She would love to tell them so, but then all would be lost. Why is that other man, Berger, not here? But she can't choose her favourite policemen to interview her. So she begins, once more, to recount that day's events.

'On Saturday, I …'

'On 31st August 1929, you mean?'

'Yes. On that day I had taken the tram from Neuss to Düsseldorf to go shopping. Shortly before seven o'clock in the evening, I left the department store Tietz and made my way back to the station. And on Oststraße, between Bismarck- and Kaiser-Wilhelm-Straße, this man approached me.'

'This Karl Bergheim?'

'Yes.'

'This is a key point. You told us before that this Karl Bergheim works for the city's gas, water and electricity works ...'

'That's what he said anyway.'

'But they don't know a Karl Bergheim there. Just a Johann Berghahn. But this Berghahn does not fit your description at all.'

'Then the man lied to me,' Karoline Heerstrass notes.

Fuhrmann nods. 'That is why we are questioning you again. We want to find out who lied, when and where. So, let's get to the interesting part of your story. The part where you spent time with the alleged Karl Bergheim. You met Bergheim at around eight o'clock in the evening and stayed with him until after midnight ...'

'Yes. But I already told you that last time. We went to the *Hofgarten* at around 9.30 p.m. and talked roughly until midnight.'

'You talked? May I ask what about?'

'This and that.'

'Also about love?'

She nods.

'And this Bergheim, did he – touch you?'

'Yes. Over the course of the conversation we got a little closer. Bergheim put his arm around me, and he kissed me on the cheek.'

'And – this is important now, just to avoid misunderstandings – did you object to this contact and the kiss?'

'Yes. I mean, no. I did not object to the kiss on the cheek, but he also wanted to kiss me on the mouth, and he wanted me to sit on his lap, and I refused.'

Fuhrmann smiles. 'Fräulein Heerstrass, you don't need to lie. We are all grown-ups here. And nobody judges you for kissing a man or for sitting on his lap. Or, indeed, for letting him slip his hand under your skirt.'

'I didn't allow anything of the sort!'

'We understand these things. We also know, of course, that you may have a greater need for affection than the average girl due to your disability ...'

'What do you mean?' Karoline Heerstrass demands, outraged. Kosinski sneers.

'I mean your deformity,' Fuhrmann says. 'I mean your crooked legs. Your crooked, rickety legs.'

'My legs are not crooked.' Karoline sobs.

'Your acquaintance, Herr Lange, is of a different opinion,' Fuhrmann continues unperturbed. 'And he – unlike us – has probably had the chance to see your legs in detail.'

Karoline Heerstrass is crying. She is no longer able to reply.

Kosinski digs deeper. 'And now the crucial part: when you wanted to return to Neuss, the mischievous Herr Bergheim simply pulled out your hairpins, ruining your hairstyle, and by the time you had fixed the damage, the last tram had left. To keep things simple, I'll assume this is what happened. But what follows, Fräulein Heerstrass, is essential, and I'm sure you didn't tell the truth the first time we asked. He suggested you spend the night at his flat on Dreherstraße.'

Karoline is incapable of contradicting the man. She simply shakes her head, desperate.

'On the way to his flat, you had sexual intercourse in the park. Consensual sexual intercourse. And after Herr Bergheim got what he wanted, he simply made off. And when you realised what had just happened, you made up this story out of anger and desperation and jumped into the Düssel – and it's no mean feat to get wet from head to toe in that shallow ditch. And then you didn't wait for someone to come to your aid, but went to Dreherstraße in the hope of meeting your lover again. Am I right?'

'No, no, no!'

'Instead, you met the nice man who put you up for the night. And since he insisted that you go to the police the following morning, you had no choice but to stick to your story.'

'No,' breathes Karoline.

Fuhrmann sighs. He gives the young woman a serious look. 'Dear Fräulein Heerstrass, I know you screwed things up ...'

Kosinski can't suppress a grunting chuckle. Fuhrmann glares at him and continues.

'... you screwed things up, but there is a way out. If you continue to makes false statements, everything will just get worse. Good Lord, we only want to help you! That's what we policemen are for, to help people in need.'

When Berger returns from Neuss, his two colleagues are highly satisfied. 'We cleared up the Karoline Heerstrass business,' Fuhrmann tells Berger. 'It was as we had suspected: a big, fat lie from start to finish. The prosecution is now dealing with it.'

*

The report to the prosecution finally results in the following penalty order:

> By feigning an assault on her, Karoline Heerstrass has displayed gross disorderly conduct. As per paragraph 360, subparagraph 11 of the Reichsstrafgesetzbuch, we find her guilty of the offence. Thanks to her own statements, we have ascertained that she has cunningly invented the assault and knowingly made a false complaint. She caused the Überfallkommando to start a pointless search and the Kriminalpolizei to investigate her case over a course of roughly six weeks. The behaviour of Fräulein Heerstrass is also reprehensible, because she has caused innocent people to come under suspicion.
>
> We sentence her to a term of imprisonment of three weeks. In addition, she will need to pay for the cost of the proceedings.

*

At first, Wilhelm Berger sees no reason to reopen the Heerstrass case. Only when Peter Kürten, the 'Vampire of Düsseldorf', is arrested in spring 1930, does he takes another look at the old files and statements.

Kürten has given a full confession, but he also admitted a murder he could not have committed. On the other hand, he left out many details. Details that could be important. Peter Kürten verifiably killed nine people and one swan. He will be sentenced to death, that's for sure.

And this alleged assault on Karoline Heerstrass – could that have been him, too? Yes. It is possible. The description the young woman had given of her attacker was accurate – in contrast to the statements of other witnesses. Peter Kürten is forty-six years old. Wilhelm Berger senses that his colleagues Fuhrmann and Kosinski bullied the woman into her confession. But he cannot prove it. And the two of them would never admit it. Berger has one last chance to solve the case.

*

'Fräulein Heerstrass, I invited you here to verify a few points that are still unclear.'

'What's left to clarify?' Karoline Heerstrass looks sad. She thinks, if Berger had interviewed her, she would never have made that stupid confession. But now? What could he do now?

'Come with me,' Berger says. 'It won't take long.' He leads the young woman down the corridor to his boss' office. Berger knocks. Then he opens the door.

The secretary shakes her head. 'Herr Berger, you can't go in there now. The *Kriminalrat* is just interviewing Peter Kürten …'

Berger continues, undeterred. He flings open the door and pushes Karoline Heerstrass into the room. The *Kriminalrat* looks up indignantly. 'Didn't I give my secretary clear instructions to …'

The man sitting in the chair opposite laughs. 'That's my girl from the Düssel,' says Peter Kürten.

KATE ELLIS

Kate was born and brought up in Liverpool and studied drama in Manchester. She is married with two grown-up sons and she first enjoyed literary success as winner of the 1990 North West Playwrights' Competition in Manchester. Her books reflect her keen interest in history and archaeology and, as well as many short stories, she has published four crime novels set in York and a stand-alone historical crime novel, 'The Devil's Priest'. However, she is best known for her crime series featuring black archaeology graduate DI Wesley Peterson, the latest of which is 'The Death Season'.

www.kateellis.co.uk

THE AIGBURTH MYSTERY

KATE ELLIS

In August 1889 Alfred John Reynolds, known as the Tussaud of the provinces and owner of a well-known waxworks in Lime Street, Liverpool, took a sketchbook into the handsome courtroom of nearby St George's Hall and proceeded to draw the woman standing in the dock.

Reynolds was forced to resort to his sketchbook because the alleged murderess's formidable mother, the Baroness von Roques, had bought up all existing photographic likenesses of her daughter before the trial. However, with the aid of his artistic endeavours, he was able to construct a lifelike waxwork of the accused to exhibit in his 'Criminal Chamber' for the entertainment of Liverpool's prurient citizens. The accused woman's distressed relatives offered Reynolds money to remove it from the exhibition, where it stood alongside the most notorious murderers of the day, but the wily proprietor refused. Florence Elizabeth Maybrick (née Chandler) was good for business.

When I was growing up in south Liverpool, I was aware of two infamous murders with a local connection. The first was the murder of Julia Wallace in which the accused's alibi hinged on the accuracy of an address very close to my home. The second was the case of Florence Maybrick who allegedly poisoned her husband in her grand home, Battlecrease House, Aigburth, which stood very near the house where my father was brought up and a stone's throw from my school. This second case was also said to have inspired a novel by one of my favourite authors, *Strong Poison* by Dorothy L. Sayers, so it has fascinated me for a long time.

The annals of Victorian crime are littered with women poisoners, ridding themselves of unwanted husbands and inconvenient family members by means of a sly dose of arsenic – it was widely known as 'the inheritor's powder' for good reason. On the face of it, the case of Florence Maybrick, who stood accused of murdering her husband, James, after taking a lover and enduring the breakdown of her marriage, was just another such tale of human wickedness. And yet, on closer examination of the facts, the case becomes more interesting, and more controversial.

The alleged victim, James Maybrick, was born in Liverpool in 1838. He was a successful and well-respected cotton broker who travelled regularly to the United States on business, particularly to Norfolk, Virginia where his company had a branch office. During his time in Virginia, James contracted malaria, an illness that had reached epidemic proportions during the American Civil War, and he was treated with Fowler's Medicine, a concoction that contained the arsenic and strychnine he would be addicted to for the remainder of his life.

On his journey back to Liverpool aboard the SS *Baltic*, James encountered eighteen-year-old Florence Chandler. Florence was a well-connected 'southern belle' from Mobile, Alabama and she was travelling to Europe with her mother, the Baroness Caroline von Roques, when she met James, who was twenty-four years her senior. The couple are said to have met in the ship's bar and by the time they disembarked eight days later, they were engaged to be married, much to the shock of their fellow passengers. It seemed that Florence, by all accounts a headstrong, impulsive girl, had convinced herself that she had fallen in love with this successful, middle-aged English cotton merchant. But some years later she was to find out that he was harbouring some rather unsavoury secrets behind that respectable façade.

The marriage took place in London in 1881 and for a while Florence and James divided their time between Liverpool and Virginia before settling permanently in Aigburth, a pleasant, leafy suburb not far from the River Mersey. There were two children, James Chandler (known as Bobo) and Gladys Evelyn, and the family eventually moved into

Battlecrease House, a grand three-storey, twenty-room mansion. With the prosperous lifestyle came a team of servants but, because of Florence's upbringing – she had travelled extensively with her three-times-married mother – she had no idea how to run a large household. Her unpopularity with her servants was later to work against her. She also found household finances a challenge and she soon built up debts, living in fear of her husband finding out how much she owed. In addition, James's cotton broking business wasn't doing well and Florence's inability to cut back on household expenses must have irritated the man who was so anxious to present a prosperous mask to the world. Florence confided to her mother that she would gladly give up the house and move somewhere else but that her husband told her 'it would be the ruin of him as one had to keep up appearances'.

These financial troubles, however, didn't prevent the Maybricks enjoying Liverpool's rich social scene, attending all the most important balls, functions and race meetings. To Liverpool society, they appeared, on the surface, to be a happy, successful couple.

However, in 1887 Florence made the distressing discovery that her husband had a number of mistresses, one of whom had borne him five children. In addition, James's drug addiction was beginning to affect his behaviour. Florence shared her worries with the family doctor, Dr Hopper of Rodney Street, telling him how her husband regularly took arsenic in a tonic and in beef tea, as well as consuming preparations containing strychnine. Dr Hopper warned Maybrick about the dangers of such an addiction, but without success.

Florence's unhappiness increased and, on learning of her husband's prodigious infidelity, she refused to sleep with him, seeking solace in the arms of Alfred Brierley, a local businessman and family friend. In March 1889, Florence and Brierley spent a weekend together at a London hotel. On her return to Liverpool, Florence attended the Grand National at Aintree racecourse with her husband but when she met Brierley at Aintree and walked up the course with him, James was furious. The Maybricks returned home separately and back at

Battlecrease House a violent quarrel ensued in which James Maybrick struck his wife. At Florence's trial, the Maybricks' nanny, Alice Yapp, testified that she overheard James telling Florence that 'this scandal will be all over town tomorrow'.

Florence once more consulted Dr Hopper, who noticed her bruises. When she confided that she wanted a divorce, the doctor made an effort to reconcile the couple and for a while it seemed he succeeded, as James agreed to pay Florence's debts.

A few weeks later on Monday, 23rd April, Florence purchased a dozen flypapers from local chemists and soaked them in a bowl, claiming that she was making a skin preparation. On Saturday 27th, James attended Wirral Races, travelling there on horseback in spite of feeling unwell. He told a friend's wife that he'd taken a double dose of strychnine that morning, having obtained the medicine in the post from London the day before. He wrote to his brother, Michael, 'I have been very seedy indeed. I found my legs getting stiff and useless but by sheer strength of will shook off the feeling and went down on horseback to Wirral races.'

When he returned home he complained that he was feeling sick and Dr Humphreys, the children's doctor, visited, diagnosing chronic dyspepsia and putting the patient on a strict diet. James seemed to recover but by the following Friday he relapsed, complaining of pains in his legs and vomiting. Although Florence had told the family physician, Dr Hopper, about her husband's drug taking, it is highly likely that these other doctors who were later called in knew nothing about it. One of them admitted at the trial that he wouldn't have considered the possibility of arsenic poisoning if James's brother, Michael, had not suggested it.

James's other brother, Edwin, was staying in the house at the time. It has been said that Florence and Edwin were lovers but, whatever the truth of this, he was sufficiently suspicious of James's symptoms to demand a second opinion. A Dr Carter was called in but he agreed with the first diagnosis. James Maybrick was suffering from acute dyspepsia and only diet would cure him.

When James's condition worsened again he was visited by a Mrs Briggs, a family friend who was told about the soaking flypapers by the nanny, Alice Yapp, who disliked Florence intensely. No doubt the mention of flypapers aroused the worst suspicions of those two women who resented James Maybrick's flirtatious and extravagant American wife. In fact Alice Yapp, on finding them, stated that 'the mistress is poisoning the master'. Just five years earlier in 1884 two Liverpool women, Mrs Flannigan and Mrs Higgins, had been convicted of murdering three people using arsenic obtained from soaked flypapers. The local case would, no doubt, have been fresh in Yapp's and Briggs's minds.

As a consequence of her new discovery Mrs Briggs sent a telegram to James's brother, Michael, who lived in London, saying, 'Come at once. Strange things going on here.' She also instructed Florence to send for a trained nurse. Florence immediately sent for a nurse from Halewood who had cared for members of the family before and, she claimed, James knew and liked.

The nurse arrived at 2 p.m. and at 3 p.m. Florence gave Alice Yapp a letter to post. The nanny was later to tell the court that she was going to the postbox with the Maybricks' daughter, Gladys, when the child dropped the letter into a puddle. Yapp claimed that she had to take the letter out of the damp envelope and that is why she read it. It seems an unlikely story, particularly as she was known to hate Florence, but after reading the content of the letter, she discovered that it was to Florence's lover, Albert Brierley. The letter is rather interesting. Florence wrote to her lover:

Dearest, Since my return I have been nursing M day and night. He is sick unto death. The doctors held a consultation yesterday and now all depends on how long his strength will hold out. Both my brothers in law are here and we are terribly anxious. I cannot answer your letter fully today, my darling, but relieve your mind of all fear of discovery now and in the future. M has been delirious since Sunday and I know that he is perfectly ignorant of everything, even of the name of the street, and also that he has not been making any inquiries whatsoever. The tale he told me was a pure fabrication and only intended to frighten the truth out of me. In fact he believes my statement although he will not admit it. You need not, therefore, go abroad on that account, dearest, but in any case please don't leave England until I have seen you once again…If you wish to write to me about anything do so now, as all letters pass through my hands at present. [A Victorian man would usually read any mail that arrived in his house.] *Excuse this scrawl, my darling, but I dare not leave the room for a moment and I do not know when I shall be able to write to you again. In haste, yours ever, Florie.*

Yapp, no doubt pleased with her juicy discovery, passed this letter to Edwin Maybrick, who showed it to his brother, Michael, as soon as he arrived at the house. Incidentally Mrs Briggs and Alice Yapp were described by Charles Ratcliffe, a friend of the Maybrick family, as 'the female serpents'.

Michael immediately took charge and tried to bar Florence from the sick room. However, she did manage to visit her sick husband from time to time. Part of the case against her was that she added arsenic to a bottle of meat juice, intended as a tonic for the invalid. Florence was later to claim that James begged her to add a little of the 'medicine' that his addiction made him crave and there was never any suggestion that he actually consumed it. As James's condition worsened, samples of his urine and faeces were taken to be analysed for arsenic but none was found.

James Maybrick died on 11th of May 1889, after prescriptions of Valentine's meat juice, Du Barry's Revalenta Arabica invalid food, sulphonal, nitroglycerine, cocaine, phosphoric acid and Fowler's solution of arsenic failed to restore him to health. On the night before his death Michael and the servants conducted a thorough search of the house, looking for evidence that might incriminate Florence. Inside Florence's trunk they found a chocolate box containing a package labelled 'Arsenic. Poison for Cats' along with bottles of white fluid and a parcel containing yellow powder. In addition a great quantity of poison was found around the house: 139 jars and bottles, some purchased from chemists and others prescribed by twenty-nine different doctors. Twenty-six more bottles were found in his office, some of which contained a 'pick me up' containing arsenic which was bought by James himself from the chemist Edwin Garnett-Heaton of Exchange Street East in the city centre, who was to give evidence at Florence's trial. I should add that arsenic and strychnine were common in most Victorian houses, not only used for domestic purposes but also in tonics, medicines and beauty treatments. The Victorians had what we would consider today to be a very casual attitude to these lethal substances and treated them as we would treat common painkillers and health supplements.

As a result of these discoveries Michael placed his sister-in-law under house arrest. It seemed that nobody else in the house came under suspicion, nor did Michael feel the need to call in the police until his brother, James, was actually dead. Reading through various accounts of the case and transcripts of the trial, it is hard not to come to the conclusion that Michael, along with the servants and Mrs Briggs, felt that Florence needed to be punished for transgressing the moral code of the day. While it was considered perfectly acceptable for James to have a string of affairs and to keep a mistress, Florence's dalliance with Albert Brierley was deemed worthy of suspicion and punishment. This attitude to her 'sins' certainly came to light when she stood trial.

Michael Maybrick himself is an interesting character. Using the name Stephen Adams, he was a famed baritone and a noted composer of the day, his success almost rivalling that of Sir Arthur Sullivan. His most famous composition was 'The Holy City'. At the time of his brother James's death, he lived in London but he was later to move to the Isle of Wight where he was to become a prominent citizen; five times Mayor of Ryde and, amongst other illustrious posts, chairman of the Royal Isle of Wight County Hospital, president of the Ryde Philharmonic Society and the Cricket Club. He died in 1913 and is described in his obituary in the *Isle of Wight County Press* as having 'a vigorous personality.' The obituary also goes on to say, 'In considering the world wide delight which "Stephen Adams" gave by his inspired music, one cannot but be struck by the absence of any recognition for his work on the part of the government, especially when one recalls the recent, rather lavish, distribution of honours, in many cases to local party politicians, which are fresh in the minds of the islanders.' Perhaps it was Michael's links with the notorious Maybrick case that prevented these, no doubt deserved, honours coming his way. We can only speculate.

Michael's 'vigorous personality' was certainly at the fore at the time of James Maybrick's death, especially regarding the strange case of James's will. In December 1888, Florence wrote to her mother to say that James had destroyed his will (made in her favour) and was threatening to write a new one. It seems that it took him four months to do so. On the evening of 10th May 1889, as James lay dying, Michael pressed him to sign papers (which Alice Yapp said was a will). James was heard calling, 'Oh Lord, if I am to die why am I being worried like this? Let me die properly.' Under the terms of a will dated 25th April 1889, James leaves his entire estate in trust for his two children, leaving Florence only the interest on an insurance policy amounting to around £125 per annum to live on, providing she resides with the children. All she possessed, her entire life, would be under the complete control of Michael and another Maybrick brother, Thomas. It is not certain

> 'Oh Lord, if I am to die why am I being worried like this? Let me die properly.'

whether the papers Yapp claims Michael was trying to make James sign was yet another will but if it was, it was never produced and the one dated 25th April was the one found at Somerset House. During the trial the newspapers referred to a 'curious will' and Michael refused to produce it at the inquest.

In some ways the unfavourable will tips the balance in Florence's favour. It gave her very little financial motive to kill James. She would have been far better with him alive and legally separated. There was always the possibility, of course, that the forceful and charismatic

Michael might have persuaded James to divorce her for her infidelity, in which case, she would have been ruined and left with nothing. However, there is no suggestion that this was James's intention at the time of his death.

A post-mortem on James's body was held on Monday, 13th May and Florence was arrested the following day while, just five days after James's death, the Maybrick brothers cleared out the entire contents of Battlecrease House and put it up for auction. The children were put into the care of a Dr and Mrs Fuller.

The first post-mortem on James's body proved inconclusive and the funeral went ahead but when the inquest was re-opened on 27th of May, there was an upsurge of interest in the case. From the beginning Michael Maybrick and the servants told the jury about Florence's hatred for her husband, leading to a great deal of attention from the press. This was to lead to the exhumation of the body on the 30th of May and a new toxic analysis of the organs found half a grain of arsenic in the spleen but none in the heart, lungs or stomach. Strychnine, hyoscine, morphine and prussic acid were also found, but these had all been in the medicines James was taking. The 'Aigburth Mystery' was now making the newspaper headlines and when Florence appeared at the inquest again on 5th June she was hissed at by women in the crowd. Again, it seemed that Florence's morals were on trial.

Although the quantity of arsenic found in James's body was not enough to kill, the inquest jury took only half an hour to reach a verdict of murder and name Florence as the culprit. She appeared before the magistrates on the 13th of June, hearing again the testimonies of her servants and brother-in-law. The only piece of evidence against her seemed to be her affair with Albert Brierley but, in spite of this, she was held in Walton jail until her trial at the next Assizes. As she left the court she was again hissed at by women in the public gallery and given a hostile reception by waiting crowds. It seemed that public hysteria was taking over and one shop even displayed a picture of Florence and Brierley together at the Grand National in its window.

On 31st of July Florence's trial began at St George's Hall. Liverpool society fought for tickets and ladies were dressed as if for the theatre, many of them carrying opera glasses. The Earl of Sefton occupied a seat on the bench and many of Liverpool's notable citizens sat in the audience. Florence expressed a hope that the trial would be held in London where she would have a more impartial hearing, but 'owing to a lack of funds' her wish was not granted.

Fortunately Florence's mother hired a barrister who sincerely believed in her innocence. He was Sir Charles Russell, one of the foremost advocates of the day, who called witnesses to testify to James's drug habit and emphasised the failure of the medical evidence to prove beyond reasonable doubt that James did indeed die of an arsenic overdose that was not self-administered. Today, the case would no doubt have been dismissed but the Judge, Mr Justice Stephen, had other ideas.

'Not only did hostile publicity prejudice the trial but the Judge's summing up was, frankly, damning.'

From the start the press had taken a huge interest in the case and at first Florence was regarded as an evil murderess. However, as the trial proceeded and the evidence was heard, opinion began to turn to Florence's advantage. But, in spite of this, inside that courtroom in St George's Hall, things didn't go well for her.

Florence was extremely unfortunate in the man who sat in judgement on her. Not only did hostile publicity prejudice the trial but the Judge's summing up was, frankly, damning. The jury had to sit through hours of varied medical evidence but it was the details of Florence's private life that must have stuck in their minds, along with the words of Mr Justice Stephen. He addressed the jury at the start of the trial with these words:

> I hardly know how to put it otherwise than this: that if a woman does carry on
> an adulterous intrigue with another man, it may supply every sort of motive…
> It certainly may quite supply – I won't go further – a very strong motive why
> she should wish to get rid of her husband.

Hardly a balanced view and an inauspicious start for the defendant.

Stephen was nearing the end of his career on the bench and had already suffered a stroke, which appeared to have impaired his judgement. He was said to have smoked opium regularly and two years after Florence's trial he was declared insane and admitted to an asylum. Although Stephen's two-day long summing up began fairly enough, it soon descended into a vitriolic attack on Florence's morals. He argued for the prosecution and slated the defence, referring to Florence as 'a horrible woman', and said:

> For a person to go on deliberately administering poison to a poor, helpless, sick
> man upon whom she had already inflicted a dreadful injury, an injury fateful
> to married life, the person who could do such a thing as that must indeed be
> destitute of the least trace of human feeling…

In other words, her infidelity with Albert Brierley automatically made her a callous murderess. It took just thirty-eight minutes for the jury to find her guilty.

Stephen, raised by a father who believed that life was a duty rather than a pleasure, was well known for his puritanical views and his dislike of women and he often used his court as a platform for his strict moral opinions. And it was his prejudice against Florence that resulted in her being found guilty of James Maybrick's murder and being condemned to death, the first American woman to be convicted of murder in a British court.

Public opinion, so keen to condemn Florence before her trial, now swung in her favour. The Liverpool crowd who had hissed her at the start of the trial now hissed the Judge instead as he drove away.

In spite of the obvious unfairness of Stephen's behaviour in the court, there was no appeal system so Florence had no recourse to legal means to save her life. However, widespread support for her cause came from both sides of the Atlantic, including a petition in Manchester signed by a number of magistrates and solicitors and requests for the US Government to intervene. Finally Henry Matthews, the Home Secretary, concluded that there was reasonable doubt that the arsenic Florence gave James was actually the cause of death. This was far from an acknowledgement of her innocence but it was enough to get the sentence commuted to life imprisonment three days before Florence was due to hang.

She was to spend fifteen years in prison, during which time there were numerous appeals, none of which met with any success. One of the reasons for this was probably Queen Victoria herself, who made it clear that she considered Florence to be guilty and insisted that the life sentence should never be overturned. After the death of Prince Albert in 1861, the Queen had shown little sympathy with women who failed to be faithful to their wedding vows and wrote to the Home Secretary that she regretted that such a wicked woman could escape on a legal quibble and that her sentence should never further be commuted. Successive Home Secretaries, knowing the Queen's views on the matter, resisted calls for Florence's release and even when Charles Russell, who had supported Florence since he defended her at the trial, became Lord Chief Justice in 1895, he found he was powerless.

Florence Maybrick was finally released in 1904 and was reunited with her mother. They travelled to the States together where she went on a lecture tour, protesting her innocence, and wrote a book entitled *My Fifteen Lost Years*. She never saw her children again. Her son, James Chandler Maybrick (who changed his name to Fuller) died tragically in Canada at the age of twenty-nine after drinking cyanide that he mistook for water. Her daughter, Gladys, went to live with her Uncle Michael in the Isle of Wight for a while before getting married and moving to South Wales. She died in 1971.

Florence herself became a recluse and died in Connecticut in 1941, penniless and alone apart from her colony of stray cats. She had reverted to her maiden name of Chandler and her neighbours were unaware of her identity.

Is there any chance that she was guilty as charged? Well, there is the fact that she did buy flypapers from two separate chemists, paying for them in cash when she had accounts with both shops and telling the chemist that she was having a problem with flies. However, it is possible that she was embarrassed about making up her own face treatment – or perhaps she wanted to avoid the chemist trying to sell her some proprietary brand he stocked. Also with her money problems, she might have thought it best not to increase the sum owed on her account, which might well have been scrutinised by a husband who was already concerned by her extravagance. There is also the fact that there was already enough arsenic and strychnine in that house to kill several husbands. Flypapers, surely, were unnecessary. Also, in 1941, a discovery was made to back up her story: on her death an old family Bible was found amongst her meagre possessions, and pressed between the pages was an old recipe providing instructions for soaking flypapers for use as a beauty treatment.

It has been suggested that she killed James to avoid the disgrace and financial penalties of a divorce, but at the time of his death there was no suggestion that a divorce was imminent and, as he had only left her a paltry sum in his will, she would have been better off sticking out the marriage or seeking a separation.

Florence sent for a nurse when James's condition worsened but, if she had been poisoning him, surely she wouldn't have wanted an extra witness. Her letter to Brierley, that the prosecution considered so incriminating, contains the words '… my brothers in law are here and we are terribly anxious.' 'We', not they'.

As for the poisons found in the chocolate box in her room, again there was so much poison already in the house, would she have needed to store more? And proving her guilt was very much to Michael Maybrick's advantage. He detested her and James's will gave him complete power over her life and property. It would have been so easy during that search he made to plant a bit of extra evidence, just in case the police didn't come to the desired conclusion.

James Maybrick habitually took arsenic, along with other poisons, and this risky habit undoubtedly led to his death. It is well known that the human body can build up a tolerance to arsenic and the relatively small amount found in James's body was hardly enough to kill even someone whose system wasn't used to it.

A strange postscript to the sad story of the Maybricks was the alleged discovery by a scrap metal merchant called Michael Barratt in 1992 of an old diary, apparently written by Jack the Ripper. The Ripper's identity isn't stated openly but everything points to him being James Maybrick. The writer of the diary claims to have confessed all to his wife but, if this was genuine, surely Florence would have used the fact that her husband was a notorious serial killer in her defence. Also she never mentions the subject in her memoirs, *My Fifteen Lost Years* – how much more sensational would a book entitled *I was Jack the Ripper's Wife* have been? It would have been a bestseller and made her a wealthy woman once more. At first the publishing and film world became very excited but then the owner confessed to the *Liverpool Daily Post* that it was a forgery. Later it was found that the handwriting was nothing like Maybrick's. However, Barratt's confession was later withdrawn and there are still some who believe the diary is genuine.

A curious end to a curious case.

> 'He detested her and James's will gave him complete power over her life and property.'

Sources

Blake, Victoria, *Mrs Maybrick*, The National Archives, 2008

Chandler, Raymond, Gardiner, Dorothy & Sorley-Walker, Kathrine (eds), *Raymond Chandler Speaking*, University of California Press, 1997

Jones, Christopher, *The Maybrick A to Z*, Countyvise Ltd, 2008

Maybrick, Florence Elizabeth, *Mrs Maybrick's Own Story: My Fifteen Lost Years*, TheClassics.us, 2013

Ryan, Bernard & Havers, Sir Michael, *The Poisoned Life of Mrs Maybrick*, iUniverse, 2000

Transcripts of the Trial of Florence Maybrick, August 1889

Whittington-Egan, Richard, *Liverpool Ghosts and Ghouls*, The Gallery Press, 1986

PAUL FRENCH

Paul is long-time Shanghai resident and the
author of the New York Times bestseller
'Midnight in Peking' (Penguin), a true crime
story of the grisly murder of a young English
woman in 1937. 'Midnight in Peking' was a
BBC Radio 4 Book of the Week, was awarded
an Edgar by the Mystery Writers of America,
and a Dagger by the UK Crime Writers'
Association. It is currently being developed
as a series for TV. He is now working on a
new book, which takes us into the dancehalls,
casinos and cabarets of wartime Shanghai.

us.midnightinpeking.com/author

MURDER IN THE SHANGHAI TRENCHES

PAUL FRENCH

Scott Road, Shanghai International Settlement
Wednesday, 18th September 1907

At 7.45 p.m. a dishevelled young woman of apparently Russian or East European origin burst into Hongkew Police Station on Woosung Road and reported the murdered body of a white woman at No. 56 Scott Road. Sergeant John O'Toole grabbed PC Cornelius Hamilton and the two Shanghai Municipal Policemen set out to the address, leaving the distraught woman under guard at the station.

When O'Toole and Hamilton reached Scott Road they found a large crowd gathered outside No. 56 including one Indian man, apparently drunk, shouting and screaming in the middle of the road. They ignored him and headed immediately inside the narrow detached house and made their way upstairs to the front-facing bedroom looking down onto the crowd below.

Sergeant O'Toole was just shy of thirty and had left Ireland and the Royal Irish Constabulary to join the Shanghai Police in 1900. Since arriving in the International Settlement, he had seen his share of dead bodies among the driftwood of life that somehow made its way to the great foreign-controlled centre of commerce for eastern China and the Yangtse Delta. For PC Hamilton, barely out of his teens and arrived in

Shanghai from rural County Limerick just months before, this was his first murder.

In front of them, on the room's only bed, was the body of a dead European woman, sprawled across the mattress and with a pillow partly covering her face. O'Toole and Hamilton then moved back out into the corridor to check the back bedroom of the house. Nobody was in that room; the window was ajar but all appeared to be in order. They heard a noise behind them, returned and found that the Indian man from downstairs had entered the house and come upstairs. He had removed the pillow from the victim's face. He started to turn the body before the policemen grabbed him and ejected him from the room, ordering him to go downstairs and leave the house. PC Hamilton went down with the man and detained him outside.

O'Toole felt for a pulse and found nothing. The woman was wearing a tattered nightdress and white stockings loosely tied with ribbons. The charge-room at Hongkew Police Station had contacted the senior detective on duty and O'Toole was to secure the crime scene, touch nothing, and await the arrival of the designated investigating officer.

Detective Sergeant Thomas Idwal Vaughan, a stocky Welshman, had joined the Shanghai Police in 1900 in the same intake as O'Toole, but had since made detective. He arrived at 8 p.m. and found a large crowd of excited and argumentative European women in the hallway of the building shouting in what he believed to be Russian. He called up to O'Toole, told him to come downstairs and clear them out of the house while Vaughan inspected the body.

Vaughan noted that the body was cold and lying on its left side, partly sprawled across the bed. It smelt of putrefaction, which indicated she had been dead some time. The autumn weather in Shanghai was still mild, the room's window was slightly open and the room stuffy, which could have accelerated the decay in the warm room. Her legs were bent at the knees, and were tied tightly together with a towel just above the ankles. Around her neck was another towel, tied in a reef knot, and a twisted curtain that had clearly been used to strangle her. There was heavy bruising around her neck. Her arms appeared to have been forcibly pulled back behind her as if they had been held there as she was strangled. There were bloodstains on the curtain and towel, which had been left slack after asphyxiating her. The woman's face was black and swollen and she had heavy bruising around her left eye and further bruising under her right eye. Her false teeth had fallen out and were lying next to her on the mattress. The dental plate was broken. Next to the bed were three more bloodstained towels. The sheet covering the mattress was also bloodstained, as were a pillow by her head and a beige shawl lying nearby.

Both the bedroom and the other upstairs back room appeared to be untouched apart from the murdered woman. Vaughan went downstairs to investigate the rest of the house. He found the downstairs back room, the house's living room, ransacked. A large travelling trunk, seemingly filled with clothing, had been upturned and emptied and the clothes strewn about the room. A tray from inside the trunk had been removed and was lying on a small bed in the corner. Clearly the entire room had been searched and all the cupboard drawers and several boxes in the room opened and the contents thrown out. However, none of the heavier furniture had been moved, no crockery or glass was smashed and Vaughan concluded that while the ransacking had been thorough it had been conducted quietly.

Completing his preliminary examination, Vaughan took hold of the corpse and lifted it up to check if there was anything underneath. He'd found no weapon that could have made the bruising around the woman's eyes so far. As he lifted the corpse he saw something drop onto the bed from inside the stocking of the dead woman – a handkerchief with one corner knotted. He picked it up and unfolded it to find two sovereigns, two American $5 gold pieces, a Korean fifty-cent coin and a small gold locket and chain.

The Shanghai Trenches

To the Shanghai Municipal Police (SMP) a call to Scott Road invariably meant two things – prostitution usually and trouble always. In 1907, Scott Road was the most notorious street in Shanghai. At its height the strip was home to an estimated three hundred brothels, mostly small houses inhabited by two, or a few more, working prostitutes. Lanes ran in between and behind the houses, allowing both punters and girls to come and go in relative anonymity and making it virtually impossible for the police to pursue anyone through the alleyways and houses of the densely packed rookery.

In 1907, Chinese, Japanese and Korean women worked alongside, and in competition with, a rising number of European women, mostly from Eastern Europe, and many of them trafficked. Among them Jewish women were prominent, having been brought into Shanghai via pimps and *souteners* working out of London and Marseilles. Most of these women were originally from Odessa, Bessarabia, Moldo-Wallachia, Romania and all the far-flung, and largely impoverished, regions of the Russian and Austro-Hungarian Empires. Many arrived via ships from Britain and began to appear in the port cities of the British Empire such as Bombay, Singapore and Hong Kong. Others came via Marseilles and popped up in Saigon, throughout French Indo-China and Shanghai. Three events had greatly increased the number of white prostitutes arriving in Shanghai in 1907 – the faster route to the Far East from Europe courtesy of the Suez Canal; the horrific anti-Semitic pogroms that flared up throughout Bessarabia and the Russian Empire in the early years of the century; and the 1906 earthquake in San Francisco, which saw an influx of working girls from the United States arrive in the Settlement.

Shanghai's main centres of foreign prostitution divided along two very different streets. In the heart of the Settlement, several blocks back from the bustling Bund waterfront, was Kiangse Road, home to several high-class foreign bordellos run by American madams and stocked with American (and occasionally French and British) girls. The so-called 'Line' was expensive and relatively exclusive with an all-white male clientele and centred on the most notorious bordello of all – former San Francisco and Yokohama madam Gracie Gale's No. 52. However, most of the trafficked women from Eastern Europe, and those Chinese prostitutes willing to service foreign men, were concentrated in the poorer districts to the north of the Soochow Creek, just outside the Settlement's full authority and on Scott Road – the 'Trenches'. In 1910, one visitor to the Trenches recorded that, 'if a drunken man or licentious European reprobate enters these quarters, the chances are ten to one against him ever coming out.'

Scott Road ran north from the junction of Szechuan Road and Dixwell Road along the side of Hongkew Park. The Hongkew docks and wharves were not far away making the area ideal for visiting sailors, while the Settlement's most easterly district, Yangtszepoo, with more docks, was also close by. Though the Municipal Police would attend murders and other crime scenes in the area, as Scott Road was technically outside the Settlement's borders, they did not subject the road's bars, opium dens and brothels to the same regulations as within the Settlement. They had tried to keep order – in 1906 a number of gambling sheds near Scott Road were destroyed but by the end of the year new sheds had been erected and gambling was in full swing again. It was a badlands, a virtual no-man's land legally and had quickly become a slum. By 1907, the tenement houses and lanes along Scott Road had become home to much of Shanghai's nefarious population, a multi-racial cluster of criminality on the margins of the city, populated by a community who lived outside the law – men and women on the run, drug and gun runners, gamblers, criminals, armed robbery gangs, pimps and prostitutes.

Immediately Detective Sergeant Vaughan entered the bedroom at No. 56 he had, despite the facial swelling and injuries, recognised the dead woman – Eliza Shapera, a Russian Jewish woman who'd lived on Scott Road for some time. Knowing who she was meant he immediately began to form theories.

Scott Road was well known to the men of Hongkew Police Station; they knew Eliza Shapera too, as a woman involved in the prostitution business of the Trenches. When Vaughan entered Scott Road he knew he was entering the underbelly of Shanghai, a city-within-a-city, a netherworld maze where the Municipal Police's writ ran thin and the local population was antagonistic to any sort of authority. He had a pretty good idea what sordid worlds the investigation of Eliza Shapera's murder would open up and was also aware that public co-operation in the Trenches, an area with its own alternative codes and loyalties, would be zero.

'I have seen two women fight with the dead woman'

Sergeant O'Toole had brought the woman who originally came to the Hongkew Police Station to report the murder to the front lower room ready for Vaughan to question. The detective, coming in from having surveyed the ransacking in the back room, also recognised her instantly, a younger woman known as Minna Nedal. He didn't know where she was from exactly but did know from previous arrests for prostitution that she was a subject of the Austro-Hungarian Empire and also Jewish. He began to question her. Nedal claimed she'd been living at No. 56 Scott Road with Eliza Shapera for over a year, that Shapera was married though her husband had left Shanghai some time ago and not returned. She had no idea when he was due back, if ever. Nedal claimed to have gone to Yangtszepoo on Monday evening to the house of some friends there to celebrate the impending Rosh Hashanah holiday, the Jewish New Year. She had stayed for two nights, returning to Scott Road at 7.30 p.m. that evening. She had found the front door locked and didn't have her own key.

She'd then gone to No. 53 Scott Road, a friend's house. With the Chinese houseboy from there she'd returned to Eliza's and tried the back entrance up the alleyway that ran behind the buildings. She entered the house and found that the living room, which she also claimed was her bedroom, had been ransacked and apparently 'searched'. She had gone upstairs and found Eliza dead in her bedroom. She had then rushed straight to Hongkew Police Station, getting there a quarter of an hour later at 7.45 p.m. and told Sergeant O'Toole of the murder. Vaughan now had a timeline for the killing, an infuriatingly long one. Eliza could have been dead since Monday night, when Nedal left for Yangtszepoo, or been killed anytime between then and 7.30 p.m. on Wednesday evening when Nedal returned.

As he was questioning Nedal, Vaughan heard a scuffle in the corridor outside and the Indian man burst in again, with Constable Hamilton attempting to restrain him. With Hamilton holding him back the Indian man shouted at Vaughan, 'I have seen two women fight with the dead woman.' The Indian gestured at Nedal implying she was one of the women brawling. Vaughan asked the man to calm down and explain exactly what he had seen but the man simply pointed at Nedal again, insisting he had seen her fighting with the dead woman. As he refused to calm down Vaughan told him to leave the house and wait outside. The Indian man left and then promptly disappeared amongst the crowd on the street and into the rookery around Scott Road. With the large mob still milling around on the street, and no other officers or constables at the scene except O'Toole and Hamilton, Vaughan could do nothing to follow the man.

Vaughan instructed O'Toole to clear the street and start looking for any witnesses and Hamilton to secure the house and not let anyone else enter.

The Protocols of Shanghai

Extraterritoriality. Every Shanghai policeman's complication. Within the Shanghai International Settlement foreigners were not subject to Chinese laws and Chinese punishments, but only to their own judges, courts and penalties. The British, French, Germans, Americans and others had all established their own judicial systems to deal with their wayward citizens and subjects. A further judicial layer was the so-called Mixed Court, established to try cases involving Chinese residing in the Settlement or cases where the defendant was of questionable nationality. In the Mixed Court the Chinese magistrate was 'assisted', in turn, by foreigners – American, British, and German. The system was messy, inconsistent and full of loopholes. If an American murdered a German and the only witnesses were British and French then the case would go before the American court. However, the American court could not compel the British or French witnesses to appear. The Americans could go to the court of the witnesses' nationality and request that court to take evidence for the witness, but this was cumbersome. In Shanghai's melting pot this convoluted system rendered an efficient and effective court system virtually impossible.

As soon as he had recognised Eliza Shapera and Minna Nedal, Vaughan knew he had a case that might be clear in its motives – robbery-murder by a client of Shapera's, or perhaps a fight over money between the two prostitutes. But he also knew he had to work within the rules of extraterritoriality that governed the Shanghai Settlement. From Scott Road Vaughan went straight to the Russian Consulate, a couple of miles away towards the centre of Shanghai where the Soochow Creek flowed into the Whangpoo River. The imposing Consulate sat on the northern Hongkew side of the Creek, opposite the Astor House Hotel. Shapera was a Russian subject and so protocol determined that the Consulate be informed.

At that time of night the Consul-General was at home but Vaughan found the Vice-Consul, Leonid Brodiansky. The Russian Consulate's doctor, who had the right to view the body *in situ*, was away from Shanghai on business but Brodiansky authorised a Dr Voelkers to examine the body on the Consulate's behalf. Voelkers accompanied Vaughan back to Scott Road and examined Eliza Shapera, pointing out several recent scratch marks on her shoulders Vaughan had not noticed before. The Detective Sergeant then called the municipal mortuary and an ambulance was despatched to Scott Road to remove the corpse. Eliza Shapera was taken from Scott Road to the Shanghai Municipal Morgue at 9.45 p.m.

Before leaving for the night Vaughan placed Minna Nedal under caution and had her transferred to Hongkew Police Station for the night, informing the Austro-Hungarian Consulate of her detention.

The 'Mohammedan'

On Thursday morning Vaughan arrived at Hongkew Police Station to be met by Detective Inspector John McDowell, who would now be the ranking officer on the Eliza Shapera murder investigation. McDowell had joined the force in 1898 and was a highly experienced detective working out of Hongkew Police Station. McDowell told Vaughan to interview Nedal again while he went to find the excited Indian from the night before. The police files referred to him as a 'Mohammedan', indicating they thought him a Muslim. McDowell knew the Trenches well and began a house-to-house inquiry. Just two doors down, at No. 58, he found a Chinese woman, Lien Yow, living in, and probably working out of, the upper bedroom. She knew exactly who the Detective Inspector was looking for.

McDowell knew a working girl when he saw one and clearly to him Lien Yow was one of Scott Road's many Chinese prostitutes who serviced the sailors and other Europeans who frequented the strip. The idea of a young Chinese woman, who wasn't a prostitute, living alone on Scott Road in 1907 was simply unheard of. She claimed to have known the Indian, who's name she told McDowell was Ameer Buchs, for about one month and that he sometimes stayed with her overnight. McDowell clearly understood their relationship to be one of pimp and prostitute. Lien Yow had no idea where Buchs was at the moment and didn't know when, or if, he would return. She was aware of the murder two doors down, claiming to know Shapera and Nedal only slightly.

Lien Yow described Buchs as an Indian who drank a lot and always wore Chinese-style straw-soled slippers, loose trousers and Chinese-style jackets – the same clothes he had been wearing when he'd burst in on Vaughan and Nedal the previous evening. She claimed that on the Monday previously Buchs had taken her for a carriage drive to a dancehall in Siccawei on the other side of Shanghai, across the Settlement and then further out to the south-west of the city's French Concession. They had returned at 1 a.m. on Tuesday morning; Buchs was drunk and went straight to sleep. On Tuesday Buchs had left the house but Lien Yow did not know when, as she had been asleep. He had returned at 8.30 p.m. and stayed the night with her. On Wednesday morning he had left the house at 8 a.m. and not returned till 7 p.m. He had sat with Lien Yow drinking beer and then, hearing shouting out on the street, had left the house, returning an hour later saying that the Russian woman at No. 56 had been murdered. She asked him for details but he didn't know how she had died but did say that the body smelt. He told her 'not to meddle in the affair and mind her own business.' He then stayed in the house for the rest of the evening drinking.

McDowell left No. 58 to continue his search. He didn't have long to wait. On Scott Road it was now 7.30 p.m. and dark, with both working girls and the flotsam and jetsam of the Trenches emerging for their night's business. McDowell headed along the strip and found Buchs, seemingly drunk and excitable, walking towards him wearing what appeared to be pyjama trousers and a Chinese jacket with black straw slippers. McDowell arrested him. Buchs protested, struggled and told McDowell, 'I savee who killed this woman. I have see two women beat her.'

Buchs claimed to have returned from his trip to Siccawei with Lien Yow at 1 a.m. on Tuesday morning and heard Minna Nedal, another woman and Eliza Shapera shouting and fighting inside No. 56. He went and banged on the door but the women refused to open it. He broke the glass in the front door window and swore at them in Russian, asking them what they were arguing about. He could see one of the women holding Shapera's hair, forcing her head down, while the other woman, Nedal, hit her. McDowell escorted Buchs back to No. 58 and Lien Yow's room, which he then searched, finding whisky and beer that belonged to the Indian.

McDowell then took Buchs to Hongkew Police Station and took his full statement. Despite Buchs being drunk, somewhat unstable and obviously a pimp, McDowell believed him. If Buchs had seen Minna Nedal at No. 56 early on Tuesday morning then her alibi of being at a Rosh Hashanah party in Yangtszepoo was questionable to say the least. By now it was early Friday morning and McDowell decided to release Buchs. He then formerly arrested Minna Nedal and arranged for her to be brought before the Austro-Hungarian Consular Court at a special session on Saturday morning.

It had been a long day. Despite exhaustive house-to-house enquires by O'Toole and Hamilton along Scott Road nobody was admitting to hearing or seeing anything. Although No. 56 was a narrow house with the adjoining residences having upstairs front windows not more than ten feet from the open window of the bedroom in which Shapera had been murdered, nobody at either No. 55 or No. 57, both known brothels and homes to working prostitutes, claimed to have heard anything, or seen Shapera enter or leave the house on Wednesday during the day.

Detective Sergeant Vaughan had been busy too. He'd been canvassing known associates of Eliza Shapera along Scott Road all day. Several Russian women had told him that they thought Shapera always kept around $200 in the house and had recently shown them a bank passbook with $900 in savings recorded. Vaughan returned to No. 56 and searched the house again. He found the passbook but there was no sign of any money on the premises at all.

Before Herr Kobr

The Austro-Hungarian Consular Court convened on Saturday morning and was presided over by the Vice-Consul Miloslav Kobr. Herr Kobr conducted a preliminary hearing *in camera* with both McDowell and Vaughan in attendance. Ameer Buch's claims against Nedal were heard, though she vehemently denied being in the house on either Tuesday or Wednesday until she returned home and found Eliza's body. She claimed to have never fought with Eliza nor to know who the mystery woman was that Buchs alleged to have seen pulling Shapera's hair while Nedal had supposedly hit her. However, she was unable to produce any of her 'friends' in Yangtszepoo with whom she had apparently been enjoying the Rosh Hashanah party and refused to reveal the address. The hearing lasted all morning and went on into the afternoon, with Nedal continually protesting her innocence. At the end of the day she was remanded back into the custody of Hongkew Police Station. But there were now doubts about Buchs's claim and, as he left the Court to return to Scott Road, McDowell arrested him.

McDowell may have been inclined to believe Buchs's story, despite recognising the man as a 'loafer', a pimp and a drunk, but nobody else on Scott Road had even hinted that they'd heard a fight in No. 56 in the early hours of Tuesday morning, or seen Buchs in the street, and several claimed the glass in the door had been smashed for several months and not repaired. Pretty quickly Buchs's story fell apart.

Police records showed that Buchs had become known to the police a couple of years previously as a witness to a murder in the Pootung district of Shanghai, the area of docks, wharves and go-downs across the Whangpoo River opposite the Bund. His testimony had ultimately proved unreliable. Over the following week McDowell and Vaughan began to investigate Buchs and his claims more closely and his alibi collapsed.

By the end of September they had enough evidence against Buchs to bring him to court – this time His Majesty's Police Court in Shanghai, as Buchs was technically under British jurisdiction as an Indian subject. While the case against Buchs was being prepared another lead came to light, one that – with Buchs in custody and new information appearing – meant Herr Kobr at the Austro-Hungarian Consular Court ordered the release of Minna Nedal.

'Loafers'

Detective Sergeant Maurice Fitzgibbon had been recruited to the Shanghai Municipal Police from his home in Limerick, Ireland in 1900. He worked out of Hongkew Police Station and was assigned to the Eliza Shapera murder case. While McDowell and Vaughan had concentrated on Nedal and Buchs, Fitzgibbon had arrested two indigent Chinese men – Lee San-foh and Sung Ling-ling. Both were described as 'loafers' in the records, and had formerly been house servants on Scott Road but subsequently been discharged by their employers and remained hanging around the district. Fitzgibbon had heard that the men had been seen in the vicinity of No. 56 on Wednesday. His sources told him the men, who were unemployed, had been seen in the notorious gambling sheds near Scott Road with money to bet.

In any robbery of European households in Shanghai, Chinese servants and former servants were immediately suspected. The Captain-Superintendent of the SMP, Clarence Bruce, a former Commandant of the British Army's Weihaiwei Regiment in Northern China, had only been appointed the force's boss in 1907 but felt confident enough to write in his first annual report to the Shanghai Municipal Council that in the 'majority of cases minor robberies can usually be traced either to servants or ex-servants.' Going so far as to murder a householder was extreme, but not unknown. Eliza Shapera was unusual among Europeans in Shanghai, even the poor and criminal, in notably not having any domestic servants.

However, since the start of the investigation McDowell had worked on the assumption that, if Shapera was not killed by Nedal and her mystery accomplice as Buchs indicated, then the killer or killers must have entered No. 56 from the back door. McDowell and Vaughan had returned to Scott Road and inspected the small passageway that ran behind Nos 56, 57 and 58 and the passages than ran between the detached houses. In the yards of the houses were the building's privies and cookhouses. The side passage between Nos 57 and 58 was open and leading from the street to the rear passageway behind the house, which allowed access to both Nos 56 and 57. However, the rear passage between Nos 57 and 58 had a five-foot high wall separating the properties. Conveniently though, leaning against this wall was a bamboo ladder making it easy to climb from No. 58 over the wall and onto the cookhouse roof of No. 57, jump down and then enter No. 56 from the rear passage. The detectives were naturally aware that Ameer Buchs was staying in Lien Yow's room at No. 58. Tiles on the cookhouse roof of No. 57 were broken, indicating someone had recently accessed the back yard of the house this way, and the policemen found freshly broken tile fragments scattered in the passage linking No. 57 to No. 56. Buchs could have accessed the house from No. 58, killed Shapera and then returned.

It was a neat theory but the problem was, given the easy access to the rear of No. 58 from Scott Road, so could anyone else.

Fitzgibbon arrested both Lee and Sung and brought them before the Mixed Court on Saturday, 28th September with Magistrate Pao Yi and the German Assessor Dr Hans Schirmer sitting. The Judge and Assessor believed the men had a case to answer and both were remanded into custody while further enquiries were made. It seemed the murder of Eliza Shapera could be as simple as a robbery gone wrong.

Means, Motive, Opportunity

Fitzgibbon's further enquiries went nowhere but McDowell and Vaughan had been busy with Buchs and now believed that they could prove he had the means, motive and opportunity to murder Eliza Shapera. Buchs was living at No. 58 and so could access the rear of No. 56 without being seen. He knew Shapera, could watch the house and know when she was alone and had probably heard the same gossip Vaughan did about the $200 she kept about the place – the means. They soon found that he had motive too. McDowell had visited a local Chinese general store and discovered that earlier in the month Buchs had signed chits (promises to pay) for $102.80. The shop assistant he questioned, Kwang Ling, hadn't been authorized to extend credit to Buchs as his boss thought the Indian unreliable, but he had done so anyway. Buchs owed the money and had not been able to settle the bill. He was broke.

And Buchs had opportunity. Asked about his whereabouts on the Wednesday Shapera's body was discovered, Buchs claimed that he had gone to an Indian food store in the French Concession to collect food he had previously ordered on Tuesday evening. He claimed to have arrived there at 1 p.m. and remained for six hours, meaning he would have returned home to Lien Yow's about 7 p.m., as she had claimed. However, the Indian shopkeeper told Vaughan when he visited the store that Buchs had left at 4 p.m. This left the hours between 8 a.m. and 1 p.m. and 4 p.m. and 7 p.m. on Wednesday unaccounted for.

Buchs claimed he had gone to the house of some fellow Indians on Hongkew's Sawgin Road for a bath, a winding road that ran alongside the rather fetid and stinking Sawgin Creek. McDowell and Vaughan visited the house on the street that was well known to them as one that housed generally undesirable and indigent Chinese and foreigners – a few months before, a major gang of Chinese armed robbers had been arrested holed up in a house on Sawgin Road. The Indians at the house denied that Buchs had come there for a bath, indeed they denied ever knowing him. His alibi was shot through with holes he couldn't explain.

Means, motive, opportunity. McDowell prepared the prosecution case for Rex *v.* Buchs at the HM Police Court before Police Magistrate J.C.E. Douglas. The British Police Court was part of the British Supreme Court for China and Korea. It dealt with minor criminal cases and committal hearings involving British subjects.

Infuriatingly, while Douglas decided there was a case to answer and agreed to a committal hearing, the Court's appointed doctor felt Buchs should go to a hospital first for psychiatric tests to assess his worthiness to be tried. The case was postponed for a week.

HM Police Court, Shanghai International Settlement Monday, 21st October 1907 – Rex *v.* Ameer Buchs

Buchs was declared fit to attend his committal hearing to decide if he should be put on trial for murder before a jury in H.M. Supreme Court. John Charles Edward Douglas was a fearsome magistrate to come before – he was barely in his thirties but was the son of a Royal Navy Admiral, had been educated at Radley School and Merton College, Oxford and had spent several years presiding over the Shanghai Court.

Formalities first. The British Court needed to formally know that the Russians had been made aware of the death of one of their own. They had, and they had ordered no inquest but left it in the hands of the SMP. Douglas decreed that Buchs's testimony before the Austro-Hungarian Court would not be accepted as evidence in the British Court – 'A statement made by a man in a criminal action in another Court was not evidence against when tried by H.M. Supreme Court.'The complications of extraterritoriality.

Detective Sergeant Vaughan was sworn in and retold his story of arriving at the crime scene and examining the body, of Buchs's outburst accusing Minna Nedal, that the Minna Nedal case had gone nowhere and neither had the case against Lee and Sung. Vaughan outlined the holes in Buchs's alibi – that he had not been at the Indian food store as long as he'd claimed, that the men on Sawgin Road did not know him and that the glass he claimed to have smashed when witnessing the fight in No. 56 had been broken months before. He also explained to the Court that Buchs had large debts with local merchants.

Vaughan and McDowell had noticed that Buchs customarily wore Chinese-style straw-soled slippers. They had returned to No. 58 and confiscated a pair that they knew to be his from Lien Yow's rooms. They had then gone to the crime scene at No. 56 and found scuffmarks on the bottom of Eliza Shapera's bed. McDowell measured the marks and determined they came from Chinese slippers of exactly the same length and breadth as Buchs's. Vaughan produced drawings of the scuffmarks and Buchs's slippers as evidence.

McDowell then entered the witness stand and produced diagrams that explained how Buchs, living at No. 58 with Lien Yow, could have used the access routes across the back passages and the cookhouse roof to enter No. 56. He produced the fragments of broken tile found in the passage showing someone had scrambled across the roof and down to the passage behind No. 56.

Douglas retired to consider the evidence.

'There is the strongest case of suspicion against the accused'

Ultimately McDowell and Vaughan had not got enough. Douglas summed up the case as he saw it. The police knew Buchs wasn't always where he said he'd been, but they didn't know where he had actually been at those times. The marks on Shapera's bed were from the same type of Chinese-style slippers as Buchs habitually wore, but then so did hundreds of thousands of other people in Shanghai. Dr Voelkers had been unable to state with any certainty the time that death had occurred. Douglas did admit that Buchs had lied, that his alibis were worthless, and that he had falsely accused Minna Nedal. He further agreed that someone had effected an entry across the cookhouse roof and the rear passage of the building and that Buchs had been in the vicinity of the house at the time of the murder. However, there was no hard evidence that it was he who had entered No. 56 and killed Eliza Shapera.

Magistrate Douglas concluded, 'There is the strongest case of suspicion against the accused, but, on the evidence being forthcoming, the decision as to whether there is a *prima facie* case to answer is in the negative.' The accused was discharged. Buchs walked free from the Court and disappeared back into the swamp of the Trenches.

Who Killed Eliza Shapera?

Eliza Shapera was probably a trafficked woman herself – lured from the Jewish shtetls of Russia, brought to Shanghai by white slavers in the late nineteenth century and forced to work as a prostitute in the Trenches. She had probably known nothing but the sordid and debauched world of Scott Road since she was a young woman. She had no husband – late nineteenth- and early twentieth-century proprietary demanded women claim they were married and often traffickers bigamously married multiple women to make transporting them easier and reduce the suspicions of immigration and port authorities regarding single women. Perhaps Eliza still sold her body, but she was older in 1907 and was most probably the madam to the much younger, and probably also trafficked, Minna Nedal.

What happened on the 18th of September 1907? Was it simply a case of two Chinese 'loafers' chancing on an open back door and the possibility of some loot, finding a woman inside who would fight to keep her money and killing her for $200? The police investigation of the two Chinese men arrested went nowhere and they were eventually released.

Did Minna Nedal, and perhaps another younger prostitute, fall out with Eliza over money or a customer? Perhaps. But while Nedal's alibi collapsed there were never any witnesses, except Ameer Buchs, who claimed to have seen her in Scott Road that night. No trace of the third woman fighting at No. 56 that evening, as he claimed, was ever found. Nedal adamantly refused to admit to being on Scott Road, but couldn't account for her whereabouts. The most likely explanation is that she was with a client and did not want to admit to prostitution or implicate her customer.

And what of Buchs? Who was he? We know little of him except that he was a Muslim from India. In 1907, the Shanghai authorities were becoming concerned about the rising number of indigent Indians in the Settlement. It was perhaps alarmist; the vast majority of Indians in Shanghai were either employed by the Police themselves or worked as watchmen, with a few more as servants and storekeepers. However, some Indians, through impoverishment or desire, slipped into the city's underworld. Buchs seems to have been one of these. He was a drunk it appears, he had come to the police's attention before during a murder investigation, he was probably living off immoral earnings as Lien Yow's pimp and maybe had other girls working for him too. His alibis all collapsed, he lied about his whereabouts – it seems he most probably also lied about the supposed fight in the early hours of 18th September. Did he not like Shapera and Nedal in competition with his

> 'some Indians, through impoverishment or desire, slipped into the city's underworld.'

girls? Did the two Jewish women refuse to work for him? He certainly seemed quick and determined enough to implicate Nedal in Eliza's murder. Revenge? Or did he simply need money and decide that he would take Eliza's savings and kill her to stop her talking? His lies to the police about Sawgin Road and visiting the food store in the French Concession and the broken glass were amateurish and easily disproved.

If he was in his right mind he must have known his tales would not stand up under police scrutiny. Buchs was unstable, dangerous, a loose cannon, probably a chronic alcoholic – perhaps that's why Lien Yow was so eager to confess her relationship with him to McDowell, why the Indian men on Sawgin Road denied even knowing him. He was a liability.

After the conclusion of the trial of Ameer Buchs all the main characters fade away from history. Neither Minna Nedal nor Ameer Buchs are ever recorded again in Shanghai police records. PC Cornelius Hamilton left the SMP in 1917; John O'Toole served until 1932, when he retired from the force. Thomas Vaughan left the SMP in 1927 and John McDowell left a few years after the Shapera case, in 1910.

Though effectively a slum in 1907, after the First World War the Trenches got a new lease of life with a massive influx of White Russian refugees from the Bolshevik Revolution flooding into Shanghai. Many turned to prostitution, taxi-dancing, gambling and running nightclubs to make a living. A rival strip of clubs and bars flourished nearby, just outside the Settlement's control on Jukong Alley, and things didn't improve. An American was shot and killed in the Trenches in 1920. The Shanghai Municipal Council and the Chinese authorities tried to suppress the Trenches but they just kept on flourishing and were still going strong by the time of the Japanese invasion of Shanghai in 1937.

Eliza Shapera's final resting place is unknown. Indeed her entire origins remain surrounded in mystery – where she was born, when exactly and how she came to leave Russia and arrive in Shanghai. She was murdered in 1907, nobody was ever prosecuted successfully for her killing and her case remains one of old Shanghai's unsolved murders.

PETER GUTTRIDGE

Peter is the author of the true
crime books 'The Great Train Robbery'
and 'Contraband' and twelve works
of crime fiction. The core of his
Brighton trilogy — 'City of Dreadful
Night', 'The Last King of Brighton' and
'The Thing Itself' — is the unsolved
Brighton Trunk Murder of 1934.

www.peterguttridge.com

THE QUEEN OF SLAUGHTERING PLACES

PETER GUTTRIDGE

June 1934. Brighton, 'The Queen of Watering Places', an hour from London on England's south coast. A town of contrasts: seedy and glamorous; gaudy and sophisticated. Victorian slums squashed in around Regency townhouses. Parts of the town being torn down to make way for street-widening projects and chain stores.

Dozens of trains a day disgorge holidaymakers. Ferries to and from Dieppe dock at the end of the West Pier daily, no passports required for the day-trippers who board or disembark from them. There are music halls and movie houses, seafront attractions and the end-of-the-pier shows, brass bands on bandstands and bi-planes from the nearby art deco airport at Shoreham trailing advertising banners across the bright blue sky. On some days Lobby Lud is lurking in town, waiting to give away his £5 when challenged by a sharp-eyed newspaper reader.

Brighton is the day-trip destination for London slum-dwellers who pour out of the railway station dazzled by the light and the blare of seaside colours. It is the weekend destination for British movie stars and theatre actors. The bisexual movie star Tallula Bankhead is a regular visitor, as is John Gielgud, who achieves matinee idol fame this year for his performance in the title role in the West End of 'Richard of Bordeaux'.

There are prostitutes and pimps, gigolos and boys for hire, music hall performers and pierrots, hoodlums and homosexual men and women, dirty weekenders and Soho gangsters.

Crime is rife. Smugglers operate by sea out of Newhaven and by air out of Shoreham. Stolen goods – antiques and jewellery – are fenced in the shops in the narrow alleys of the Laines. Local and London razor gangs fight running battles on the seafront and at the racecourse for control of the lucrative penny arcade and bookmaking rackets.

Cynical private eyes and photographers have set up shop to cater for the divorce trade as the town is the destination of choice to fabricate grounds for divorce – Fred Astaire and Ginger Rogers are doing just that in a Hollywood version of Brighton in one of the year's top movies, *The Gay Divorcee.*

And, still, the lingering presence of the Great War. Limbless veterans, men with lungs wrecked by gas attacks, men with melted faces – they haunt the seafront and the backstreet pubs and the public lavatories.

There is a hidden history of Brighton involving the homosexual and lesbian communities living or visiting there in the 1930s. Radclyffe Hall visited in the 1920s and by the end of the decade there were already women-only tea dances at the Royal Albion Hotel. In 1929, Lillia Arkell-Smith was sentenced to nine months in prison for passing herself off as Colonel Sir Victor Ivor Gauntlett Blyth Barker (man-about-town, huntsman and cricketer). She married a local woman, signing the register as a bachelor, and honeymooned at the Grand.

Graham Greene was a regular visitor that summer of 1934, staying at the Grand with a mistress. In the bar he observed the Soho gangsters, the Sabini brothers, who controlled the rackets on most of the racecourses in Britain. *Brighton Rock* was brewing.

Hindsight tells us that the unusually hot summer of that year was dominated by significant events in the rise of fascism across Europe. In Germany, Hitler committed the atrocity against his own comrades known as the Night of the Long Knives. In Austria, Nazi sympathisers assassinated liberal Prime Minister Dolfuss. In Britain, Sir Oswald Mosley's Blackshirts showed their true nature at a rally in Earls Court where they subdued protesters with razor, cosh and boot.

There was also big news from Chicago, where John Dillinger, Public Enemy Number One, was shot to death by the Feds as he came out of the Biograph cinema.

But first in June, then in July, the stories that dominated British newspapers – and some European ones – were that of one and then a second gruesome murder in the town. Brighton was suddenly 'The Queen of Slaughtering Places'.

On a sweltering Sunday, 17th June police were called to the left luggage office of the railway station at the top of town to investigate a trunk, deposited on Derby Day, 6th June. It was giving off an overpowering stench. In it was the decomposing torso of a woman, wrapped in oiled brown paper. No arms, no legs, no head. The legs and feet were found the next day in a suitcase at King's Cross left luggage office.

Detective Inspector Donaldson of Scotland Yard immediately took responsibility for the case and asked Sir Bernard Spilsbury, the country's most celebrated pathologist, to examine the remains, referring to it as a 'bits and pieces' case.

Spilsbury in turn described it to a colleague as 'another cut up case'. Some seven years earlier he had done the autopsy on the dismembered remains of a woman discovered in a trunk at Charing Cross station.

The police surgeon first called to the scene had judged the victim's age to be around forty. A person's age is most easily determined by examining the sagittal and coronal sutures in the skull. The first fuses fully by the age of thirty-five, the second by the age of forty. In the absence of a head, the surgeon and Spilsbury could only rely on a secondary test on the join between the ribs and the sternum.

Spilsbury concluded that the Brighton victim was in her mid-twenties and certainly no older than thirty. He added that she was 'well-nourished', took care of her appearance and was three months pregnant. Spilsbury's view prevailed over that of the police surgeon and the police focused on that narrow age range.

Spilsbury had as much ego as talent. He regarded himself as a Sherlock Holmes of pathology and in consequence often drew conclusions beyond his actual remit. He was the first and last pathologist to be knighted whilst still working. He was the last because it became evident that juries were unduly swayed by his knighthood.

The porter who had taken the trunk in had no memory of the man who had deposited it. Even so, Donaldson had high hopes of finding the killer by identifying the woman through the contents of the trunk. There was brown paper with part of a handwritten word on it and a quantity of olive oil, something not commonly available in Britain at the time. He hoped to find which shop had sold the trunk itself and to whom.

Donaldson set up a special incident room in the Royal Pavilion, in rooms adjacent to the Music Room, because there was insufficient space in the police station. (This was the police station where, ninety years earlier, Chief Constable Henry Solomon was bludgeoned to death with a poker by a prisoner he was interviewing about the theft of a roll of carpet. It is now Brighton Town Hall but the Victorian cells can still be visited in the basement.)

The police came up with a list of almost 750 missing women in Britain. Remarkably, in a matter of weeks in those pre-computer days of handwritten, carbon-copied reports, they traced all but seventy of them. Donaldson believed the dead woman was the mistress of a married man who killed her when he found she was pregnant to avoid a scandal. She might have been French or German, brought here (dead or alive) on the West Pier ferry. European police forces were asked to help.

Witnesses came forward with a host of sightings of men carting trunks about: on trains, on railway stations, on the Downs near Roedean School. Indeed, over the next two months the public response to the appeal for information overwhelmed the police. By the start of September the investigation had received 12,000 letters, cards and telegrams and countless phone calls.

Only a handful of the written communications survive because, in 1964, the files were destroyed under a thirty-year rule. The files that still exist, usually copies of copies, provide an eccentric mosaic of life in Brighton at the time.

Of the people who contacted the police, there were mad men and women with loopy theories, others with scores to settle. Neighbour reported neighbour. Wives reported husbands or, more usually, ex-husbands. B&B owners reported their guests. The authors of anonymous letters signed 'Londoner' and *Pro Bono Publico* were of particular interest – and then proved not to be.

All leads seemed to go to dead ends. The partial word on the brown paper led nowhere. The trunk was too common for its source to be located. The olive oil could not be tracked to its source either. Knives were discovered dumped in Hove that might have been the murder weapons – but weren't. Empty houses were searched and back gardens dug up all over the area, although there was no actual evidence the crime took place anywhere near Brighton.

Girl Guides had seen a man burning something suspicious and horribly smelly on the Downs. He said he was burning fish, they didn't believe him. Nothing came of this. Witnesses reported hearing screams coming from a luxury boat moored off the West Pier. On investigation it transpired the owner was turned on by strangling a chicken before having sex. This had come as an unwelcome surprise to a female guest.

Police were, of course, hampered in their efforts to identify the poor woman by the absence of her head. What the newspapers did not report for another thirty years but what the police files in the Archives reveal, is that a head had in fact been found in a rockpool at Black Rock, a mile or so to the east of Brighton's other pier, the Palace Pier, two weeks *before* the torso was discovered at the left luggage office, around the time the trunk was being deposited there.

A young courting couple had stumbled on it, partly wrapped in newspaper, but the boy had insisted they leave it there. He said it was probably that of a suicide and that the police had dumped it there to wash out to sea, having taken all the parts of the body they needed. Word of this find percolated down to the police three weeks later, by which time the tides had washed the head away. In the memo to his superiors reporting on his questioning of the couple, Donaldson could scarcely contain his frustrated anger at their stupidity.

A throng of reporters stayed at the Grand on generous expenses of £3 per day and bribed policemen to give them information. In the National Archive there is a bulky file relating to an attempt to prosecute the head of Hove CID (or at least withhold his pension) for leaking information – true and false – to the press. The press virtually laid siege to the station, where interviews were carried out, harrying whoever came in or out for information. They followed Donaldson and his team wherever they went, on however routine a mission, and ensured the crime stayed on the front pages of the national newspapers by making up imagined leads.

Then, almost exactly four weeks after the discovery of the torso in the trunk, another woman's body was found in a second trunk in a basement bedsit in Kemp Street, close to the station.

The *Daily Mail* was not the only newspaper to go berserk but it did excel itself. It's headline on 16th July declared, *'Trunk Murder Sensation, Second Woman's Body Found'.* So far, so true. The subheadings declared, *'Discovery of first victim's head and arms; all packed in black box; death room's signs of fierce fight; bloodstained hammer.'* All false.

There was only the poor woman and some bloodstained sheets in the trunk. Fully clothed, possessing all her limbs. She wasn't killed in the room in which she was found although she had been killed by a blow to the head, probably inflicted by a hammer. No hammer, bloodstained or otherwise, was present.

She was identified as Violet Saunders, aka Violette Kaye. She was one of a family of sixteen and had worked as a dancer in a provincial music hall with Miss Watson's Rosebuds and The Parisian Pinkies before doing an end-of-the-pier show called 'Kay & Kaye' in Brighton. Until early 1933 she had lived with her dancing partner Tony (also known as Kay) Fredericks but may already have been working as a prostitute. Her last court appearance for soliciting was in August 1933. She drank and was addicted to morphine.

In 1933 she left Fredericks and in London met a waiter in a Piccadilly restaurant. They moved in together then, in late 1933, moved down to Brighton. She was forty-one, he was twenty-six. He was a petty thief and hustler who went by many names, including Jack Notyre, Hyman Gold and Tony Mancini. His real name was Cecil Lois England.

England, born in Deptford but brought up partly in Hull (his father was a shipping clerk), had drifted into petty crime in provincial cities and served short spells of prison time with hard labour before he joined the RAF then deserted. He drifted to London and Brighton. He was embroiled in some way with the conflict between Jewish and Italian gangs in London, hence the Jewish and Italian aliases. (He once gave his profession as clothes-presser, so perhaps worked for one of the Jewish tailors in Soho.)

He was best known as Tony Mancini, although he had stolen that identity and a reputation from an Italian gangster, Tony 'Baby' Mancini, who managed a billiards club for the Sabini brothers in Soho. The reputation included the fact that Mancini, a former boxer, had forced the hand of one rival gangster into a meat grinder, chopped off another gangster's hand with an axe and was himself hospitalised after a razor attack by a rival gang.

Notyre/Mancini lived off Violette's earnings whilst he hung around the Brighton amusement arcades and dance halls with a shady mix of crooks, rent boys, prostitutes and hustlers. The girls loved him, his excellent dance skills making up for his stutter.

In May 1934 he started work as a waiter at the Skylark café under the arches on Brighton beach. He quickly started an affair with one of the girls there. He also hung out at the skittles stall in the nearby Aladdin's Cave. Sometime around the 10th of May, in a violent, drink-fuelled argument in their basement flat, he hit Violette Kay with a hammer and killed her.

Leaving her on the blood-soaked bed he went out and bought a trunk, stuffed her and the bloodstained sheets inside and hid it in a cupboard. The waitress from the Skylark moved in with him for a few days. He told her (and others) that Violette had gone off with a bookie. He gave the girl some of Violette's clothes, saying Violette wasn't able to fit them in her suitcase. He sent Violette's sister a telegram, ostensibly from Violette, saying that she had got a job in Paris and would be in touch soon.

A few days later he moved, enlisting a friend to hire a handcart to shift the trunk through the streets of Brighton to new digs in Kemp Street, near the station. He moved into a bedsit with three beds side-by-side.

He put the trunk at the bottom of his bed. He entertained men and women in this bedsit. They used the trunk as a seat.

This was almost a month before Brighton Trunk Murder No. 1 was revealed – or indeed had happened. As weeks went by, his friends complained about the smell. He made various excuses to explain it.

When the first trunk murder victim was discovered at Brighton railway station, Violette's sister and a client reported her missing. The police were focused on women in their twenties so they took little notice. A couple of weeks later a friend of hers also went to the police. The police brought Jack Notyre in for questioning on Saturday, 14th July. He answered their questions but that night did a midnight flit. He spent the evening and half the night in the company of Robin Taylor, a male professional dancer and interior decorator at the bedsit, then in an all-night café, and at 7 a.m. he took a train from Preston Park station to London.

A decorator working on the exterior of the house in which Notyre/Mancini had his bedsit phoned the police the next day about a terrible smell coming from the basement. Oddly, neither the landlord nor the landlady had a sense of smell. The police visited. They found the trunk. They found Violette Kaye.

Four days later, at about 1.30 a.m., two alert policemen spotted Notyre/Mancini walking on the Maidstone road near Sidcup. He looked 'nervous and hesitant'. He was taken back to Brighton where he claimed that he had found Violette Kaye dead when he came home one afternoon.

The press, of course, were saying he was a double murderer. *The* Brighton Trunk Murderer. He wasn't. The two trunk murders were coincidental but not connected.

Notyre/Mancini was put on trial for murder at Lewes Assizes. The trial lasted four days. In the courtroom next door, Sir Oswald Mosley was on trial for a riotous assembly of his Blackshirts at Worthing. Notyre/Mancini's barrister, Norman Birkett (later Lord Birkett), argued his innocence successfully in the face of apparently overwhelming – though in parts circumstantial – evidence. He was found not guilty.

Notyre/Mancini continued his life of petty crime. On the 27th of September 1935 he was sentenced at Trowbridge, Wiltshire to three months' imprisonment with hard labour on a charge of stealing a gold watch from a jewellers. Thirty years later he confessed to a Sunday newspaper that he had killed Violette with a coal hammer.

The police were convinced of his guilt so did not look for anyone else, focusing instead on murder number one. Detective Inspector Donaldson was by now also working on a second possible scenario: that the death was the result of an abortion gone wrong.

He felt he had a viable suspect for the second scenario: a society abortionist with premises in the elegant Brunswick Square, Hove. (Abortion was, of course, illegal.) In early July, his attention had been drawn to Edward Says Massiah, a mixed race doctor from Trinidad in his mid-fifties, partly because of a letter from one of his domestic staff about the disappearance of another member of his staff. It was a malicious letter as the woman had been fired by Massiah, but nevertheless it drew Donaldson to Massiah.

Donaldson put him under covert surveillance to see what firm evidence could be found against him. However, as police files in the Archive reveal, a senior Hove policeman (possibly the same one selling false stories to the press) took it upon himself to visit Massiah and pretty much accuse him of the crime. As the policeman made his accusations, Massiah wrote on a notepad. He passed the pad over to the policeman.

He had written a list of names of aristocratic and establishment families for whom he had got rid of unwanted pregnancies. He said that if he were accused of the murder these names would come out as part of his defence, with obvious consequences.

No charges were ever laid against Massiah, who returned to Trinidad in 1938 to live out his remaining years.

Although he is not mentioned in the police files, there is one other potential suspect – and a celebrated one at that. The author Graham Greene. At least, that is, reading between the lines of a hostile biography, *The Man Within*, by Michael Shelden.

Shelden certainly makes a plausible case for Greene's obsession with the murder and mutilation of prostitutes – and in particular with the Brighton Trunk Murders – with reference to Greene's fiction, dream journals and poetry both from the 1930s and later. And Greene was a regular visitor to Brighton in the '30s for sexual adventures. However, whether that puts Greene in the frame is another thing again.

Nobody was ever charged with the first killing. The first trunk murder was never solved. Months went by, the witness statements stacked up, the suspicious characters multiplied but the victim was never identified so the killer was never caught.

By September 1934, Chief Inspector Donaldson had moved back to Scotland Yard from the Royal Pavilion. By November, he had been reassigned to another dismemberment – this time of a man. The man's torso had turned up in the Brentford canal; his legs and feet (still in socks and shoes) were discovered under a seat in a railway carriage at Waterloo. The head and arms and hands were never discovered. The photographs of the legs and feet standing in the carriage and against a wall in the pathology lab are misfiled among the Brighton Trunk Murder documents.

Also misfiled are crime scene photographs from 1936 of an unconscious Arthur Cyril Jefferson Peake and his murdered chauffeur, Arthur George Noyce. A little digging in the newspapers of the time reveal that Peake, described variously as a 'former sports promoter' and 'an interior decorator' was a married man who kept a separate apartment in Hove. In 1934, he employed the much younger Noyce as secretary/ chauffeur. Noyce's mother ran an antiques shop in the Laines.

Two years later, Peake's wife threatened to expose him as 'an invert'. Peake strangled Noyce with his belt and tried to kill himself with an overdose and then with gas. He survived and was tried and sentenced to death for Noyce's murder. At the last moment the sentence was commuted on the grounds of insanity and Peake was committed to Broadmoor for the remainder of his life.

In 1938, Graham Greene published *Brighton Rock*. The Ida Arnold character was the kind of 'brass' Violette Kaye might have been before her decline into addiction and alcoholism.

In 1941, the real Tony Mancini, 'Baby', the Soho gangster, was the first person hung by newly appointed Official Executioner, Albert Pierrepoint.

He had knifed a Jewish gangster, Harry 'Little Hubby' Distleman, to death in an altercation in his Wardour Street billiards club when Distleman and another man had attacked him with billiard balls and cues.

Pierrepoint went on to execute a number of Nazis convicted of war crime at the Nuremburg trials in 1946. These war criminals were convicted by Lord Birkett, the Judge who, twelve years earlier, had successfully defended Jack Notyre – the *other* Tony Mancini – at Lewes Assizes.

In 1958, criminal proceedings were brought against Brighton's Chief Constable Charles Ridge for corruption. Although acquitted he was undoubtedly guilty. He was dismissed by the police authority without being given the opportunity to defend his actions. This led to a landmark legal judgement (Ridge *v.* Baldwin) in 1964 when Ridge successfully appealed for reinstatement of salary and pension, plus damages backdated to the year of his dismissal.

Ridge had been in the Brighton force since 1926. By the time of the Brighton Trunk Murders he controlled some backstreet abortions (and probably knew Massiah), took money from prostitutes and their pimps and ran his own protection rackets along the seafront. The thought of such a man's involvement in the these investigations inspires all sorts of giddy notions.

The few remains of the first murder victim were buried in a pauper's grave at parish expense in January 1935. We probably will never know the identity of this woman reduced to a torso and a pair of dismembered legs. The pathologist, Spilsbury, commented on the fact she took care of her feet. We know she dyed her hair blonde. We know what her last meal was. We just don't know who she is.

But her remains are still in the ground. Her grave is unmarked but its location is known. Perhaps if there are ever compelling reasons to do so, an exhumation would allow familial (mitochondrial) DNA tests to be done on her bones. Such tests would provide information which at the least would help to identify her place of origin and probably much more. Might she actually be identified? And if so, might her killer finally be named?

BRIAN INNES

Brian was a musician, publisher and author, who died in July 2014, shortly after submitting his contribution to this anthology. After spending a number of years first working in a laboratory and then as an artist, he came to fame as co-founder of, and percussionist with, the Temperance Seven jazz band, which had a number one chart hit with 'You're Driving Me Crazy' in 1961. Later, he helped to found the part-work publisher Orbis and started writing true crime, with very occasional forays into fiction. In recent years, he chaired the CWA's Non-Fiction Dagger judging committee.

(4 May 1928–14 July 2014)

THE HEADLESS CORPSE

BRIAN INNES

It was early on the late-summer morning of 31st August 1986, on the A22, which runs between Nutley and Wych Cross, some ten miles south-east of East Grinstead, West Sussex. The sun was up, but there was still very little traffic on the road, except for a lone motorcyclist, taking a 'spin' in the fresh morning air.

So early in the morning, it was still cool, and soon the motorcyclist felt the need to relieve himself. The A22 runs through an area known as Ashdown Forest. (This is not thick with trees – the word 'forest' means originally a tract reserved for the monarch to hunt – but still a relatively isolated area, largely covered by a widespread growth of bracken and other scrub.)

The rider parked his bike at the side of the road, and pushed a few steps into the bracken. He soon noticed a cloud of flies not far away, and in particular a disgusting stink of putrefaction. Penetrating a yard or two further into the undergrowth, he found what appeared to be lumps of flesh wrapped in pieces of fabric. Fortunately, he decided to inform the local police at once, and soon a patrol car from East Sussex Police arrived at the scene.

Four or five years later, I was able to spend an afternoon with CID Superintendent Bryan Grove – then retired – who was the Senior Investigating Officer (SIO) in the case. 'At first,' he told me, 'we thought it was the remains of an animal, but it was a human body.' Not a whole body, however. The pieces were buried in two shallowly dug graves, some five feet apart. One contained a torso, from which all the skin had been stripped, together with the upper arms and both thighs, wrapped in some curtain; the other contained an abdomen and various fragments bundled up with another curtain, a cream-coloured nightdress and a pink negligee.

The head, hands and feet were, however, missing. 'This,' said one of the first officers on the scene, 'is a murder with a body, the like of which I have never seen before in all my life.'

The grisly fragments were assembled in the local mortuary, where they were examined by Home Office pathologist Dr Michael Heath. The head, hands and feet had clearly been severed to conceal identity, and therefore the first steps in identification were to establish whether the victim was male or female, and then make some estimate of his/her height. It was fortunate that the entire abdomen was present, because the form of the pelvis is the most obvious way of determining sex: in the female it is broader and slightly shallower, and the opening larger (to ease childbirth) than in the male.

Dr Heath was able to declare confidently that the body fragments were female. In addition, the victim was sexually mature, and slight scarring of the pelvis indicated that she had borne a child. A residual scar in the flesh of the lower abdomen indicated that she had been operated on, possibly for the removal of an abscess of the vagina, or perhaps during childbirth.

The long bones of the thighs – the femurs – can also provide an indication of sex: those of a female are generally less sturdy than those of a male. Their length can establish roughly the body's height: forensic tables provide a relationship between this and the overall stature. Dr Heath was able to inform the police that the victim was a woman, probably in her mid-twenties, and approximately five feet three inches (160cm) tall.

Her blood group was O – the commonest, and therefore difficult to pinpoint. Her skin colour, however, was of increased pigmentation, and possibly of Mediterranean origin. Time of death – always impossible to determine accurately – Dr Heath put at least two weeks, although maybe a little longer, before the discovery of her remains. This suggested that she had died, at the earliest, around the 17th of August.

All the woman's internal organs, apart from the heart and lungs, had been removed. But the state of her thorax indicated that she had died from having her throat cut before her head was severed, and Dr Heath also found a number of stab wounds to her body. This was, undoubtedly, a murder committed in a passionate rage.

'With most murders,' Superintendent Grove told me, 'the deceased is known, and that in turn leads possibly to the offender, and certainly to witnesses.' But the absence of head and hands made the immediate solution of the problem of identity seem, to the police, almost impossible.

Teams searched nearly a half square mile of Ashdown Forest without finding any further grisly remains. Over the next fortnight, more than 800 local residents within a wide radius of the site were interviewed, without success. Police files were searched for reports of missing persons: there were more than 150 to be investigated, but eventually the list of possibles was reduced to five.

One of the most promising of these leads was the report of a girl who had disappeared from a refuge in nearby Portsmouth. She was said to be extensively tattooed over her body – which would explain why the murderer, to make the corpse unidentifiable, had removed the skin from the upper parts.

But this trail, as with the other four possibles, led nowhere. The police could find none of the missing women, and there were no known circumstances to connect them to the site where the corpse was found, nor the condition in which it was discovered.

Toward the end of September, the investigating team began to feel that they were up against a brick wall. Leaflets were therefore printed, and inserted in the pay packets of every milkman and postman in the area, asking for a report of any housewife who had not been seen recently; and local TV rental shops were persuaded to include a recorded appeal among the demonstration tapes that they screened. There were no helpful results.

Grove was beginning to ask himself whether he would have to extend the inquiry nationwide – and then he received a further setback. Another serious crime required half his team to be taken from him for a separate inquiry, and among those who remained morale was at a low ebb. So he asked the BBC to feature the murder in their *Crimewatch* television programme.

'You may be able to identify the victim, or her killer,' announced the police spokesman, 'if you recognise the materials that were used to wrap her remains … These curtains, one with a floral pattern, the others blue acrylic. If you look here, you can see that somebody once took up the hem by hand.'

A woman living in Godstone, Surrey, reported that she was sure that she recognised the stitches in the blue curtains as hers: she had altered them for her son's flat. But some months previously she had sold them at a car boot sale opposite the railway station in nearby Crawley.

On measurement, the curtains exactly matched the dimensions of her son's window. Later in the investigation, it was found that these were not the identical curtains, but at the time the police realised that they should look a little further afield from the crime site, and the inquiry was switched to the town of Crawley, which was still in the vicinity. It soon flushed out a suspect.

The previous year, a Moroccan, Kassem Lachaal, had travelled to his home country with Fatima, another member of the local Crawley community, in order to marry her under Islamic law. On their return by boat to Newhaven, he had been arrested with a quantity of cannabis in his luggage. He had served a term in Ford Open Prison, before being released on parole some two weeks before the discovery of the corpse. Lachaal lived in Greenwich Close, Crawley, with Fatima and their children.

Under Islamic law he was allowed two wives (but required to sleep with them on alternate nights): his other wife, Latifa, with a son by a previous marriage, lived close by in Ramsey Court – but she was no longer there. She was twenty-six years old, and five feet three inches in height: the police already had her photograph on file, because she had earlier been convicted of shoplifting.

Enquiries immediately began with the Immigration Service, and the local doctors and hospital.

Learning of the police inquiries in Crawley, Lachaal had consulted a local solicitor, stating that, in the circumstances, he feared that he would almost certainly need legal representation. A week or so later, the solicitor wrote to the police on his behalf, announcing that he was representing him.

DC Eyre and WPC Fitzgerald of Crawley police called on the Lachaals, who told them that Latifa had announced that she was leaving for Morocco on the 18th of August to obtain a divorce from Kassem, but they had now learned that she had not arrived there. 'After ten days,' Superintendent Grove told me, 'we'd carried out all the inquiries we could make. We'd found five houses where Latifa had lived, so I took the decision that, on a single day, we'd arrest the occupants of all five houses for questioning. It was a gamble …'

Most were released after only a brief interview. But DCI Roy Winton decided on a longer interview with the Lachaals. They told a plausible tale of how Latifa had bought her own air ticket for cash, how she had left her young son in their charge – and, on the 18th of August, they had woken to find the boy's benefit book and Latifa's house keys pushed through their letterbox.

But not one of fifty local travel agents had any record of having sold Latifa a ticket – and there was, indeed, no flight to Morocco on the 18th of August – and some neighbours said they had been told by Kassem that his wife had gone to France …

And then there was the question of the two bags of 'rubbish' that Latifa had asked Kassem, he explained, to take to the local tip. Grove seriously considered the necessity of excavating the tip, in the wild hope of finding the missing remains, but was advised by his Scene of Crime Officers (SOCOs) that this would be an almost impossible task.

With so many doubts already raised, Grove knew that the time had come to obtain a warrant to carry out a thorough forensic examination of the last house in which Latifa had lived. But it was a council house, and he was dismayed to learn that, immediately after her alleged departure on the 18th of August, Kassem had asked Latifa's brother to remove all her furniture, and informed the council that she would not be returning to England. And new tenants were already in possession.

However, with warrant in hand, the SOCOs, DCs Mark Dudeney and John Taylor, were given, as they said, 'carte blanche to turn the place upside-down, starting at the front door and working our way in, and taking as long as necessary.' Fortunately for the wife of the new tenant, DC Taylor soon asked her, almost idly, if she had noticed anything unusual when she moved in, 'She came out with the classic comment, "only the blood in the bathroom".'

The new tenants were moved to alternative accommodation, and Dudeney and Taylor concentrated their attention on the bathroom. The bath itself had already been replaced by the council – it was said to have had a deep scratch in its surface – but there were still tiny stains on the wooden floor and on the bath panelling, and spot tests indicated that these were probably human blood.

Dr David Northcott of the Home Office Central Research Establishment at Aldermaston was sent for, and he asked for numerous items for further examination: 'the lavatory seat, the washbasin, even the floorboards'. In all, Dr Northcott counted 140 small stains, and his careful analysis established that these were definitely of the human blood group O.

The police had also found a scrap of blue carpet with the remains, and three similar-looking pieces were discovered, caught beneath the bathroom skirting board. Dr Northcott confirmed that these were all identical.

Grove, after the usual bureaucratic delay, obtained permission to interview Latifa's family, and obtain blood samples from them, which they willingly provided. By detailed serological analysis, Dr Northcott was able to establish that the blood from the corpse, the blood in the bathroom, and that obtained from the family, were all closely related in their profiles.

Grove was also given, by a family friend, photographs of Latifa standing in front of some blue curtains. Knowing her height, it was possible to calculate the length of the curtains – and this matched the length of those wrapped around the corpse, and their weave appeared to be the same.

As for the other curtain – in a floral pattern of blue, turquoise and cream – one of Latifa's friends recalled that she had ordered such curtains from a mail order catalogue. The suppliers confirmed that Latifa had placed an order of the appropriate value – although, unfortunately, they had no record of what she had bought.

Other police inquiries, at the local hospital and among the medical profession, made it possible to track down – in faraway Sri Lanka – the surgeon who had operated on Latifa for a vaginal abscess. And he agreed that the appearance of the scar in the flesh of the abdomen could match the incision he had made for the operation.

There was now sufficient circumstantial evidence for Kassem and Fatima Lachaal to be formally charged with the murder of Latifa, and committed in custody. This was in January 1987, following nearly six months of continuous inquiries after the discovery of the body remains. The police remained, however, uncomfortably aware that they had no solid proof that the remains were those of Latifa, nor that the Lachaals were responsible for her murder, but both they and the Crown Prosecution Service considered that the evidence was already sufficient to take to trial.

Among the Moroccan community Kassem was known widely as a persistent womaniser. One girl with whom he had an affair told the police that on one occasion, during a violent argument, he had attacked and raped her and said, 'If you're not careful, I'll cut off your head!'

There was, however, one other piece of alleged evidence that the prosecution were sure the defence would make the most of – that is, after all, what they are retained to do. Latifa's brother in Morocco reported that he had received a letter, apparently from her, that he said was dated 18th September. However, both he and his sister suggested that this could be a forgery, as they thought that it was not in her usual style.

Grove therefore applied once more to the Moroccan authorities for permission to visit their country officially, and obtained a copy of the letter: it was, in fact, dated 18th August. Under examination no prints similar to Latifa's (raised from possessions that she must have handled) appeared, but a clear print of Kassem's thumb was found close to a fold on the paper.

Moreover, the print was at an angle, which could be only explained by assuming that it was he who had folded the letter.

Grove could find no British handwriting expert with sufficient knowledge of Arabic script. He therefore, through Interpol, was able to get in touch with a French expert: his final report, however, came to no definite conclusion whether the handwriting was Latifa's or a forgery.

It was now only a few weeks before the date set for the trial, and the prosecution had already entered the evidence they intended to present, but the appointed Judge agreed to accept the letter, with its telltale thumbprint, as further evidence. However, he warned Grove that he wanted no more last-minute submissions. But then, with only two weeks in hand, a dramatic piece of evidence turned up that was to clinch the case.

A fierce hurricane hit southern England in October 1987, and brought down many trees. A woodman was clearing a stretch in woodland close to Worth Abbey – halfway between Crawley and the site of discovery of the body remains – and uncovered a skull in the undergrowth.

> 'a dramatic piece of evidence turned up that was to clinch the case.'

The police already knew that Kassem had, at one time, worked as an odd-job man at nearby Worth Abbey School. Could this be Latifa's skull, from the missing head?

Time was running out before the trial began. Latifa's dentist was contacted, and by chance he had once taken a full X-ray of her jaw. She had also attended the local hospital on an occasion after Kassem had assaulted her, and they still had an X-ray of her skull in their records.

Expert odontologist Bernard Sims took X-rays of the skull, and mapped the shape of the frontal sinus, an open space in the central forehead. This had become a standard technique for over half a century, since it had been first employed in the trial for murder of Dr Buck Ruxton in 1935. Sims also observed the line of the chin, the angle of the jaw, and the orbits of the eyes. Compared with the X-rays held by Latifa's dentist and the hospital, there was an exact match.

The trial of Kassem and Fatima Lachaal opened at Lewes Crown Court on the 29th of February 1988. Grove and his investigating team had spent eighteen months putting together all the evidence in the case, which was certainly very strong – indeed, virtually undeniable. At the opening of the trial the defence, whose main contention had been that Latifa was still, somewhere, alive, were forced to concede that she was now undoubtedly dead. Were the accused unquestionably responsible?

In view of the formidable forensic evidence presented by the police, the jury had little doubt in reaching their conclusion, and they agreed unanimously upon a verdict of Guilty. Kassem was sentenced to life imprisonment on the 24th of March, and Fatima to eighteen months for assisting in the disposal of Latifa's body.

Dogged persistence by Grove and his team, combined with that final fortuitous discovery, had at last brought identity and justice to the headless corpse.

DIANE JANES

As well as being the author of several crime
novels, including 'The Pull of the Moon',
which was shortlisted for the John Creasey
Award, Diane Janes has also written three
factual books examining real life British
murders which occurred in the first half of
the twentieth century. When not researching,
writing on, or speaking about the darker
side of life and death, she greatly enjoys
reading, watching tennis and travelling.
   Originally from Birmingham, she has
lived in various parts of the north
of England and by way of a change is
currently domiciled in Devon.

www.dianejanes.50webs.com

BABY FACE

DIANE JANES

Like many young men in 1939, Harry Livings found himself in uniform soon after war broke out. He saw active service in France, was evacuated off the beaches at Dunkirk, and after a whole series of close shaves and fortuitous escapes, earned himself the nickname 'Lucky Livings' among his army pals. In one sense of course, Harry was not fortunate at all. At the outbreak of war he was just twenty-three years old, newly married and had recently begun training as a dental mechanic, but the service of his country took a six-year bite out of his life, sending it in directions he had never wanted or expected. When he returned to Civvy Street there were no suitable openings which would have enabled him to continue his training, so instead Harry joined forces with his brother Arthur, pooling their army gratuities to start a taxi business in their home city of Birmingham.

A good many of the men driving taxis in the immediate post-war period were ex-servicemen, many of whom had acquired their driving licences in the army. In comparison with today there were fewer taxis on the road and a strong camaraderie existed among the drivers, who mostly knew each other to a greater or lesser degree. An unwritten code of honour ensured that the rule of the rank was strictly observed. This meant that taxis waited in the order of their arrival and fares were always directed to the man at the head of the line.

On Tuesday, 29th April 1947, sometime around 10.15 p.m., Harry was at the head of the rank in Stephenson Place, outside New Street Station, waiting for what he had decided would be his last fare of the night. Another driver had strolled up from a few cabs back to chat with Harry and the two men were standing on the pavement when they were approached by a young airman, wanting to be taken to Derby. Although the majority of the fares from the station rank were likely to be heading for addresses within the city or the suburbs of Birmingham itself, a request to be taken on a journey of some forty miles was not exceptional. A serviceman on a forty-eighty-hour pass, who had perhaps just missed his train and was desperate to get home and meet up with family or a sweetheart, was likely to take a taxi if he could afford it – indeed Harry had recently accepted a fare from Birmingham to Doncaster in just such circumstances.

On this occasion, however, Lucky Livings had already been working all evening, and had no desire to make a round trip well in excess of two hours, so he passed the fare to the next cabby in line – George Tyler – knowing that George, who was engaged to be married and saving hard, would be glad of a long-distance run. At twenty-six years old, George Tyler was a little younger than Harry Livings, but their route to the taxi business had been almost identical. George had served as a mechanic in the RAF and on demob he had joined forces with his friend, David Taylor, also an ex-RAF man, to start a partnership – again using their gratuities to purchase their cabs. George and David were particularly close. George's parents were both dead by the end of the war, so David Taylor's father and mother had taken George into their home when he left the Air Force, and treated him as a son. Likeable and popular, George was frequently described as the best looking driver on the rank.

With his latest passenger safely installed in the rear, George Tyler pulled out of Stephenson Place and initially drove to a nearby garage, to pick up petrol. Mr H.C. Evans, the attendant at Pearce Garage in Great Charles Street, remembered the sale (in fact he probably recognised the young cabby, as Pearce's was regularly used by taxi drivers). While filling up the car, he did not notice much about the passenger in the back, except that he was wearing an Air Force uniform, appeared to be asleep when the car arrived at the garage, but awoke briefly before immediately dozing off again, and sinking right down in the seat.

After this brief delay, George Tyler headed north. Once beyond the city centre there would have been relatively little traffic. Lighting up time that night was not until 10.28 p.m., so the taxi must have driven through the gathering dusk, then on in the darkness, steadily eating up the miles. George Tyler and his passenger were not destined to reach Derby that night however.

Mr and Mrs Hood, who lived at 3 Meadow Villas, Clay Mills, had retired to bed for the night at just after 11 p.m. Meadow Villas was an isolated row of houses on the main road to Derby, about two miles north of Burton-upon-Trent and just south of the turn for the village of Rolleston. The Hoods were still awake when, between 11.20 and 11.30, they heard some loud bangs. Mrs Hood thought it might have been a car tyre bursting. The couple's dog, Dash, began to bark loudly and Mr Hood got up and parted the bedroom curtains to look outside. He could see that a car had stopped on the opposite side of the road, a few yards north of the little row of houses, and informed his wife that it was 'a car gone wrong'. The dog continued to bark for some time, but in spite of their pet's considerable agitation, Mr Hood took no further interest in the strange car or its occupants. Mrs Hood was similarly unperturbed. As she lay in the darkened bedroom she heard sounds which she took to be someone trying to restart the car and noticed that the car lights appeared to be switched on and off a couple of times, but that was all.

Their next-door neighbours, the Hardwicks, were similarly untroubled by whatever was occurring within a few yards of their front door. Mrs Hardwick was aware of the car stopping, and of what she took to be various car doors banging, while her son, Joseph, did not hear the car at all, though he did hear the dog barking. The other residents of Meadow Villas, the Janney family, heard nothing at all. Of all the potential witnesses to this episode, only Dash the dog appears to have been concerned that anything serious might have been going on.

Mr Hood was on an early shift and when he rose for work and looked out on Wednesday morning at 5 a.m. he remarked to his wife that the car was still parked across the road. Given that some five and a half hours after its arrival, the car headlights were still switched on, one might have thought that Mr Hood's curiosity would be aroused, but Mr Hood was evidently not a curious man and when he left for work that morning, he did not look inside or take any further notice of the car at all, in spite of crossing the road as he left the house and walking within inches of it.

Local Co-op bakery roundsman, William Mitchell, exhibited marginally more interest in the unfamiliar vehicle, when he arrived to deliver bread to Mrs Hood at nine o'clock that morning. He remarked on the car's presence to Mrs Hood, who said that she thought it must have broken down the night before and been left there when it couldn't be restarted. Mitchell walked across to the car and noticed that not only had the headlamps been left on, but the keys were still in the ignition. Being a helpful sort of chap, he opened the driver's door, switched off the headlights (in order to save the battery) and also decided to remove the keys from the ignition, placing them within easy reach on the dashboard, before closing the door again. Unfortunately this brief interaction within the interior of the vehicle failed to encompass the fact that there was a body lying in the rear foot-well, a bullet hole in the windscreen, and a pool of blood, which had dripped through the floorboards of the car and was clearly visible on the road underneath the chassis. Mitchell went on his way without raising the alarm – indeed without being aware that an alarm needed to be raised. (One imagines Dash the dog, lying in his basket across the road with his head on his paws, emitting a despairing sigh.)

By now the Derby Road was busy with lorries, cars, and buses full of people heading for school and work. George Tyler's car represented quite an obstruction, parked on a well-used main road so that every vehicle travelling north had to pull round it, and literally hundreds of people must have seen it as they passed, but none of them noticed anything out of the ordinary. It was almost ten o'clock that morning before PC Challinor, who was undertaking a routine patrol on the Derby Road, was alerted to the presence of the car and went to investigate. Almost twelve hours after the fatal shooting, Staffordshire Police finally became aware that a murder had been committed on their patch.

The post-mortem established that George Tyler had died from shock and haemorrhage. He had sustained three bullet wounds, each of which had penetrated vital structures – his heart, left lung and head, but the pathologist, Professor Webster, did not consider that any of the gunshot wounds would have been sufficient to have killed him outright. The pattern of the wounds suggested that two had been fired from close proximity, while George Tyler was still upright in his seat, and a third shot had been delivered into his back when he was already slumped over the wheel of his cab. A further wound on the side of his neck suggested that the shot which went through the windscreen had grazed him as he was turning in his seat. There was no sign of any preliminary struggle. The other minor injuries found on the body were consistent with its being moved from the front to the back of the vehicle. The implication of the medical evidence was that the assailant had been in the back of the vehicle when he fired the gun, and had then dragged the young cabby out of the front of the taxi, and thrust his body into the back, between the front and rear seats. The pathologist took the view that George Tyler had bled to death, while slumped in the rear of his vehicle.

A local legend would grow up, to the effect that George Tyler's eyes had been shot out. This was undoubtedly due to an old wives' tale – clearly still current in the 1940s – which had it that a dying person's eyes recorded the last thing they had seen in life, thereby creating a kind of photographic image which could be used to help track down a killer – not only was this theory entirely without foundation, but the victim in this case was not in fact shot in the eyes.

Though the enquiry had been slow to get off the mark, Superintendent Tommy Lockley and his team wasted no time once they became aware of the incident, and it did not take them long to establish that George Tyler's last fare had been an airman. If the airman had simply walked up to the first taxi in the rank and climbed in, he might have gone unnoticed, but as chance would have it, Harry Livings and his fellow driver had both seen the airman close up and Harry had spoken with him. Lockley was also unusually fortunate in that Harry was a keen amateur artist – a man to whom accurate observation came naturally. In less than twenty-four hours the police were able to circulate a reasonably detailed description of their suspect.

The airman was estimated to be five feet eight inches tall, round faced, clean shaven, with a fresh, rather pale complexion. He had dark hair and dark eyes and spoke with 'a middle class Midland accent'. Though estimating his age at about twenty-five, the witnesses said he was young looking: 'baby-faced'.

Nor were the airman's movements in the immediate aftermath of the killing to remain a mystery for long. Half a dozen long-distance lorry drivers came forward to say that they remembered seeing an airman walking along the Derby Road that night at various times between 11.30 p.m. and 3.00 a.m. It emerged from the testimony of these witnesses that the young man had initially set off in the direction of Derby – positive sightings took him at least two miles north of the crime scene – but at some stage he had turned back and retraced his steps in the direction of the taxi. He must have walked back to within sight of the car, its headlamps still illuminating its presence opposite Meadow Villas, and at this point perhaps the young man's courage failed him, because rather than walking past the abandoned vehicle, he turned down Clay Mills Road and began walking towards Rolleston.

Somewhere along this road he must have stopped and killed time. It is possible that he rested on one of the platform benches at Rolleston-on-Dove station, which was still operational in 1947, though it would have been deserted for the night. The tiny halt on the Tutbury line (now long dismantled) was one of the few places on the airman's route which would have offered the prospect of easy shelter. Certainly by about 6.30 a.m. he had covered less than three miles since leaving the main road. At this point he can be placed at Horninglow crossroads by Albert Cheetham, a local man who lived at Beacon Hill, Rolleston, and was cycling home after working a nightshift at the British Tyre and Rubber Company in Burton. Albert Cheetham's attention was drawn to the young airman when the latter abruptly ran across the road and knelt down on the grass verge, where he appeared to be looking for something. Mr Cheetham noticed that he was also fumbling with an object in his hand, but he was too far away to see what it was. Police later searched the ground at this point and discovered two live bullets in the grass, which suggested that what Mr Cheetham had observed was the young man breaking open his gun and either ejecting the bullets onto the grass, or dropping them while reloading. Fortunately Albert Cheetham did not hang around to find out what the airman was doing, and merely continued on his way home.

The next sighting occurred at a bus stop on Horninglow Road North, where Arthur Barker, a gas fitter who lived in nearby Wyggeston Street, was waiting for the bus on his way to work. At approximately 6.55 a.m., he was approached by a young airman, who appeared dishevelled and tired, and asked him for directions to the railway station. To Mr Barker the young man had a Derby accent, rather than a 'middle-class accent' – which the Birmingham cabbies had also described as a 'posh Birmingham accent'. It is a fact that accents are subjective, depending on the listener. Citizens of Birmingham who are unfamiliar with a Derby accent may well think it sounds like a fellow Brummie, affecting some sort of posh voice, whereas a Burton man would recognise a native of nearby Derby immediately. Putting the Staffordshire and Birmingham ends of the story together, it can be virtually certain that the witnesses are all describing the same young man, and that he definitely spoke with a Derby accent.

The airman arrived at Burton-upon-Trent Railway Station at 7.40, where he bought a ticket to Derby, prior to purchasing a cup of tea and two slices of cake in the station refreshment room. The waitress recalled that he drank his tea, but left the slices of cake. He sat in the refreshment room until about 8.15, when he left to board the 8.20 train for Derby. It was a busy train and no one particularly noticed the scruffy young airman with the 'baby face'. From this point onwards, reliable sightings ran out.

Not surprisingly, given the numbers of airmen then stationed in Britain, numerous sightings of mysterious airmen were reported in the days that followed. One possible lead originated in central Nottingham, where, on the day of the murder, Dr Andrew Smith and his new bride, en route from their home in Newcastle-upon-Tyne to honeymoon in Cornwall, parked their car outside the Black Bull Hotel while they went inside for lunch. On leaving the building at 1.30 p.m., they discovered that their car had been stolen. The car – an Austin 8 – was later abandoned in the Leicestershire village of Markfield. Among the items missing from their luggage was one of Dr Smith's suits, and a theory ran that this could have been purloined by the airman, in order to disguise himself. However, there was never any confirmation that the car thief and the airman were one and the same, and when the police reunited the Smiths with their car the next day, they did not tell the couple that its theft might have been linked to a murder enquiry.

Within hours, however, came more tangible evidence back in Horninglow. At 8.30 that evening two local girls, June Stanbridge and Doreen Harrison, both aged thirteen, set out to pick some wild flowers for a school project they were engaged in. The girls lived within a few doors of each other in Horninglow Road North and they headed into the open countryside, towards Rolleston. Unaware that they were retracing the route taken by the killer earlier that day, they were intrigued when they reached the place where the brook went under Rolleston Road and spotted two torn pieces of what initially appeared to be a book, floating on the water. The girls retrieved them and realised they were fragments of clothing coupons. Interest aroused, they began to search nearby and found more pieces of torn paper, stuffed into the brickwork of the arch which carried the road over the brook. Excited by their find (while not exactly gold doubloons, the discovery of discarded clothing coupons in the immediate post-war period of rationing was pretty remarkable) the girls hurried back to Doreen's house, where they attempted to interest her mother in the unexpected results of their foray, but Mrs Harrison was doing some painting and took little notice. (The Harrisons were distantly related to William Mitchell, the bread man, who had failed to notice the victim's body when he leaned into the car to extinguish the headlamps – the family do not seem to have been genetically predisposed to detective work). However, the girls managed to create more of a sensation with their discovery when they arrived at the Stanbridge household, where Mr Stanbridge observed that the torn papers – clothing coupons and identity papers – bore the name of the murdered taxi driver, whose death he had just been reading about in the local newspaper. He went immediately to a local telephone kiosk and dialled 999.

In the days that followed, the police searched the surrounding lanes, the banks of the brook, and even dragged some local ponds and the nearby canal, but they found nothing else to assist in the enquiry. In spite of this there was no shortage of clues and the early days of the investigation promised much. In 1947, the process of demobilisation was well under way, but there were still well over half a million officers and men serving in the Royal Air Force. Superintendent Lockley requested and was provided with a complete list of RAF men stationed in Britain who had been absent – with or without permission – from their bases on the night in question. As well as some 300 men who were legitimately on leave, a further 200 were absent without leave – either for that night only, or over a longer period of time. In some circumstances a list of 500 suspects might appear daunting, but Lockley and his team had plenty of information with which to narrow down the list. A physical description and 'home' address were standard information to be found in the record of every British serviceman. Staffordshire Police were looking specifically for a dark haired, dark eyed, clean shaven man in his twenties, who stood about five feet eight inches tall, had a Derby accent and could feasibly have been climbing into a taxi in the centre of Birmingham at 10.30 p.m. that night. Some men were palpably unable to have reached Birmingham from their bases that night. Any men who had blonde or auburn hair could be immediately excluded, as could exceptionally tall men, short men, and those who wore the RAF trademark handlebar moustache. Irishmen, Cockneys, Welshmen, indeed any airmen likely to have a non-Midland accent were instantly ruled out. With help from the RAF, it took a mere two days for Lockley and his team to narrow the field to just one suspect.

The airman in question was brought to Burton-upon-Trent police station and placed in an identity parade on the 2nd of May. At least five witnesses had got a reasonably good look at the killer, including the Birmingham taxi men, Albert Cheetham, Arthur Barker and the waitress in the refreshment rooms, though the latter was clearly handicapped by the fact that there was nothing remarkable or memorable in serving one more RAF chap a cup of tea, so it was always a long shot that she would be able to pick him out.

The situation with the Birmingham witnesses was more promising. Harry Livings and his fellow driver arrived together to view the line-up, but as was good practice, they were asked to sit in separate rooms at the police station and each went in to view the parade of RAF men separately, having been told to walk along the line as many times as they wished and to then touch the man on the shoulder if they recognised him. When Harry entered the room he immediately recognised the man who had asked to be driven to Derby. He walked straight up to him and touched him on the shoulder. It was about as emphatic an identification as it was possible to get.

Only when both men had been through the identification process did they have the opportunity to confer again. The second driver had also been able to pick out the person he believed he had seen that night and one of the detectives now confided that both drivers had picked out the same man, and that this man was indeed the suspect, rather than one of the men chosen to make up the numbers.

Harry assumed that this would lead inevitably to the 'baby-faced' airman being arrested and charged with the murder, so he was very shaken when the policeman explained that they did not yet have enough evidence to bring a charge. As he and his fellow driver left the police station, they were accosted by waiting pressmen, who attempted to interview the two drivers. Someone had clearly alerted local reporters to the possibility of a scoop – though they had been given to believe that these witnesses had merely been looking at photographs of suspects. Harry was a very quiet, private person, and also a man with an eye to self-preservation. As a cab driver listed in the telephone book, who happened to have an unusual surname, Harry was taking no chances. The airman had killed once and could do so again. He gave the reporters a false name. It is possible that his fellow driver took similar precautions. The press reported that cab drivers named Walsh and Platt, or Platts, attended the police station – at least one, and possibly both these names are incorrect. Mr Walsh appears to have made no comment at all to reporters, while Mr Platt, or Platts, informed the reporters that he had not recognised any of the faces in the photographs. A couple of papers provided their readers with a somewhat longer version of an interview with Mr Platt/s, which included enough errors to suggest that the piece contained as much journalistic imagination as it did genuine comment from a key witness.

In 2006, Staffordshire Police confirmed to the present author that their records relating to the George Tyler murder have been destroyed, but even without the records it is not difficult to conjecture why – in spite of the apparently compelling evidence from the Birmingham drivers – 'Baby Face' walked free. Both Birmingham drivers had the advantage of seeing and speaking with the young man close up, in daylight. Albert Cheetham also encountered the suspect in broad daylight, but he only caught a passing glance as he cycled by, and had little opportunity to commit the young man's face to memory. Though he thought the man he had seen that morning was in the line-up, he could not be completely certain. No firm evidence survives regarding the success or otherwise of the identification process in Arthur Barker's case, but it is possible that he had not registered enough about the young man who asked directions to be sure of identifying him a couple of days later.

It is not of course necessary for every witness to identify a suspect before there is sufficient evidence for him to be charged. The testimony of the Birmingham drivers was strong – and in 1947 it was far from unknown for the police to bring charges based on identification evidence alone – if the young airman had been unable to account for his movements that night, the case might well have gone to court. It is therefore almost certain that the investigation came up against a stumbling block in the form of an alibi. Someone – a wife, or girlfriend, a family member, or just a good mate – was willing to vouch for Baby Face that night. Someone somewhere was prepared to say that by 11.30 p.m. on the night of 29th April, Baby Face was safely tucked up in bed and nowhere near Clay Mills.

What Tommy Lockley and his team needed was a magic bullet which would smash that alibi apart, exposing it for the lie it was. Alas forensics proved useless – the car was covered in fingerprints, none of which could be definitively matched to the airman. (Even if they could, a defence lawyer would no doubt point out that as the vehicle in question was a hire car, his client might legitimately have travelled in it at some point previous to the murder, just like the owners of all the other prints found in and on it.)

The present author is convinced that as early as the 2nd of May, Lockley knew the name of his man and exactly where to find him. On the 2nd of May – the day of the identity parade – although the superintendent managed to keep secret the presence of a suspect within the police station, he confidently told reporters that he expected to be able to provide them with a solution in the next thirty-six hours. Three days later Tommy Lockley was a little less upbeat, but stated that 'the answer will be found in Derby' and that yes, he believed the suspect was still in the Derby area. He and some of his colleagues travelled to Derby on the 5th of May, and in the face of questions about this from reporters, Lockley responded that he wanted to establish whether the wanted man had friends in Derby – a very curious statement to make unless he had some idea of who the airman was.

If Tommy Lockley's purpose in seeking out the airman's Derby friends was to shake someone's statement regarding Baby Face's whereabouts when George Tyler was shot, then he met with no success. As days turned into weeks there was no further public intimation of an imminent arrest. At the conclusion of the inquest on the 6th of June (a verdict of wilful murder against person or persons unknown was recorded), Superintendent Lockley appealed to the public, saying:

'Someone, somewhere, knows who this man is.' The plea fell on deaf ears. In spite of repeated forays to pursue enquiries in Derby, Lockley never got the breakthrough that he was hoping for.

In October 1948, his hopes must have risen with news of an important discovery. George Brown of Tatenhill was working on his brother's smallholding, which bordered Rolleston Road, when he caught his foot on something while clearing a ditch. The place was only about 250 yards from the point where Albert Cheetham had encountered the airman on the morning after the murder, and when Brown bent to get a better look at the object in the mud, he discovered it was a gun which had been shoved, barrel first, deep into the side of the muddy ditch. He immediately reported his find to the police.

Superintendent Lockley persuaded the press to maintain silence about the discovery while the weapon was taken to the lab for cleaning and testing for prints – no need to alert his man to the discovery and give him a chance to run for it.

'Someone, somewhere, knows who this man is.'

The gun was a Smith & Wesson .38 revolver, still loaded with live bullets, and a perfect match for the murder weapon – but in the end the gun revealed nothing. The serial number identified it as one of a consignment shipped to Britain in December 1941 under the Lend Lease Program – one weapon among many which had managed to find its way into unauthorised hands, its provenance immediately prior to 1947 untraceable. No fingerprints had survived the eighteen months buried in the mud. (The large numbers of unauthorised ex-service revolvers in circulation at this point is underlined by reports during the week of the murder of .38 revolvers being handed over to the investigation after being found respectively in a railway carriage and lying on a public pavement.)

George Tyler's funeral was a huge affair: the cortege included thirty Birmingham taxis and hundreds of people lined the route to the cemetery. His fiancée Doreen eventually married and went to live in America, where she died at the comparatively young age of fifty-two.

When Tommy Lockley retired from the police force, he was succeeded in his role as head of CID by Frank Tucker, who had worked alongside him during the Tyler investigation. Like all the senior officers involved in the case, both men have long since died.

Harry Livings, one of the most important witnesses in the case, has also been dead for some years. After George Tyler's murder he did not continue for very long as a taxi driver, dissolving the partnership with his brother, Arthur, and finding work in a local factory. Harry was conscious that just as he knew the killer's face, so too the killer knew his. It would not be terribly difficult to lure a taxi driver to his death, in order to remove an inconvenient witness. There was also the issue of Harry's young wife, left alone in the evenings while he was out driving. He did everything he could to keep his identity out of the newspapers, and warned her to close the door on any reporters who managed to sniff them out. When giving up the taxi business, he also had the telephone – and thereby his directory entry – removed, and the family remained without a telephone for many years afterwards.

Harry never forgot the murder and although entirely blameless, he always felt that he had been in some way responsible – as if in passing on the fare, he sent George Tyler to his death. Being the 'lucky' survivor can sometimes be a terrible burden.

And Baby Face got away with murder. It is impossible to say why he decided to kill George Tyler that night. The police established with reasonable certainty that George was not known to his killer – like so many taxi murders (it remains a statistically dangerous job to pursue) it was a case of being in the wrong place at the wrong time. The killer had no way of knowing that George Tyler would be on the rank in Stephenson Place – in fact George had started his shift on the rank at Snow Hill, but his penultimate fare must have brought him to the city's other principal railway station.

Robbery may have provided a motive. The killer took George's papers and some – though not all – of the money he was carrying. It is impossible to know how much money was taken, since there was no record of how many fares had been carried that night – but at the inquest George Tyler's partner, David Taylor, suggested that the sum was probably a relatively small one. He knew that his partner always started a shift with £1 for petrol and thirty shillings for small change, and that he had probably undertaken several journeys before his final run – but these would have netted him relatively small sums – the meter had only clocked up thirty shillings on the journey from Stephenson Place to Meadow Villas, and the fact that George Tyler had purchased five gallons of petrol would have accounted for about ten shillings. Taylor did confirm that before undertaking a long-distance run, neither man would have been likely to ask for any money up front, unless something about the person wanting to make the journey had appeared suspicious, so we can also assume that nothing in the airman's initial demeanour gave George Tyler cause for concern.

The location of the murder is another source of mystery. The car was found parked neatly at the kerb, just twenty-four feet from the nearest dwelling, with no suggestion that the driver had become alarmed and brought his vehicle to a sudden halt, preparatory to an attempted escape from a madman with a gun. If something in his passenger's behaviour had alerted George Tyler to the possibility of trouble, there is a faint chance that he spotted the houses and hoped to get some help from within – though nothing in the evidence supports this and there were apparently no lights burning, which would have made the houses stand out.

It is more likely that the airman readied his gun in the darkness, then asked the driver to stop, believing he had chosen an isolated spot, well away from any habitation. He then shot George Tyler and moved his body into the back, with the intention of driving the taxi on towards his destination himself. It is clear that the murderer had not chosen the location because he knew it well. His behaviour in walking several miles towards Derby, then turning back and walking an almost circular route, via Rolleston and Horninglow, before catching a train from Burton-upon-Trent (having first needed to seek directions for the station) cry out that he was not familiar with the geography around Clay Mills. The police said that they believed the airman to be a competent driver –

something they can only have based on the theory that he initially intended to drive the taxi himself. However, the airman was not *that* competent, because he only succeeded in turning the headlights on and off, before giving up and starting to walk instead.

What is clear throughout is that the main objective in the mind of our suspect was his desire to reach Derby. Was it merely the prospect of a night with his girl, or a taste of home cooking which drove him to such desperate lengths that he took a taxi he could not afford, with the deliberate intention of robbing and killing the driver en route? Or is it possible that the innocent taxi driver was not the only intended victim? That perhaps the gun was originally taken along with a view to using it on someone else? Whatever the original thinking behind it, the journey did not pan out as intended. Rather than getting to Derby by midnight, the young man found himself wandering around deserted rural roads, with blood on his hands and a death on his conscience. By early morning he had decided to rid himself of both gun and remaining ammunition. Instead of arriving in Derby by car, complete with a loaded gun, he travelled there by train, unarmed, got off at 8.40 in the morning … and went where? By now he must have assumed that the police were already looking for him. (He had no way of knowing that George Tyler's body would be lying clearly visible, yet still undiscovered, where he had left it in the car.)

Even the most amateur of criminals knows that what they need in such circumstances is an alibi – and the chances are that our man immediately went in search of one, extracting a promise from someone that very morning, who would forever afterwards steadfastly insist that he had been with them all night.

It is unquestionably the case that the person who lied for Baby Face knew what he had done – if not on the day when they made him that promise, then very soon afterwards. The murder was all over the local and national newspapers; he fitted the description and was taken in for questioning. It is inconceivable that the person who alibied our man did not know about the terrible crime he had committed – but their story remained unshaken all the same.

Did the young murderer flinch when Harry Livings strode up to him so confidently: did he feel that touch on his shoulder and perhaps sense the shadow of the hangman's rope nearby? Did he ever pass the spot on the Derby Road again and remember the night of 29th April 1947?

It is probable that this man from Derby is long gone – as I write this in 2014, his estimated age would now have reached ninety-two. The theoretical person who provided his alibi – and I feel confident that there was such a person, for without an alibi of some kind, there would surely have been an arrest – is equally likely to have passed on by now, taking their secret beyond our reach. It is sobering to think that Baby Face might have gone on to become a friend or neighbour to any one of us, perhaps even a loving grandfather by the end of his days, with no one suspecting that for reasons we will never know, still less begin to understand, on an April night in 1947 he robbed an innocent young man of his own chance to live.

*

In writing and researching the foregoing account, I have relied on a variety of archival sources, including more than a dozen different newspapers. I am grateful to Staffordshire Police and Smith & Wesson for checking their archives, and also to the families of the late George Tyler, Albert Cheetham and Dr Andrew Smith; and particularly to the family of the late Harry Livings, whom it has been my great privilege to count as friends and family for almost half a century.

JOAN LOCK

Joan's first book, 'Lady Policeman', described her six years as a policewoman. The next, her training as a nurse. Nine non-fiction, police/crime books followed including three on Scotland Yard's First Detectives and a history of the British Women Police, a subject on which she is an authority. Her fiction includes one modern ('Death in Perspective') and seven Victorian crime novels featuring the charismatic Scotland Yard Detective, Ernest Best. Joan has also written short stories, radio plays and documentaries, and many features for 'Police Review' and 'Red Herrings', the journal of the Crime Writers' Association.

www.joanlock.co.uk

A CRIME OF CONSEQUENCE

JOAN LOCK

'There has been a tragedy in surrey', announced *The Times* on the 3rd of October 1850.

The tragedy was a murder but one aggravated by the fact that not only had the county of Surrey no police to investigate the crime but that fact had brought about the tragedy in the first place. Nearby London had police, as had the local small town of Godalming and city of Guildford. Consequently, claimed *Times'* correspondents, the countryside in between had become 'a prairie of predatory excursion' and warned that its inhabitants were all arming themselves.

Of course, the homes of the wealthy were prime targets but in quiet rural villages the less-guarded parsonage was often the most substantial house and sometimes even had church plate on the premises. The home of fifty-four-year-old Perpetual Curate Reverend George Edward Hollest was just such a house, set back in its own grounds, on the edge of sleepy Frimley.

On Friday, 28th September 1850 he and his wife Caroline were asleep in their four-poster bed on the first floor while along the corridor were their two teenage sons just home from boarding school. At about 3 a.m. they were awoken by the sound of footsteps, a light shining in their eyes and masked figures pointing pistols at their heads. Thinking they were his two sons playing jokes, Reverend Hollest told them not to be so silly at this hour and to go back to bed.

His wife realised this was no joke and screamed, whereupon the masked intruders threatened to blow their brains out if they made another sound. But Caroline was a spirited woman. She leaped out of bed and reached for the bell rope to warn the servants, causing one of the men to rush around the bed, seize her with such force that the rope broke, and lie on top of her holding the pistol close to her eyes.

Though older, Reverend Hollest was also a fighter. He too had jumped out of bed and was bending down picking up the poker by the fireplace when his assailant fired his pistol, hitting him in the stomach. The shock of the report caused the man holding Mrs Hollest to release his grip momentarily. She rushed to the fireplace, seized a large handbell and rang it several times. The men fled. Reverend Hollest rushed into the next room, picked up the gun he always kept loaded and gave chase, firing off a shot at the fleeing figures as he did so. Only as he returned to his wife did he realise that he had been shot.

Even today a gunshot wound in the abdomen is liable to be life threatening. In those days before antibiotics and modern surgery it was an almost inevitable death warrant. The local doctor, who found Hollest in good spirits when he arrived half an hour later, nonetheless concluded from the direction the bullet had taken that the wound was mortal. Sure enough, on the evening of the following day, the Reverend Hollest died in agony. By then, Sergeant Edward Kendall of the Metropolitan Police Detective branch had arrived on the scene.

DS Kendall was one of the newer men in the Detective Branch, which, since its inception in 1842, had suffered much vehement criticism about its crime-solving attempts from the press, public, magistrates and coroners. Make a rapid arrest and they were acting too quickly. Take their time and they were clearly out of their depth and the Bow Street Runners should be recalled.

Their investigations were of course not then aided by fingerprinting, blood or DNA analysis, or reliable poisons tests. They had no transport with which to pursue and if they made use of the limited omnibus system or railways they had great difficulty in recouping their costs from the Commissioners. There were no typewriters or telephones. Communication was mostly limited to messengers, Her Majesty's Postal

Service and their own internal route paper system, through which they passed information from division to division via horseback riders.

But things *were* beginning to look up. The magic new electric telegraph was speeding up *some* communication. They had had a recent success in the handling of the Mannings murder, and a kinder eye was being cast upon the detectives by Charles Dickens, who had practically fallen in love with them that summer when he met them over brandy and cigars in his *Household Words* office.

These working class men not only had power and confidence, 'led lives of strong mental excitement', enjoyed a wonderful camaraderie and an unselfish appreciation of each other's talents, but also had some fascinating tales to tell. He passed his enthusiasm on to his public.

Dickens found Cornishman Edward Kendall to be 'a light-haired, well spoken, polite person', who was 'a prodigious hand at pursuing private enquiries of a delicate nature'.

When DS Kendall arrived at Frimley he examined the parsonage's scullery window where the men had gained entry, found the mark of a naked foot in the doorway and a trace of blood. There were more naked footprints in the garden and under a tree and marks on the ground 'such as would have been made by a corded jacket or trousers', and he discovered a small piece of baize, which turned out to be of the same material as the burglars' home-made masks.

The thieves had made quite a haul: three watches (two gold and one silver), various small silver items, two lads' rough blue-cloth overcoats (with the names marked on tape), a bag of copper coins collected for the Parish Clothing Fund, and a gold ring set with a bloodstone and on which 'Forget Me Not' was engraved in Old English lettering.

Frimley did in fact have two parish constables (householders taking their turns at the duty) and they had already gone over the scene and removed an umbrella and a stolen telescope from under a tree in the garden.

Also deciding to become involved were the chiefs of Guildford police (Inspector Hollington) and of Godalming's tiny force (Inspector Biddlecombe) and they had the benefit of local knowledge. Hollington soon decided who was probably to blame, and went off in search of three likely suspects: Levi Harwood, James Jones and Hiram Smith. When he discovered that they had been absent from their homes on the night in question he arrested them. A fourth suspect was soon added to the group: Samuel Harwood, cousin of Levi.

So now four varieties of police were involved, none with ultimate authority but all doubtless keen to demonstrate their superior methods. Not a recipe for success.

The seeds of possible dissension were quickly sown when *The Times* credited the Scotland Yard man with the decision to arrest the suspects. The fact that the Coroner kept deferring to the Yard man can't have helped. But Kendall was clearly aware of the potential problems. At the inquest, he stepped forward every now and then to prevent too much information being made public (Westminster's famous Coroner, Thomas Wakley, had been haranguing police about letting out too much information at inquests) but when the Coroner asked Kendall to relate the circumstances of the case he said diplomatically, 'I beg your pardon, Sir, but Inspector Biddlecombe was at Frimley before I arrived, and perhaps you would obtain a more correct history of the case by taking his evidence first.'

It seemed that despite Kendall's efforts to be diplomatic, trouble was brewing as *The Times* reported next day:

Nothing fresh whatever has transpired calculated to throw light on the perpetrators of the crime. The police are still actively engaged in their inquiries – Sergeant Kendall on the spot, Inspector Hollington at Guildford, and Inspector Biddlecombe between the two places. There is no doubt that each officer is using his best exertions, but from what transpired today there is too much reason to fear that a degree of jealousy mars their united operations.

But something fresh had in fact transpired. Hiram Smith had turned Queen's evidence, or in current parlance become 'an approver'. The actual murderer was not allowed to escape justice in this fashion even though

The Times thought Smith was probably the ringleader. Besides which he had a sallow, unhealthy skin, an extremely forbidding expression, sharp, prominent features and a hesitating glance which marked him out as a rogue. But Smith insisted that it was not he who had fired the fatal shot but Levi Harwood.

He proceeded to relate chapter and verse on the lead-up to the tragedy. According to him, on their walk from their homes to Frimley the four men had armed themselves with two horse pistols[1] and loaded them with stone marbles. They broke into the parsonage through the scullery window and, while three of them feasted on bread, beef, wine and spirits the fourth, Samuel Harwood, kept watch outside fortified by a decanter of wine and sheltered by an umbrella taken out to him when it began to rain. Then, reassured that their presence had not been noticed, all four went up to the Hollest's bedroom, Samuel remaining by the bedroom door because he had no mask. And indeed young Samuel Harwood was found Not Guilty due to lack of evidence but soon after was rearrested for a similar burglary elsewhere, for which he was convicted and transported for life.

The other two defendants simply denied all the charges. The ruffian-looking Levi Harwood, whose 'coarse and rugged features betrayed violent passions', claimed he couldn't have done it because he had been in London, and James Jones, whose whole physiognomy, *The Times* felt, expressed a life of depravity and crime, claimed he had been out on the Downs watching the snares he had set for rabbits.

Witnesses identified Smith as having been in the village a few days earlier on the pretext of selling crockery – presumably for the purpose of spying out the burglary prospects – and many people claimed to have seen the men on the road to Frimley that night.

'coarse and rugged features betrayed violent passions'

---

1   A large pistol carried in a holster by men on horseback.

Caroline Hollest's view of the whole room had been obstructed by the bed curtains but during her spirited evidence she firmly identified Levi Harwood's voice as that of the man who had held her and approver Smith as the man who had fired the shot. She also identified a penny found on one of them as having been amongst those in the missing bag of parish clothing fund coins. It had been very worn – the King's nose being so battered that it had almost been discarded.

Kendall gave evidence of finding a cut on Levi's foot, which tied up with the blood found beside the footprint. The measurement of another footprint corresponded with Smith's right foot.

James Jones and Levi Harwood were found guilty and hanged. Harwood, after much pressure, confessed at the last minute that he indeed had been the one who had fired the fatal shot.

One consequence of the murder was that Surrey got its County Constabulary. Indeed, the matter had been long mooted but the murder proved a tipping point. Within a month a Rural Police Committee had met in Reigate, Surrey, and the new force became operational in January 1851 whilst the Frimley murder suspects were awaiting trial.

Amongst its seventy recruits were William Henry Biddlecombe, who became one of the first five Superintendents as, shortly afterwards, did Guildford's chief, Charles Hollington. Oddly, one of Hollington's earliest acts in his new capacity was to write a furious letter to *The Times* in response to a magistrate's claim that the credit for breaking up the Frimley Gang was due to Inspector Biddlecombe of the Godalming Police. He (Hollington) had apprehended no less than six[1] of them, he insisted, entirely on his own suspicions!

Whilst Kendall had been at Frimley, Scotland Yard's other new detective, Sergeant Smith, was down in Frome, Somerset, helping out another police-less county with another home invasion murder (that of a fourteen-year-old girl). Somerset was not the only other crime-plagued area. After a Surrey man claimed a dozen burglaries within ten miles

---

1   He was including two other local burglars who were convicted and transported for life.

of Frimley within a few months, another *Times'* reader exclaimed: 'Why, Sir, we have had half a dozen in Birkenhead alone in the last few days!', whilst a Cambridge man claimed a plague of highwaymen attacking villagers returning from market and university men visiting friends. All reluctant regions were to get police, whether they wanted them or not, when the County and Borough Police Act came into force in 1856.

Another consequence of the Frimley murder was in April 1851, when the Reverend Joseph Smith of Walton in Cumberland became frightened by continuous knocking at his parsonage window at around midnight. He reached for the six-barrelled revolving pistol he had acquired following the Frimley murder, opened the door and fired blindly into the night. The next morning, the body of William Armstrong, a respected local landowner, was found just inside the parsonage gate whence he had staggered. (Apparently Armstrong was drunk after a long market day and may have been trying to visit Ann Glendinning, a servant at the parsonage, who had previously been his servant.)

The third major outcome, and this time a joyful one, was on 16th October 1852, at St Botolph's Church in the City of London, when forty-two-year-old Caroline Hollest, 'a woman with a warriors heart'[2], married the 'light-haired, well-spoken, polite', thirty-seven-year-old Inspector[3] Edward Kendall.

---

2 Caroline was so described in a broadsheet ballad, one of several which PlanetSlade. com suggests that you might like to set to music, and record singing and playing, as part of The Gallows Ballard Project!

3 He was promoted to Inspector following the Frimley murder.

PETER LOVESEY

Peter has published thirty-six novels and
five collections of short stories. His work
has been adapted for radio, TV and film and
is translated into over twenty languages.
He won the Gold Dagger for 'The False
Inspector Dew' in 1982 and in 2000 he was
honoured by the Crime Writers' Association
with the Cartier Diamond Dagger. He is
a Grand Master of the Swedish Academy
of Detection and a winner of the French
Grand Prix de Littérature Policière.
The latest in his award-wining Peter Diamond
series is 'Down Among the Dead Men'.

peterlovesey.com

THE TALE OF THREE TUBS: GEORGE JOSEPH SMITH AND THE BRIDES IN THE BATH

PETER LOVESEY

I first read about the 'Brides in the Bath' in a book called *The Life of Sir Edward Marshall Hall*. Odd reading for a ten year old whose friends were working their way through Enid Blyton and Richmal Crompton, but my house had recently been destroyed by a V-1 flying bomb and we had almost nothing left. This was a damaged copy belonging to my father that must have been salvaged from the bombsite. At an age when my inner world had been transformed by reading, I picked up the book and was enthralled. Marshall Hall was the renowned defence lawyer involved in many of the sensational trials of the past fifty years. And what evocative titles they had: the Green Bicycle Murder; the Camden Town Murder; Seddon the Poisoner; the Yarmouth Beach Case; and Madame Fahmy at the Savoy. Then I came to the Brides in the Bath. For some mysterious reason the Bath was in the singular, as if the same tub had been used over and over. But the book soon put me right. Three 'brides' were murdered in baths as far removed from each other as Herne Bay, Blackpool and Highgate.

This was a complex case involving scores of locations. The serial bigamist, George Joseph Smith, could not risk staying in one place for long. He is known to have made at least six illegal marriages. A hundred and twelve witnesses gave evidence at his trial. That he was guilty of wilful murder was agreed by the jury in just over twenty minutes, despite

Marshall Hall's best efforts. Smith did himself no favours by several times interrupting the Judge during the summing-up. He was described by the author of his entry in the *Notable British Trials* series as 'the most atrocious English criminal since Palmer'. On the other hand, his first victim wrote, 'He is a thoroughly good husband, and I am as happy as any woman breathing, in fact, everybody seems to take to him.'

More than anything, it was Smith's formula for making money – his 'system', as it was termed at the trial – that made the case exceptional. Three women were destroyed by it. Shortly before their deaths each was persuaded to make a will in Smith's favour. Two took out life insurance policies and the other had a substantial trust fund that passed to Smith after her death. All three were induced to visit a doctor complaining of headaches and the same doctor was called in soon after to confirm that they were dead. Each woman took a bath in an unlocked room. On each occasion, Smith drowned her, went out briefly to buy food, returned and made sure someone else in the house was with him shortly after he 'discovered' the body. Used once, the system was artful and efficient. Twice, and it was risky. Three times, ruinous.

So much has been written about the personalities in the case – Smith, Marshall Hall, the expert witness, Bernard Spilsbury, and the victims – that I thought it might be different to approach it obliquely by focusing on the baths and their part in the case and after. They have an intriguing history.

Let us start in an ironmonger's shop in the seaside town of Herne Bay in July 1912. This is a time when poorer houses weren't equipped with bathrooms. A customer is examining a bath, not a hip bath, but a cast-iron, five-foot bath with a plug. The shop owner, Adolphus Michael Hill, forty-one, recognises him as Henry Williams, a slim, handsome man about his own age who has leased a house in the High Street for at least a couple of months. We know him as George Joseph Smith. The bath is second-hand, Hill explains. 'How much do you want for it?' the customer asks. 'Two pounds,' Hill says. The customer says he will think about it – which any shopkeeper knows is often a get-out – and leaves.

But two days afterwards, Mrs Bessie Williams comes into the shop and says *she* is interested in buying the bath, but not for as much as two pounds. She is willing to offer half-a-crown less. Hill ponders the matter and notices that the lady is pitifully agitated and excited. 'Mr Williams told me to say you must let us have it,' she says. Hill is sympathetic and agrees to the reduction. He promises to deliver it to the house in the High Street the next day. No money changes hands. These are people he has met and trusts.

It slightly undermines the 'brides in the bath' tag to reveal that Bessie was not a recent bride. Smith had met and married her eighteen months before, in 1910. She was one of the string of hapless women he cheated out of their savings in bigamous marriages, before disappearing from their lives. She had inherited £2,500 from her father, a bank manager. Her uncles, as trustees, had placed this considerable sum (worth more than a quarter of a million pounds in modern money) into a trust fund for Bessie, enabling her to draw £8 a month in interest. Within a week of their register office wedding in 1910, Smith realised he stood no chance of getting his hands on the capital sum. Instead, he demanded £138 that he said was legally due to Bessie in excess interest. When the trustees' cheque arrived at Bessie's solicitors he insisted on having it cashed. He then deserted her. Devastated, Bessie sent a telegram to her Uncle Herbert, 'Husband left me today. Taken money. Please send me some. Writing. Bessie.'

As if being abandoned was not cruel enough, Bessie received a letter the next day from Smith that began, 'Dearest, I fear you have blasted all my bright hopes of a happy future. I have caught from you a disease which is called the bad disorder, for you to be in such a state proves you could not have kept yourself morally clean.' He added that this would cost him a great deal of money to be cured and might take years.

She called the police and wrote to her uncle, 'I do hope my husband will be caught … I quite see now what I have fallen into, and I feel I have disgraced myself for life.' There her ordeal might have ended were it not for a twist of fate, a coincidence you would not expect to find outside a Thomas Hardy novel.

In March 1912, eighteen months after Smith deserted her, Bessie took a short holiday in Weston-super-Mare. While walking on the promenade she chanced to meet her errant husband. But instead of calling the police, she allowed herself to be persuaded that he still loved her and had been looking for her and that he had been mistaken about the sexually transmitted disease. The £2,500 was still being held in trust and Smith had thought of a new way of getting his hands on it. The couple were reconciled. Fast forward to Herne Bay in July 1912.

When he arrives to deliver the bath, Adolphus Hill, the ironmonger, is surprised to be told he and his assistant must carry it upstairs to the back bedroom. This is strange for a bath that won't be plumbed in. The only water supply is downstairs. Bucketfuls of heated water will have to be carried up two flights of stairs and later the process will go into reverse when the bath needs to be emptied. The room where the bath is to go is about as far away from the copper downstairs as it is possible to be. Unusually, the couple have their bed downstairs in the dining room. On the first floor there's a vacant bedroom with a lock, but Hill and his assistant are told to pass that and go up more stairs to this small room that doesn't have a lock. Later it is calculated that when Mrs Williams half-filled her bath the trips up and down the stairs with the bucket must have taken forty-two minutes.

Four days later, Smith returns to the shop and asks Mr Hill to collect the bath from the house, as he wishes to return it. He says he will be leaving Herne Bay shortly. The bath has still not been paid for, so the shopkeeper retrieves his property. He only hears later that Mrs Williams died in it, apparently of an epileptic fit.

The sequence of events over that week in July 1912 became the blueprint for George Joseph Smith's 'system'. On 8th July, the couple had attended a solicitor's and completed the process of making wills leaving all their worldly goods to each other. On the 10th they had visited a doctor and reported that Bessie had a fit the previous day. On the 12th the doctor was called to the house at 1.30 a.m. because, the husband said, Bessie had had another fit. The doctor prescribed more medicine, deciding she might be epileptic. On the 13th, Smith called the doctor out again because Bessie was dead in the bath. This was early Saturday morning. An inquest was held on the Monday and the Coroner concluded she drowned accidentally while suffering another fit. The funeral was Tuesday.

All remarkably quick. And because there was no post on Sunday, there wasn't time to invite Bessie's family to the funeral. They lived in Wiltshire, almost two hundred miles away. Smith disliked them anyway, and the feeling was mutual. The Mundys had been suspicious from the start that he married Bessie for her money.

The inquest on Bessie was at best perfunctory. It was held in the Herne Bay council chamber at 4.30 in the afternoon and was concluded the same day. The Coroner, Rutley Mowll, when questioned at Smith's trial, couldn't remember many of the details. He couldn't be sure whether the jury, who visited the house, had been shown the bath. He thought the body was seen in a coffin upstairs. No post-mortem had been ordered. No measurements had been taken of the body or the bath. The Coroner's officer, PC Kitchingham, was better informed. He had been called to the house on the day of the death and seen the body upstairs lying naked on the floor and the bath three parts full of soapy water. When the inquest jury had visited, the body was in a coffin in the dining room downstairs. They hadn't gone upstairs to see the bath and hadn't asked to see it. The only other witness at the inquest, apart from Smith, was Dr French, who had been called to the house on the morning of the death.

Under questioning in 1915 at Smith's trial for murder, Dr French explained why he had concluded that the cause of Bessie's death was asphyxia caused by drowning in the course of an epileptic fit. He had been told at the first consultation that she had suffered a fit and he had been called out in the night to see her because of another. 'The following day I am called in and I find her drowned in a bath. Again I have no suspicion; I have no reason for suspicion that there is any foul play.' She was a tall woman, at five feet nine inches, and she was lying on her back in the five-foot bath with her face submerged and her feet out of the water resting against the sloping end. The bath was about two-thirds full. He had removed the body from the bath and tried artificial respiration. There were no marks of violence. Her right hand was still clutching a bar of Castile soap.

If Smith had settled for one profitable murder, the crime was unlikely ever to have been detected. However, the system had worked so efficiently that when an opportunity arose he couldn't resist using it again.

So the Herne Bay bath was returned to the ironmonger's. Whether it was bought by anyone else in the two and a half years before the law caught up with Smith, I cannot say with any certainty. It seems unlikely that a cheap, used bath would have been allowed to take up room in the shop all that time. In 1915, its whereabouts were traced and it was transported to London, to Kentish Town police station, where a murder enquiry was under way. Two more baths had been brought there, one from Blackpool, the other Highgate. The sensational story of the 'Brides in the Bath' was about to break.

The Blackpool victim was Alice Burnham, a nurse. She had met Smith in mid-September 1913 (two months after Bessie's death), in the Congregationalist chapel in Southsea, near Portsmouth. He liked to portray himself as a devout man. His letters – of which many survived – are peppered with sanctimonious sentiment. He was also a past master at charming the ladies. He must have felt confident with Alice because he used his own name when he introduced himself. Within two months she married him, on the 4th of November 1913. But they didn't have a chapel wedding. He preferred the local register office.

The system powered into action again: demands and threats to the family for money. Alice wasn't an heiress like Bessie, so the best way to capitalise on her coming death was to take out life insurance. A honeymoon by the sea in Blackpool. This time, the house where they lodged was furnished with a plumbed-in bath. A visit to a local doctor, to get something for Alice's headaches. On the third evening, the 12th of December, Alice announces she would like to take a bath and the landlady's daughter runs the taps for her. Smith goes out briefly, returns, shouts for assistance and asks the family to fetch the doctor – who discovers Alice dead in a bath filled to the top with soapy water. Smith is supporting her. Between them, they lift her out and try artificial respiration, but it is too late. The police are called and a sergeant inspects the body downstairs, but doesn't look into the bathroom. The inquest, the next day, is got through in half an hour. This time the doctor has already carried out a post-mortem and found the symptoms of drowning. He describes Alice as 'well nourished, very fat' and observes that the heart was enlarged and the valves diseased. This, he feels, probably contributed to her collapse. The verdict of the jury – who listen to statements, but don't visit the house – is that she 'was probably seized with a fit or a faint'. Another accidental death.

Smith profited by £140 of Alice's money, plus life assurance of £500. It wasn't enough to fund him for long, so he fitted in another bigamous marriage – his fifth – before resorting to murder again. He met another Alice in Woolwich and deprived her of her savings of £78, her piano, furniture and spare clothes, and then deserted her while out walking in a park. Alice Reavil lived to tell the tale.

The next bride did not. In December 1914, Smith decided to use the system again. He married a Bristol woman, Margaret Lofty, in – of all places – Bath. She was less well off than either of the previous brides, but she was an easy catch, having recently been badly let down by a fiancé who had turned out to be married already. Smith, now masquerading as John Lloyd, persuaded Margaret to take out an endowment insurance policy for £700. The system required that the murder must take place a long way from Bristol, so he travelled to London in advance and found lodgings in Orchard Road, Highgate. He was seen by one of the lodgers there, a Mrs Heiss, who sometimes handled arrangements for the landlady, Mrs Lokker. When shown the vacant room, he asked if there was also a bathroom. The bath was rather small for his purpose. He studied it with calculation and finally commented, 'I daresay it is large enough for someone to lie in.' He paid six shillings as a deposit, but when asked for a reference said the ready money ought to be reference enough. He would return with his wife on the following Thursday.

Everything was in place once more, the insurance, the register office wedding, the trip to London for the honeymoon and the lodgings furnished with a bathroom. But there was a hitch. When the couple arrived at the house about three in the afternoon, the room wasn't ready. They were asked to come back about six. Smith was annoyed and made his feelings clear. They left their luggage in the hall and returned a little after five-thirty and knocked several times, but no one came to the door. They had to wait until six. Mrs Lokker was cautious about who she took on as lodgers, and Smith sounded troublesome. She had arranged for a male friend, who happened to be a detective sergeant, to stand in for her and tell this unpleasant man that as he hadn't provided a reference he was not a desirable lodger. 'Mr Lloyd' said, 'This is a funny kind of house. I want my deposit back.' The couple were forced to walk the gas-lit streets of Highgate looking for another place to spend their wedding night.

Smith wasn't deterred from his plan. They parked their bags – a holdall and a Gladstone bag – at Highgate tube station and started the search. On the way, they passed a doctor's surgery in Archway Road, duly noted. Eventually they found rooms to let at 14 Bismarck Road. Miss Blatch, the landlady, carrying a lighted candle, took them up to the attic on the second floor and showed them the furnished room. On the way downstairs, Mrs Lloyd asked if there was a bathroom and Miss Blatch pointed to a first-floor room with a bath and w.c. The bath was slightly longer, at five foot six, plumbed in and cased in wood. Smith agreed to take the room at seven shillings per week and paid in advance. Then he went off to collect the luggage while Miss Blatch made tea for Mrs Lloyd. Later, the couple went out again to visit the doctor and get something for a headache Margaret had developed.

The murder next day went according to plan. During the afternoon Mrs Lloyd enquired whether she could have a bath later. Miss Blatch got it ready for her about seven-thirty, heating some water in the kitchen and providing towels and soap. The Lloyds had been for a walk and were in the sitting room downstairs. Soon after, Miss Blatch was ironing in the kitchen below the bathroom when she heard someone go upstairs. 'A few minutes after that I heard a sound from the bathroom. It was a sound of splashing. Then there was a noise as of someone putting wet hands or arms on the side of the bath, and then a sigh. The splashing and the hands on the bath occurred at the same time. The sigh was the last I heard. The next sound I heard was someone playing the organ in the sitting room.'

Mr Lloyd was playing *Nearer My God to Thee*. Quite a musician in his way, he filled the house with music for ten minutes, and then Miss Blatch heard the front door slam. Presently the doorbell rang and she opened it to find Lloyd there with a paper bag in his hand. He told her he'd been out to buy tomatoes for Mrs Lloyd's supper and forgotten he had a latchkey. He asked if his wife was down yet. He went upstairs and called her name.

The process followed the usual pattern. A shout from Lloyd, 'She is in the bath. Come and help me.' After finding him in the gas-lit bathroom holding his wife's upper body above the water, Miss Blatch said she would go for help. It was pretty obvious to her that the woman was dead. Lloyd said, 'Fetch Dr Bates. I took her to him last night.' By chance, Miss Blatch met a police officer on patrol duty only fifty yards away. PC Heath ran to the house and discovered Lloyd kneeling beside the body on the floor. The constable tried artificial respiration until Dr Bates arrived. The doctor decided the woman must have died from asphyxiation caused by drowning. Later he would say at the inquest that she might have fainted in the hot bath. He had thought she may have had a mild form of influenza, which was rife at the time.

The inquest and funeral followed, although not so rapidly as after the previous deaths. Smith was obliged to remain at 14 Bismarck Road longer than he had planned. The inquest was four days after the death, on the 22nd of December, and then adjourned until the 1st of January because Miss Blatch had injured her knee and was unable to get there.

However, the Coroner allowed the funeral to take place on the 23rd of December. The only mourners were Smith and one of the Lofty family, a cousin. Like the other dead wives, Margaret was buried in a common grave. Rather than remaining at Bismarck Road over Christmas, Smith left for what he said was a cycling tour. He returned for the resumed inquest and it went according to plan. Mrs Lloyd, the jury decided, had died accidentally, from suffocation by drowning.

All done. It remained only to cash in. On the 4th of January 1915, Smith visited a solicitor and produced the marriage certificate, the life policy and the will, and instructed him to obtain probate. The system appeared to have worked for a third time in three years. But there was something he had not factored in: the power of the press.

The story of a bride found dead in her bath was perfect material for the *News of the World* with its reputation for scandalous and suggestive human interest stories. 'FOUND DEAD IN BATH: BRIDE'S TRAGIC FATE ON DAY AFTER WEDDING,' ran the headline on the 3rd of January. The paper would be seen by more than two million readers, and one of them was Charles Burnham, the father of Smith's second victim. Burnham's dislike of Smith was absolute. He had fought to prevent him getting his hands on Alice's modest savings. This, of course, had incensed Smith. When Burnham had requested information about his background, Smith had replied on a postcard,

> Sir, In answer to your application regarding my parentage etc. My mother was a Buss horse, my father a cabdriver, my sister a rough rider over the Arctic Regions. My Brothers were all gallant sailors on a Steam roller. This is the only information I can give to those who are not entitled to ask such questions contained in the letter I received on the 24th inst. Your despised son-in-law, G. Smith.

Charles Burnham read the account of the Highgate incident in the *News of the World* and couldn't fail to notice the similarities to Alice's drowning, even though the names of the husbands were different. He took out a cutting about his daughter's tragedy he had kept from a local paper: 'BRIDE'S SUDDEN DEATH: DROWNED AFTER SEIZURE IN A HOT BATH.' He showed both to his solicitor, who sent them to the police. Meanwhile, Joseph Crossley, the son-in-law of the Blackpool landlady, was also a *News of the World* reader and he, too, wrote to the police.

The true horror of what had been committed was about to be exposed. The newspaper clippings were attached to a memo headed SUSPICIOUS DEATHS and forwarded to Detective Inspector Arthur Neil, who was based at Kentish Town police station and actually lived in a flat in Archway, the Highgate street 'Mr Lloyd' had walked along on his way to Bismarck Road. Neil spoke to PC Heath, the officer Miss Blatch had called to the house the night Margaret Lloyd had died. Heath had discovered the lifeless woman lying naked on the floor in the bathroom doorway. He had tried unsuccessfully to resuscitate her. He had formed a bad impression of the husband – having to tell him 'in pity's name' to fetch something to cover her modesty.

Inspector Neil decided to see the Bismarck Road bathroom for himself. He swiftly decided it was 'a physical impossibility' for someone to drown accidentally or through fainting in a bath of this size. Its entire length was five feet six and the inside length, where someone taking a bath would recline at the base of the sloping end with their feet against the vertical end, was four feet two. Moreover, it had a wooden top shaped to the curves of the bath that overhung the bath by five inches at the head end and two and a half inches at the head end.

Intensive enquiries were set in motion. As well as interviewing Miss Blatch – who thought it impossible for Mr Lloyd to be in any way responsible – the Inspector spoke to Dr Bates and the cousin who had been at the funeral. None of them appeared to have any doubts that it had been an accidental death. But no one seemed to know where Mr Lloyd was living now.

At this stage, there were suspicions of two murders. The motive: financial gain. The Blackpool police had discovered that Smith had insisted he needed a number of extra copies of Alice's death certificate, which was likely to mean he had claims with several insurance companies. Inspector Neil traced the Bristol insurance company Mr Lloyd had used in connection with Margaret's death and, through them, a Mr Davies, the solicitor who was acting on Lloyd's behalf, and had obtained probate. Lloyd had given Davies an address that was no longer current, but he had recently called at the solicitor's to enquire about his legacy. It hadn't been ready. More documents were required before the money could be released. Smith had been annoyed at the delay. This was quite a breakthrough, because it gave the police a chance – in modern parlance – to stake out the solicitor's office on the Uxbridge Road in confidence that Lloyd would be back.

Days passed while the police kept surveillance, first from the street and later from a room over the pub opposite. Finally, on the 1st of February 1915, a man answering Lloyd's description was seen entering the solicitor's office and was arrested as he came out.

'Are you John Lloyd?' Inspector Neil asked.

'Yes.'

'Your wife died in a bath at Bismarck Road, Upper Holloway, on the 18th December last – the day after she was married to you.'

'Quite right.'

'You are also said to be identical with George Smith, whose wife died under similar circumstances on the 13th December 1913, at Blackpool and to whom you were only married a few weeks.'

This was too much. 'Smith? I'm not Smith. I don't know what you're talking about.'

When pressed – informed that Alice's father was prepared to come down and identify him – the prisoner owned up to the double identity, insisting that the deaths of his two wives were 'a phenomenal coincidence'.

With Smith in custody, held on the lesser charge of causing a false entry to be inserted in the marriage registry, a spate of police activity got under way. Tracing the bigamous marriages and stashes of money in banks and post offices was a huge challenge, involving forces all over the country. And within a week came the astonishing news from Kent of a case two years earlier involving the sudden death of another young woman in a bath – Bessie Williams, in Herne Bay. The picture of the husband, known as Henry Williams, bore a striking resemblance to George Joseph Smith.

The notion of coincidence had stretched beyond breaking point. For Inspector Neil, the investigation moved to a new, more challenging phase. If Smith had murdered the women, how had he done it? A quick-acting poison? Brute force? There had been no attempt at concealment except for the changes of name. Two of the murders had been carried out in guesthouses where other people were present. In all three cases a doctor had been called. There had been no sounds of violence, no screams. There were almost no marks on the bodies, just some slight bruising of the third victim's arm.

The victims were exhumed for post-mortem examination by Dr Bernard Spilsbury, a rising forensic pathologist who had been an expert witness at the trials of two notorious murderers, Dr Crippen and Frederick Seddon. Both had been poisoners, but in Smith's case no traces of poison were found in any of the victims. They had drowned, but how?

While Spilsbury was giving his attention to the post-mortem results, Inspector Neil arranged to have a closer look at the three bathtubs. He had them all brought to his police station at Kentish Town. The ones in Blackpool and Highgate were disconnected and removed from the respective boarding houses and the bath from Herne Bay was also traced and transported there.

To Neil's eye, it was difficult to imagine anyone drowning naturally in any of these baths. The largest, the Highgate one, was only four feet two inches (1.27m) along the bottom. He was unable to work out how the women could have been held under water without grabbing the sides and struggling – in which case their bodies would surely have taken some bruising. He decided to experiment. Another drama was about to be enacted. He sought the help of a young woman swimmer 'used to diving, plunging and swimming from early girlhood'. All three baths were filled and 'in each one demonstrations were given by this young lady in a swimming costume in many positions'.

The volunteer must have been courageous to agree to climb into each bath in turn, knowing that a woman had died there, and was probably murdered. After a series of experiments to see whether there was a risk of accidental drowning as the woman lowered herself into the water and then leaned forward as if to wash her hair, she was asked to lie back and allow Neil to put pressure on her forehead and force her head under the water. It wasn't the answer. She grabbed the sides to save herself.

The next experiment almost resulted in another drowning. Neil wanted to test sudden immersion, so without warning he grasped the young woman's legs and lifted them. She slid below the water and showed no resistance.

To his horror, Neil realised she had lost consciousness. He raised one of her arms and it was lifeless. He and his colleagues lifted her limp body from the bath. 'For nearly half an hour my detectives and I worked away at her with artificial respiration and restoratives.' That must have been one of the worst half-hours of Neil's life. Eventually, the life-saving efforts worked. Some colour returned to the subject's face. When able to speak, she said the water had rushed into her mouth and up her nostrils and she remembered nothing else until her consciousness returned.

'He raised one of her arms and it was lifeless.'

The experiments ceased at once. Bernard Spilsbury's biography makes clear that he had not witnessed what went on and had disapproved of it. However, he certainly profited from Neil's discovery. He was able to make a convincing case in court that Smith's *modus operandi* was to reach into the water and raise the legs high.

When the trial opened in June 1915, the only victim named in the charge was Bessie Mundy, the Herne Bay victim. Even so, all three bathtubs had been brought to the Old Bailey and stored under the courtroom. They would all be exhibits in the case, for early in the trial the Judge, Mr Justice Scrutton, ruled that evidence of Smith's alleged system of murder would be allowed. This enabled the prosecution to point to similarities between all three drownings and it effectively sealed Smith's fate. The trial was one of the longest on record, with one of the swiftest of verdicts.

So the baths had their day in court. On Day Three, when Adolphus Hill, the ironmonger, gave evidence, the Herne Bay bath was brought in and set on the end of the solicitors' table in front of the jury, the first time such a bizarre exhibit had ever been seen in the Central Criminal Court. At one stage, the foreman of the all-male jury asked that someone should be put in the bath 'for ocular demonstration'. The Judge was having none of it. 'I can only suggest to you that when you examine these baths in your private room you should put one of yourselves in. Get some one of you to try who is about the height of five feet nine.'

Imagine the thoughts of the jury at this minute, eyeing each other to see who was the nearest in height. Marshall Hall, appearing for the defence, suggested that the prosecution should provide someone in open court, but the Judge dismissed the suggestion. 'It is much better the jury should try for themselves, Mr Hall. There are disadvantages in the French system of reconstructing a crime.'

On Days Four and Five the court's attention turned to the drowning of Alice Burnham. The Blackpool bath and its wooden casing were brought into court. Dr Billing was given a red pencil and asked to mark the place where he thought the dead woman's buttocks had been positioned. Unusually, she had been lying with her head – supported by Smith – towards the taps when he was called to the house.

The Highgate bath appeared on Day Six, when Miss Blatch, the landlady at Bismarck Road, gave evidence and recalled hearing noises from upstairs when she was ironing in the kitchen. 'It was a sound of splashing. Then there was a noise as of someone putting wet hands or arms on the side of the bath, and then a sigh … The next sound I heard was someone playing the organ in the sitting room.'

The evidence of the pathologists, Spilsbury and Dr William Willcox, took up most of the next day. After explaining at length why he did not believe Bessie Mundy had died from some form of fainting or fit (she would have recovered consciousness at the moment of submersion), Spilsbury asked for the Herne Bay bath to be brought in again (by which time the court functionaries who did the heavy work must have been silently cursing), to demonstrate how a person might be drowned in a half-full bath in only nine inches of water when the feet were pulled up and the head pressed down. The inrush of water through mouth and nostrils would cause a shock resulting in immediate loss of consciousness. Willcox endorsed the theory. Nothing Marshall Hall extracted in hours of cross-examination undermined the expert witnesses.

When the Judge summed up on the ninth day, he was compelled to point out that there was no direct evidence that Smith murdered Bessie. If they arrived at a guilty verdict, it would be based on circumstantial evidence. But as the circumstances were gone over in minute detail, including all the financial manoeuvrings and the so-similar deaths of the other brides, the case against Smith became so overwhelming that the prisoner himself started interrupting the Judge. Wisely, Marshall Hall had kept him silent up to then, but he shouted repeatedly, 'You may as well hang me at once the way you are going on'; and 'Go on, hang me at once, and be done with it'; and 'What about it? That does not say I done a murder. It is a disgrace to a Christian country, this is. I am not a murderer, though I may be a bit peculiar.'

'I am innocent.'

The jury agreed that he was a bit peculiar. But they also decided he was a murderer. They retired at 2.48 p.m. and returned their verdict at 3.10 p.m.

An appeal was heard and dismissed on the 29th of July and on the 13th of August, Smith was hanged at Maidstone. His last words were, 'I am innocent.'

Curiously, while under sentence of death, he succeeded in convincing the chaplain at Maidstone Prison that indeed he had been wrongly convicted. The chaplain asked the Bishop of Croydon to come and meet Smith, and he, too, became convinced that although the man had 'been steeped in every villainy' for over twenty years, he was not a murderer.

Marshall Hall, who corresponded with the bishop, wrote back: 'That he did not drown them in any of the ways suggested by the evidence, or the *ex parte* suggestions of the Judge, I am convinced; but I am equally convinced that it was brought about by hypnotic suggestion. I had a long interview with Smith, under very favourable circumstances, and I am convinced that he was a hypnotist.' Hall didn't go on to suggest that the chaplain and the bishop had been hypnotised, but instead surmised that Smith had satisfied his own conscience that the act of drowning was induced by his will and was, 'to all intents a voluntary act on the part of the woman.'

Edith Pegler, one of the bigamously married 'wives' who survived, told the *Weekly Dispatch* shortly after the execution, 'He had an extraordinary power over women. The power lay in his eyes. When he looked at you for a minute or two you had the feeling that you were being magnetised. They were little eyes that seemed to rob you of your will.'

Professional hypnotists insist that nobody in trance can be induced to do anything harmful to themselves. Drowning oneself in a bath while hypnotised would surely be impossible. Smith was a controlling man who demonstrated time and again that he could persuade women to trust him absolutely, and this must surely have facilitated his 'system'. All three of his victims went with him to a doctor complaining of headaches just when it suited him, and each decided to take a bath within forty-eight hours of the consultation – events remarkable enough to suggest that his willpower had been impossible to resist.

Whatever were the secrets of his persuasiveness, Smith had paid with his life and few, if any, would miss him. But his notoriety held an enduring fascination, particularly for writers. The bestselling novelist Edgar Wallace reported on the trial for *Tit-Bits*. The playwright George R. Sims, who also attended at the Old Bailey, was inspired to write *The Bluebeard of the Bath*. William Bolitho produced a small masterpiece of irony, an essay headed *The Self-Help of G.J. Smith*. And in due course the case was written up by Eric R. Watson for the *Notable British Trials* series. Among crime writers who referred to Smith in their books were Dorothy L. Sayers, Agatha Christie, Margery Allingham, John Dickson Carr, Graham Greene and Patricia Highsmith. George Orwell wrote nostalgically about the harmonium-playing in *Decline of the English Murder*. Eric Ambler went in search of the boarding houses where the murders took place. William Trevor's short story, *The Child of Dynmouth*, reworked the plot. As recently as 2010, a new account of the case by Jane Robins, *The Magnificent Spilsbury and the Case of the Brides in the Bath*, was published to critical acclaim.

After their court appearances, the three baths could no longer remain in the bowels of the Old Bailey and they would not have been welcomed back to Kentish Town police station or the guesthouses that had housed them originally. However, there was interest from Madame Tussaud's for their Chamber of Horrors, which was basically a section of the waxwork show intended to chill visitors' spines. The macabre extra element was that some of the exhibits were relics of notorious crimes. For many years the wax figures were dressed in the actual clothes of murderers, acquired after execution from the public hangmen, who considered this one of their perks.

Tussaud's did a deal for the bath from Bismarck Road, Highgate. Soon after Smith's execution, it was exhibited at Marylebone Road and became a feature of the show for many years, labelled as the bath in which Smith's final victim, Margaret Lofty, had been murdered. If I may become personal again, I recall being impressed by it – and by Smith's figure beside it – on a visit there in the 1940s.

Another of the baths was retained by Scotland Yard for what was then known as the Black Museum. Many years later, on a privileged visit with members of the Crime Writers' Association, I saw the dusty old bath stored in a small room along with a fine collection of macabre items such as death masks, hangmen's nooses, Jack the Ripper's letters and Charlie Peace's burglary instruments. One of our party sat on the edge of the bath while we were being given a lengthy explanation about some other gruesome exhibit. When told its story, the lady shot up as if it was red-hot.

With the passage of time and the arrival of new exhibits for both exhibitions, the two baths were put into storage. The third, the Herne Bay bath, had long ago been turned into scrap. You might think this was the end of the story, but it isn't. There is another twist.

Newspaper accounts of the Black Museum from the 1930s onwards suggested that *their* bath was the one from Bismarck Road. This seems to have gone unchallenged until a family historian, Gordon Lonsdale, decided to investigate a story that his great-grandfather, William Ashforth Drabble, a Blackpool Detective Inspector, assembled evidence for the trial, including the bath Alice Burnham had died in, and travelled with it by train to London. The family legend was that he had scratched his initials, WAD, on the bath. Gordon Lonsdale emailed the Crime Museum in June 2013, to see if there was any way the story could be checked. Paul Bickley, the curator, and formerly a Detective Inspector in the Flying Squad, had no reason to doubt the provenance of the bath in the Yard's possession, but he decided to investigate. For at least a quarter of a century, the bath had been stored in a warehouse at Charlton, but it was no longer there. Paul eventually traced it to a disused room at Hendon Police Training College. And when he examined it, he found Drabble's initials scratched quite small on the inside. The family story was confirmed and Scotland Yard concluded that their bath was, after all, the Blackpool one. As extra confirmation, a second set of initials, JC, was found. They are assumed to have been put there by Joseph Crossley, the son-in-law of the Blackpool landlady. Crossley was one of the people who had seen the *News of the World* item and written to the police. The whole story was written up in the *Blackpool Gazette* of 10th December 2013 and appeared on the Internet.

For the latest thinking on the tale of the tubs, I consulted the historical researcher and actor, Keith Skinner, who is a part-time volunteer at the Crime Museum. He told me that the discovery had prompted a fresh inspection of the files. They showed that when Inspector Neil decided to bring the three baths to Maida Vale early in 1915, two of them (from

Herne Bay and Blackpool) were bought from the owners and became the property of the police. The third (from Highgate) was acquired on loan and the astute owners waited until it was returned to them and then sold it to Tussaud's along with a few extra items relevant to the case. This bath was removed from the Chamber of Horrors some years ago and is now apparently in storage.

After Smith's trial and execution the former owner of the Blackpool bath contacted Scotland Yard and offered to buy it back, but this was seen as a possible attempt to exploit the crimes and rejected. The Black Museum didn't have the space for two baths, so the one from Herne Bay was destroyed. The Blackpool bath was retained for the museum – which wasn't open to the public – and somehow in the years between the two world wars it was mistakenly assumed to have been the one from Bismarck Road, Highgate.

In 2013, the surviving (Blackpool) bath made another journey, on extended loan to the Galleries of Justice museum in Nottingham. And there, in September 2014, it went on display as part of a First World War: Heroes and Villains exhibition. No need to ask which category Smith represented. The irony that so many hours were spent in 1915 deliberating over his fate while thousands of innocent soldiers were losing their lives had not been lost on the court – and was commented on by both the Judge and Marshall Hall, who called it 'a tribute to our national system of jurisprudence'.

So the Blackpool bath was exhibited along with Sir Bernard Spilsbury's forensic evidence cards as well as the actual dock from Bow Street Magistrates' Court where the accused man stood when he was committed for trial. With nice timing, the exhibition was due to end in August 2015, exactly a century after George Joseph Smith's notorious life was brought to a close.

Sources

Bolitho, William, *Murder for Profit*, Dobson, 1926
Browne, G. & Tullett, E.V., *Bernard Spilsbury: His Life and Cases*, Douglas, 1951
Fido, Martin & Skinner, Keith, *The Official Encyclopedia of Scotland Yard*, Virgin Books, 1999
Hodge, Harry (ed.), *Famous Trials 2*, Penguin, 1940
Marjoribanks, Edward, *The Life of Sir Edward Marshall Hall*, Victor Gollancz Ltd, 1929
Neil, Arthur Fowler, *Forty Years of Man-Hunting*, Jarrolds, 1932
Robins, Jane, *The Magnificent Spilsbury and the Case of the Brides in the Bath*, John Murray, 2010
Watson, Eric R. (ed.), *Trial of George Joseph Smith* (Notable British Trials series), 1922

With thanks to Bev Baker, Joan Lock and Keith Skinner.

LINDA STRATMANN

Linda is the author of sixteen books of crime fact, crime fiction and biography, including the popular Frances Doughty Mysteries, and an acclaimed biography of the notorious Marquess of Queensberry. She is currently working on the next Frances Doughty book and a history of nineteenth-century poison murders. In her spare time she enjoys cooking.

www.lindastratmann.com

THE CASE OF THE GREEK GIGOLO

LINDA STRATMANN

Nicolas Kostolo was a Greek from Constantinople, tall, handsome, and with an easy charm that both recommended him in society, and disarmed suspicion. He was also vain, duplicitous and utterly without shame. The question that came before the Paris Court of Assize in November 1823, however, was whether or not he was a murderer.

Kostolo, then aged thirty, had lived in France for six years and although he often claimed that he was looking for work, there was no evidence that he had ever been engaged in regular employment. Since 1822 he had been living off the generosity of his mistress, the Dame Olivereau.

That summer Kostolo made the acquaintance of a seventy-one-year-old widow by the name of Flamand, and told her a heart-rending tale of the sufferings of his family, his own poverty and desire to obtain a post as a *valet de chambre*. The widow Flamand, moved by the plight of the seductive Greek, arranged an introduction to her niece, Marie Boursier.

Marie Adelaide Bodin had married Guillaume-Etienne Boursier in 1809. Shortly afterwards he opened a grocery shop at the corner of the Rue de la Paix, Paris. The trade prospered, and in 1823 the business was making 11,000 francs a year with excellent prospects. Boursier planned to continue in business for another four years, by which time he expected to be able to retire on an income of 15,000 francs, (then £600 or about £50,000 in 2014). Marie, by then the mother of five children aged between five and twelve, took an active role in the business.

Monsieur Boursier could be both quick-tempered and excitable, but he also had a robust sense of humour and many good qualities that had earned him numerous friends. The family shared their house with the widow Flamand, a cook, Josephine Blin, who in the summer of 1823 had been in their service for four months, two shop men and a shop woman, Mademoiselle Reine.

Into this bustling and contented household came the handsome adventurer, Nicolas Kostolo, whose pleasing manners so captivated both Monsieur and Madame Boursier that he became a frequent visitor. The supposed purpose of his visits was to enquire whether the lady of the house had obtained a situation for him, but his real reason was to worm his way into her affections so she would give him money. Kostolo had mastered the art of flirtatious talk, saying whatever he knew would most please and flatter a lady in a light-hearted and teasingly suggestive manner. In the case of Madame Boursier, however, he may have gone too far.

Madame Boursier was a diminutive woman, four feet five inches in height, with no pretentions to beauty. Her features were plain and irregular, her complexion reddened and marked with smallpox. She was undeniably gratified by the attentions of the tall, young Greek with his exotic good looks, and readily gave him the money he requested. When he suggested that they meet privately she was eager to do so.

To avoid suspicion Madame Boursier told her husband that she intended to take a walk for her health, then, accompanied by Mademoiselle Reine, she departed early one morning and strolled to the Champs Élysées where, by prior arrangement, they met Kostolo and went to his lodgings in the Rue de Grammont. This was nothing more than an innocent friendly visit, but on the second and third of her healthy walks, Madame Boursier went indoors with Kostolo alone and told her companion to call for her later.

On another occasion Madame Boursier formed a party for a carriage trip to Versailles, together with Mademoiselle Reine and another friend, hotelier Monsieur Alberti. On the way they encountered Kostolo as if by chance, and the carriage stopped so he could join them. Kostolo accompanied Madame Boursier throughout the day, the two walking together arm-in-arm. This pleasant outing was kept secret from her husband. When Madame Boursier attended the baptism of her niece's child, it was Kostolo who accompanied her.

The betrayed husband suspected nothing, or he would not have planned a journey to Havre, whereupon his wife, delighted at the freedom his absence would allow, invited her lover to spend the night at her house.

On the 28th of June, Monsieur Boursier rose early in good health and spirits. Marie had been unwell the previous night and had been prescribed an emetic, which she had taken, so remained in bed rather longer. Boursier decided to play a practical joke on his sick wife, and, creeping into her room as she lay asleep, drew a moustache on her upper lip with the black pomade he used for his hair. He then asked Josephine Blin to wake her mistress and give her a looking glass. When Madame Boursier saw her face in the mirror she was very angry, which only made her husband laugh the more. She pouted a great deal as she was dressing, but when she came into the shop all seemed to be forgiven and the couple embraced.

The family breakfast was rice pottage thickened with egg yolks, which was prepared by Blin in an iron stew pan. That morning Blin, after reserving portions for herself and the youngest child, carried the pan into the dining room just behind the shop at nine o'clock and placed it on a desk not far from where Madame Boursier was sitting. Monsieur Boursier was not in the room, but at the shop counter reading the newspapers. Blin returned to the kitchen to eat her breakfast, and about five minutes later Boursier came into the dining room and helped himself from the pan.

As soon as Boursier had eaten a little of the pottage, he called Blin to him and complained that it was bad, saying it had a nauseous, poisonous taste. Blin protested that this was impossible, as she had already eaten some herself; in fact, she declared, it ought to be better than usual as that morning she had used three egg yolks instead of two.

Boursier, who seems to have been remarkably compliant, allowed himself to be persuaded that the breakfast was wholesome. 'Since it is good,' he said, 'I must eat it.' He ate a few more spoonfuls, but stopped and declared that the pottage was certainly bad and it was impossible for him to eat any more. The words were hardly out of his mouth when he was seized with an attack of vomiting which was so violent that he brought up not only the rice but green bile from his stomach.

Madame Boursier went to prepare a glass of sugared water to help alleviate her husband's distress, but his sickness continued with such force that the vomit was streaked with blood. Boursier was taken to bed, complaining of pains and weakness in his bowels, and there followed many repeated and particularly foetid evacuations.

Boursier had planned to take a trip with his friend Alberti that day, but when the hotelier arrived he found Boursier too ill to stir from his bed. Boursier complained to his visitor that the pottage had burned his throat.

While her husband lay on his bed of pain, Madame Boursier was not idle. She removed the stew pan of rice from the dining room, threw away its contents, rinsed it under a fountain, and ordered the servant to clean it thoroughly. Blin did so, scouring it with sand and ashes.

A medical attendant, Sieur Bordot, was summoned to the sick man and Josephine Blin told him that both she and the child had eaten the rice without harm. Had Bordot suspected poison, he might have tried to wash his patient's stomach with copious draughts of fluid, a simple remedy that could have saved Boursier's life, however, Bordot decided that Boursier was simply suffering from indigestion, so he ordered some soothing potions, and left.

Kostolo arrived for his usual visit at three in the afternoon, and appeared surprised at the sudden and alarming illness of his friend. He asked Boursier what ailed him, but Boursier, who must have believed his doctor, said it was nothing. Kostolo returned to his lodgings.

By the time Bordot returned at six, Boursier's condition had worsened. The doctor applied leeches and a mustard seed poultice, neither of which made any difference to his patient's sufferings.

Kostolo came back the same evening and seeing that Boursier was in considerable distress, volunteered to stay with him overnight. Madame Boursier refused at first but he persisted and she agreed. When Boursier complained of thirst his wife prepared some lime flower water, which Kostolo gave him. Next morning when there was no improvement, another doctor called Tartra was called in. Madame Boursier told him that she had eaten some of the breakfast rice after it had been brought in by Blin, and by now her husband was too ill to confirm or deny her statement. Tartra ordered additional medicines, and Kostolo, ever attentive, remained by the sickbed to administer them.

As Boursier's condition worsened, a medical student called Toupié was hired to sit by his bedside overnight, but at four o'clock the next morning the patient's agonies were over.

Toupié noticed that the extremities of the corpse were unusually cold, and that the nails had a bluish discoloration, a sign to which Kostolo also drew attention. When Bordot and Tartra arrived neither could account for their patient's sudden death and the appearance of the body gave them cause for disquiet, since discoloration of a fresh corpse was believed to be the sure sign of an unnatural death.

'discoloration of a fresh corpse was believed to be the sure sign of an unnatural death'

Madame Boursier was asked if she would allow a post-mortem examination, but refused. The medical men appealed to her on behalf of her children, saying that it was important to know if their father had died of some hereditary disease, but despite the most earnest entreaties she would not be moved. Her sister-in-law also urged her to allow it, but Madame Boursier replied that the cause of her husband's death was already known; he had died from a flow of blood to the head.

The chamber in which the corpse lay was low ceilinged and, in the Parisian summer, very warm and close. Madame Boursier, claiming that she was concerned that, due to her husband's 'full habit of body', putrefaction might commence immediately and damage the stores of the shop, urged that burial should take place that very same evening, and asked two of her late husband's friends to apply for permission. This was not granted, but on the following day Monsieur Boursier was buried in a private grave in the cemetery of Père Lachaise.

It was not long before Kostolo's continued daily visits to Madame Boursier gave rise to scandalous reports. A grocer friend of her late husband was told that Kostolo was already speaking openly of his intention to marry the widow, and rumours began to circulate that Monsieur Boursier had died from poison.

There had certainly been poison in the Boursier household. That March, the grocer, concerned at the rats and mice swarming in his cellars had bought half a pound of arsenic from a neighbouring druggist and some ratsbane (rat poison) in the form of a malleable paste. He and his assistant, Bailli, had made up some balls with the arsenic and placed them in the cellar. The symptoms Boursier had suffered in his last illness – a burning of the throat with severe abdominal pains and violent vomiting and diarrhoea – were those associated with acute arsenical poisoning.

Monsieur Demoutiers, an examining judge of Paris, was appointed to investigate the case, and Bailli, who had appeared troubled and agitated at Monsieur Boursier's funeral, was questioned closely. Bailli told Monsieur Demoutiers that it was public opinion that Madame Boursier had poisoned her husband, but said that he did not know what had become of the arsenic that remained after the balls of rat poison had been made up, as his master had taken charge of it.

Demoutiers also questioned doctors Bordot and Tartra. Despite being ordered to be discreet, they were unwise enough to warn the widow Boursier about the enquiries that were being made concerning her possible role in her husband's death. As soon as she knew about this, the daily visits from Kostolo ceased. Soon afterwards the police took over possession of the grocery shop, and also Kostolo's lodgings in the

Rue de Grammont. Both were searched minutely but no traces of poison could be found.

Weeks had now passed since the death of Monsieur Boursier, and it was then almost unheard of to exhume a body to look for poison within more than a few days of burial. Many doctors still believed that the bodies of people who had died from poison decomposed more quickly than in cases of death from natural causes, making exhumation not only unpleasant and dangerous but useless. The preservative effect of some mineral poisons was not yet fully appreciated. In Germany, a few exhumations of long-buried bodies had been carried out which had provided proof of poison, but this was not widely known outside that country.

Demoutiers decided to call in the man who was undoubtedly the leading forensic toxicologist in France, and most probably the world. Mathieu Orfila was Professor of Medical Jurisprudence at the Medical Faculty of Paris. His groundbreaking two-volume treatise on poisons, published in 1814 and 1815, had brought him international renown and he was inevitably consulted in any poisoning case that presented difficulty.

On the 30th of July, a month after the death of Monsieur Boursier, Demoutiers asked two important questions of Monsieur Orfila – was it possible after the lapse of so much time to detect poison in a body, and if it was, was it safe to attempt an exhumation? The absence of reliable antiseptics and any real means of fighting infection made the second question especially pertinent. Orfila, with the authoritative confidence that was his usual manner, replied that in the case of mineral poisons it was easy to detect them after a month or even longer. Exhumation was undoubtedly dangerous, but it could be made safe if precautions were taken.

On the following day the *procureur du roi* (public prosecutor) ordered the body of Monsieur Boursier to be exhumed. A team of expert analysts led by Monsieur Orfila was appointed to examine the remains, and at seven in the morning a deputation of police and the medical team attended the cemetery together with some friends and relatives of the deceased. The body was removed from its coffin and after formal identification, placed on a table for examination.

The exterior of the body was in an advanced state of putrefaction, and it was necessary to sprinkle it with a liquid that would dissipate the bad smell. The doctors then proceeded to open the body and found the interior to be in a remarkable state of preservation. Monsieur Orfila applied a ligature to the upper and lower ends of the alimentary canal and the whole was removed to the School of Medicine for further examination.

Although the delicate tests to reveal the presence of arsenic in organic tissue had yet to be devised, there were in 1823 several methods by which the experienced examiner could determine its presence in a corpse. Usually all available methods were applied in order to arrive at a firm conclusion. Powdered arsenic, as many a murderer has discovered to his or her cost, does not dissolve easily in water. Its gritty, coarse crystals will mix well in food, but were often to be found as visible deposits on the interior of the victim's intestines, when they could be scraped off and subjected to testing. Arsenic is also a powerful irritant, and on the interior surface of Monsieur Boursier's stomach were angry red patches, which were clear signs of inflammation. In the lower intestines was an undissolved white powder mixed with balls of fat.

The simplest and most time-honoured test for arsenic at the time was placing the suspect substance on a fire, where it would burn with a characteristically garlicky smell. In recent years a number of more sophisticated methods had been developed, based on the discovery that certain chemicals added to a solution of arsenic resulted in the formation of brightly coloured precipitates. Monsieur Orfila and his team were able to entirely satisfy themselves that the white powder in the intestines was arsenic, and present in sufficient quantity to account for Monsieur Boursier's death.

The team also reported that there was no evidence of any rupture of blood vessels or ulceration to suggest that death might have occurred from natural causes.

Monsieur Boursier had undoubtedly died from poisoning with arsenic, but Demoutiers now had to consider if it was the result of crime, suicide or accident.

Demoutiers thought suicide unlikely. Boursier was a successful, popular and prosperous tradesman, expecting to retire in comfort in four years' time, and the father of five children. He knew nothing of his wife's infidelity. His cheerful practical joke on the morning of his illness was the act of a man untroubled by anxiety. If he had administered the poison to himself he would hardly have called attention to the bad taste of the rice.

There was no evidence to suggest that the arsenic could have got into the ingredients of the rice pottage by accident, or other poisonings would have followed. The inevitable conclusion was that Monsieur Boursier had been murdered.

Blin and the child had eaten some of the pottage before it was served, but before Boursier ate his, the rice pan had stood for five minutes in a room in which the only occupant was Madame Boursier, giving her ample opportunity to poison the dish. Kostolo, although not present at the breakfast, had later been in a position to add poison to Monsieur Boursier's medicine, his friendly attentiveness now looking decidedly suspicious. Madame Boursier and Nicolas Kostolo were arrested and questioned.

From the beginning Madame Boursier's responses were a tangle of contradictions, evasion and downright lies. Initially she claimed that her husband had never mentioned having arsenic on the premises, but later she declared that he had told her of his purchases. When she was asked for the names of people who frequented the house, she omitted to mention Kostolo. Obliged to admit that he was a frequent visitor, she vehemently denied any criminal intimacy between them.

Kostolo, however, dropping all pretence of being a respectable friend of the family, boasted openly and brazenly about his amorous conquests of both the Dame Olivereau and Madame Boursier, neither of whom were aware that they had a rival. When Madame Boursier was confronted with this, she finally confessed that she had looked upon the handsome Greek with interest and pleasure, and later abandoned herself to his desires. She admitted supplying Kostolo with money, insisting that it had been a loan, but since she knew he was unable to repay any loans it was clear that she was paying him for his company and sexual attentions.

The mere fact of the affair did not in itself prove the existence of motive, but this was provided by Kostolo himself with brutal and shocking frankness. He told Demoutiers that soon after the death of her husband, Madame Boursier had suggested that they marry. She had been anxious to do so as soon as possible before her young paramour changed his mind.

Desperate to wriggle out of the charge, Madame Boursier now stated that her husband had poisoned himself. She said that one of her husband's friends, Henri Clap, had told her that he had heard that Boursier had died from poison because he was tired of life. Monsieur Clap was duly questioned, and told Demoutiers that while he had heard the rumours that Boursier had died from poison, he had never circulated any report that Boursier had become weary of existence.

The trial of Madame Boursier and her lover for the murder of Monsieur Boursier opened on the 27th of November at the Court of Assize and was the sensation of Paris. From an early hour the front of the courthouse was besieged with dense crowds, and when the doors opened the court filled to capacity within minutes.

The appearance of the two accused attracted particular attention. The diminutive Madame Boursier wore, in accordance with her status as a widow, a plain bombazine dress with a black gauze bonnet and black veil, her eyes modestly cast down. Her handsome paramour was dressed in a fashionable mourning suit. In a court of law, it was expected, not unreasonably, that accused persons should show some sign that they appreciated the importance of the tribunal and the seriousness of their position. Kostolo, however, shocked everyone by displaying no respect for the proceedings. As he was brought in he looked about the courtroom with a cool and confident expression approaching outright impudence, exciting considerable hostility amongst the spectators. He appeared to be completely indifferent to the fact that he was on trial for his life.

The Act of Accusation citing the charges against the prisoners was read aloud, and when the couple's criminal intimacy was described, Kostolo smiled and cast a saucy look at his co-defendant, whose eyes remained downcast. An audible murmur of disapproval ran around the court.

Unlike English murder trials of the period, where the accused was obliged to stand silently in the dock, the defendant in a French trial could be questioned, although Kostolo was required to leave the court during Madame Boursier's examination.

The widow admitted that Kostolo, who she had known for only a month before her husband's death, was a frequent visitor to the house. When pressed as to the nature of the relationship, she admitted after much confusion and hesitation, and in a voice so low and quiet as to be scarcely audible, the intimacy between herself and the attractive Greek. She said she had loaned Kostolo between 250 and 300 francs, something her husband knew nothing about, and had taken no security for the loans, as she had implicit faith in his promises that he expected to receive some money from Constantinople. He was, she explained, in great financial distress at the time, having pawned all his available property. She insisted that the loans were in the amount she had stated despite Kostolo having made a counterclaim that they were in the region of 600 and 700 francs.

'Kostolo smiled and cast a saucy look at his co-defendant, whose eyes remained downcast.'

Contradicting her previous claim that her husband was tired of life, Madame Boursier now told the court that on the morning of his illness he was in high spirits and singing. In her initial examination before Monsieur Demoutiers she had said she didn't remember where her husband was when breakfast was served. Now she said she could remember perfectly and disputed the evidence of Blin, who had said he was in the shop. Madame Boursier said she was now positive that he had been sitting across the counter facing her, explaining that the reason she had not recalled this when first questioned was that she had been ill and tired. She admitted, however, that the desk where the pan of pottage was placed was near where she had been sitting, and that no one else had gone into the room between the stew pan arriving and Boursier eating his breakfast.

Madame Boursier told the court that after her husband complained that the rice was bad, she had tasted it, and it was good. She had never suspected poisoning, as – and this was a new suggestion – her husband had previously been indisposed in the same way.

She explained that the scouring of the pan was to demonstrate to her husband that there was no verdigris in it.

Madame Boursier made a very poor impression in court, introducing numerous changes to her story and being repeatedly caught out in lies. Despite evidence to the contrary, she claimed that it was on the advice of her relatives that she had not allowed the post-mortem, and denied that she had pressed for the body to be buried on the day of her husband's death. Even the story of her taking an emetic on the day before Boursier's illness was called into doubt, as there was no mention of the prescription in the druggist's books.

Madame Boursier had already admitted intimacy with Kostolo a fortnight after her husband's death, saying that she had yielded to the power her lover had already established over her, and had signed a statement to that effect. In court, however, she retracted this admission. Her excuse was that Demoutiers had pressed her so much on that point that she had told him to write down whatever he thought proper and she had then signed the statement without knowing what she did.

Understandably, the suggestion that the investigating judge had falsified a witness statement went down badly with the trial judge, who pointed out very firmly that investigating judges knew their duty too well to write down responses that had not been made.

Madame Boursier now appeared to be blaming the murder on Kostolo, since she said that her husband's death was neither suicide nor accident, and she attached no blame to Blin.

When Kostolo was brought into court to be examined, Madame Boursier was allowed to remain. She often interrupted his testimony with angry shouted denials, and no attempt seems to have been made to stop her from doing so.

Kostolo said he had come to France after having fought against the Turks in Greece. The Dame Olivereau had been his mistress and he had been intimate with her. This intimacy had continued up to the time of his arrest. After having become acquainted with Madame Boursier he was a frequent visitor, and was often asked to dinner. He insisted that the money given to him was 600 or 700 francs.

He had met Madame Boursier by appointment on the boulevards three times, and on two of those occasions she had gone with him to his apartment. Asked if she was intimate with him there he replied, 'Yes,' a reply that resulted in a flurry of movement amongst the onlookers.

There was a moment of unintended hilarity when Kostolo was asked when Boursier had proposed making his visit to Havres and solemnly replied, 'Before his death,' at which the audience, forgetting the gravity of the proceedings, burst out laughing.

Kostolo then described the events in the Boursier household during the grocer's last illness, and admitted administering drinks prepared by Madame Boursier to the patient, but said that he had not given him any other drinks.

He said that he had commented on the blue nails of the corpse because he had seen the same symptoms before on the body of Prince Callimachi of his own country, who had been poisoned. (Since Callimachi had died less than two years previously, at which time Kostolo was living in Paris, this claim seems unlikely. Perhaps Kostolo believed that some royal name-dropping would assist his case.) Confronted with an allegation made by Madame Boursier that he had told her he had dreamed of her husband dying of poison after horrible sufferings, he made an absolute denial.

Kostolo openly admitted that Madame Boursier had been intimate with him fifteen days after her husband's death, a statement that caused murmurs of outrage in court, and Madame Boursier burst out loudly that it was she who had told the truth.

Realising that the prospect of marriage to a wealthy widow gave him a motive for murder, Kostolo now made light of his former statements. He admitted that he had asked Madame Boursier if she would like to have a husband like him, but it was only in pleasantry, '… on these occasions one says all sorts of things. I spoke as it were for the sake of speaking. I did not love this woman; I had no thought at all of marrying her.'

Madame Boursier, according to Kostolo, had replied that she didn't dare, that the law forbade it before a year; '… we said all this in jest; you know well, that on these occasions, a woman never says at once, *yes*.' He denied, however, that he had ever spoken of marriage before her husband's death, and he had never seriously proposed marriage at all, adding, 'How could I have desired to marry a woman with five children, and especially one whom I did not love?' At this, there were exclamations of disgust from the onlookers, and someone was heard to murmur '…happily he is not a Frenchman.'

'Nevertheless,' said the Judge, his extreme distaste for Kostolo apparent in every word, 'you made protestations of attachment; you received money – constantly excited her to abandon herself to your brutal passion. Your conduct not only shews [*sic*] great immorality, but the utmost baseness. I am forced to tell you this.'

'I ask everybody a thousand pardons.'

Kostolo suddenly changed his tactics and made a great show of weeping. He agreed that he was at fault, saying that he had been carried away by Madame Boursier's great attachment to him. Turning to the contemptuous and sceptical crowd in the public galleries, he cried out between sobs, 'I ask everybody a thousand pardons.'

Relentlessly, the Judge pointed out that at the same time as Kostolo's intimacy with Madame Boursier the accused was also having relations with another woman who supported him.

'Yes, yes, I am a great wretch,' admitted Kostolo, weeping still more bitterly. To the indignation of the onlookers he protested that what he had done was very common, saying that he had no way of existing other than accepting the favours of Madame Boursier, and that he had only spoken to her of marriage in jest. After Boursier's death she had said that while it was very unfortunate to have lost her husband, it was best that this had taken place before any discovery of her guilty liaison. He had suggested that his visits should be less frequent as the other members of the household regarded him with unfavourable looks, but she had replied that she was mistress of the house and he should come as usual.

Kostolo stood down, and in the medical testimony that followed, the experts who had examined the body left the court in no doubt that Monsieur Boursier had been poisoned. Doctors Bordot and Tartra, who had attended the deceased, were obliged to admit they had told Madame Boursier of the suspicions against her, and were sternly reprimanded since they had given the suspects the opportunity to remove every trace of the crime.

The maid, Blin, confirmed that when the rice had been taken in, Boursier was at his own counter reading the newspaper, to which her mistress shouted out an angry denial. Blin also stated, contrary to Madame Boursier's most recent claims, that the grocer had not been in the habit of vomiting.

Mademoiselle Reine, who had accompanied her mistress to the door of Kostolo's lodgings, declared that she had no idea of any intimacy between the two, although Madame Boursier had told her she loved the Greek well for his society – a comment that produced a general laugh from the galleries – and that Kostolo had told her he loved Madame Boursier.

The Dame Olivereau also appeared and confessed her connection to Kostolo, saying that she had known nothing of his affair with Madame Boursier.

The shop man Bailli, who had once been so suspicious of Madame Boursier, had changed his tune since Monsieur Demoutiers first questioned him. He had subsequently made frequent visits to the widow, and also called on her defence counsel, after which he had suddenly become eager to declare her innocent. He had also come into the possession of an unusually large sum of money, which he claimed had been given to him by his sister.

Bailli now said that it was he and not Monsieur Boursier who had had charge of the leftover arsenic, and it had been securely locked away. Before the trial, Bailli had been made to look for this arsenic in the presence of witnesses and produced a bag of ratsbane and a bag of arsenic from a locked compartment in the shop. In court the conflicting nature of the witness's statements became more glaring the more he was questioned.

The defence could do nothing except bring witnesses as to the good character of Madame Boursier, although their testimony referred to a time before she had been intimate with Kostolo.

At the end of the second day of the trial the charges against Nicolas Kostolo were withdrawn, however, the prosecution had done everything necessary to prove that Madame Boursier had poisoned her husband short of producing an eyewitness to the act. Her fate rested solely on the eloquence of her counsel, Monsieur Couture, who made a long and impassioned appeal on behalf of his client. He maintained that the case for the prosecution was mere possibility and presumption and there was no evidence on which the jury could condemn a fellow creature. Despite the errors of her conduct there was nothing to suggest that Madame Boursier was capable of such an atrocity. Her behaviour on the morning of the 28th June, he maintained, was that of a person with a mind at ease, and not labouring with a terrible design.

The jury deliberated for an hour before delivering their verdict. Later commentators stated, '…all believed her guilty, except the jury, who acquitted both Madame Boursier and Kostolo.' The Judge, before liberating the widow, spoke to her very severely:

The jury have declared you not guilty of the crime of which you are accused; may you find the same absolution in the testimony of your conscience; but never forget that the cause is in the dishonour which covers your name – the irregularity of your conduct, and the violation of the most sacred ties. May your future conduct justify your past life, and may repentance replace the honour which you have lost!

Of Kostolo he said, 'Debauchery is his only means of existence, the desire of money his only passion, and he is sincere only in his ingratitude. Kostolo will be allowed to depart from this court, but he will leave it with ignominy! […] Acquitted by the court of assize, he will be punished by public contempt!'

Madame Boursier fainted away and was carried from the court, however, her recovery was rapid and, surrounding herself with her rejoicing friends, she enjoyed a night of celebration. The grocer's widow was a celebrity, no less famous for the accusation of murder than her criminal relations with a man who now attracted only general hatred and scorn. Next morning she appeared in the shop as usual, and seemed quite happy to be the object of the fascinated stare of the crowds that assembled outside. For several days afterwards the curious of Paris pressed around her door.

Kostolo and the widow were not reunited; neither was the Dame Olivereau forgiving, and the young Greek with no other resources than his undoubted physical attributes found himself homeless and without a means of income. He was arrested as a vagrant and ordered to leave France.

Madame Boursier did not remarry and died in 1837.

There can be little doubt that Monsieur Boursier died from eating poisoned pottage, the only question being who administered the arsenic? The only person with access to the pottage other than Madame Boursier was Josephine Blin, but if Madame Boursier was innocent why did she claim to have tasted the pottage, refuse permission for a post-mortem, try to hurry the burial and make so many conflicting and demonstrably untrue statements? The conclusion must be that Madame Boursier poisoned her husband in order to supplant him with the flirtatious Kostolo, who, she had imagined, might marry her. The jury must have seen her as Kostolo's victim and been unwilling to condemn her when the manipulative charmer walked free.

Sources

The Annual Register for 1823, Law Cases, pp 19-21
Edinburgh Annual Register for 1823, volume 16, part III, pp 190-3
Fraser's Magazine, 1833, volume 8, pp 455-470
Journal des Debats
The Times
National Archives of France

Rice Pottage

This is the author's adaptation of a recipe from *Domestic French Cookery* 1836. (The original recipe used a quart of milk for the same amount of rice, 4 ounces of sugar and flavoured the pottage with peach kernels or peach leaves.)

Ingredients to serve 4
6 tablespoons or 100g long grain rice
1 pint milk plus one tablespoon
Sugar (about 2 ounces but adjust to personal taste) or equivalent
    sweetener of your choice
A few drops almond essence
2 egg yolks
1 level teaspoon cornflour (my optional addition; this helps stabilise
    the mixture)

Boil the rice in a pint of water till soft. Drain through a sieve then return rice to the clean pan, add the pint of milk, essence, and chosen sweetener to taste. Simmer about five minutes till thickened. Beat the yolks in a small bowl with a tablespoon of milk and the cornflour if used, till smooth. Stir into the pottage and cook gently for a minute until thick. Do not add arsenic. Serve.

ANDREW TAYLOR

Andrew is a British crime and historical
novelist, winner of the Cartier Diamond
Dagger (for lifelong excellence in the
genre), the Historical Dagger (three times)
and other awards. He has also been
shortlisted for the Edgar and the CWA
Gold Dagger. He has written more than
thirty novels. They include the number
one bestseller, 'The American Boy';
the Roth Trilogy (filmed for TV as 'Fallen
Angel'); the Lydmouth and Dougal series;
'Bleeding Heart Square'; 'The Scent of
Death'; and 'The Silent Boy'. He is the
Spectator's crime fiction reviewer.

www.andrew-taylor.co.uk
Follow on twitter: @andrewjrtaylor

DISTRESSING CIRCUMSTANCES: THE MOAT FARM MURDER OF 1899

ANDREW TAYLOR

Crime novelists routinely plunder the past, the real past, in order to create their fictional worlds. Whether the past is five minutes old or five hundred years old, we cannibalise it for our sinister purposes.

We suck like vampires on past crimes. That's where our creative nourishment comes from. Indeed it's both a characteristic and a strength of the genre that it reflects concerns about real crimes, real murders, real social breakdown.

A few years ago I wrote a novel called *Bleeding Heart Square*, which was inspired by the circumstances of a late Victorian murder case. The novel had other ingredients as well, and I took many liberties with the historical case – not least in moving it from the end of the nineteenth century to the 1930s. But the book was, from first to last, my attempt to revisit this real-life murder and, in particular, to give a voice to its victim.

It was my grandmother who first told me about the murder. She talked about it with modest proprietorial pride. As far as she was concerned, it was always 'our murder'. I was twelve years old, and my experience of homicide derived largely from Agatha Christie's detective stories.

The Moat Farm Murder had been a very well known case in its time. The farm was in Essex, near Saffron Walden. Its very name sounded pleasingly romantic, redolent of antiquity. The farm used to belong to my great-great-grandparents, the Savills, and, in the 1890s, my grandmother and her sister Fanny would go down from London to stay there. I saw a photograph of them once, two little girls in white pinafores standing in a garden with a gloomy house in the background.

More than twenty years later I found myself making a living by writing novels with corpses in them. I don't think there was a cause-and-effect connection between this and the Moat Farm Murder, though the novels of Agatha Christie probably had something to do with it. In the course of work I found myself flicking through one of those compilations of famous murder cases that regularly trickle into print. And suddenly there it was, no longer confined to childhood memory: the Moat Farm Murder of 1899.

What caught my eye was a double-page spread of photographs that accompanied the short account of the case. There was the house itself, with a stretch of the moat, which had been drained. Two men, one in a bowler hat and the other in cap and shirtsleeves, were searching it, presumably for bodies. There was the timbered interior of the farm's great barn, where the inquest had been held. There was the murderer: a bearded man, rather like Edward VII. His name was Samuel Herbert Dougal. And there was his victim, Miss Camille Cecile Holland – first as a pretty, middle-aged woman posing by a sofa in her Sunday best and smiling shyly at the camera; and then in death as a sodden bundle wrapped in sacking and stretched across three dining chairs in the greenhouse at Moat Farm.

That's where my novel started, with my grandmother's memories and two photographs of Miss Holland – first as a sweet-faced woman and then parcelled up in a greenhouse. She seemed almost incidental to her own murder, for her larger-than-life killer dominates her even in death.

When I began to research the case, I had a stroke of luck: it had been covered in the Notable British Trials series, which fed the pre-war public appetite for homicide that George Orwell immortalised in his essay 'The Decline of the English Murder'. Each of these plump red volumes concentrates on a single murder case, providing transcripts of court proceedings, copies of other relevant documents, photographs, and a substantial introduction by an expert. F. Tennyson Jesse, the distinguished criminologist (and the great-niece of the poet Tennyson) wrote the introduction to *The Trial of Samuel Herbert Dougal*, which was published in 1928.

Miss Holland met Samuel Dougal in 1898. She was a genteel fifty-five-year-old spinster with a small fortune of her own and a rather touching pride in her own attractions. He was three years younger, a former soldier, a womaniser and a convicted forger who had narrowly escaped prison for a string of other offences that included arson, larceny, bigamy and possibly murder. He posed as a retired army officer. He must have been a charmer, for he swiftly overcame Miss Holland's religious, moral and social scruples. Within three months they were living together as man and wife. But they didn't marry.

There is no doubt that Dougal's motives were entirely mercenary. As F. Tennyson Jesse puts it in her inimitable prose, '…there can have been no physical pleasure for him in his conquest of this timid, precise, elderly woman. His taste was rather for buxom country wenches whom he was yet to garner so plentifully.' He persuaded Miss Holland to use nearly a quarter of her capital in buying a farm – which is where my grandmother's family made their brief appearance in the story. The patriarch, William Savill, had recently died. The family put the farm, then known as Coldhams, up for sale. Dougal – or rather Miss Holland – bought it.

> 'His taste was rather for buxom country wenches'

It is not difficult to come up with reasons why they both wanted to make a fresh start in a place where neither of them was known. But it is impossible to say for certain why they wanted this place in particular. Miss Holland had spent her life in cities. Perhaps she had romantic ideas about living in the country, particularly in a farmhouse encircled with a moat like the gloomy but romantic grange of Tennyson's 'Mariana'. Perhaps she hoped that Dougal would settle down and farm; that he would stop leering at buxom wenches and drinking too much brandy. As for Dougal, perhaps the loneliness of the farm's location was a recommendation.

During negotiations for the purchase, Dougal had the contract put in his sole name. Miss Holland showed a flash of common sense by insisting that it be put in her name instead. But she didn't have enough sense to walk away from him. Perhaps she felt she had finally found a man to love her. She wouldn't have wanted to lose him or indeed her treasured family furniture and possessions, which were now installed at Moat Farm. Or perhaps she believed her reputation was now so compromised she had to make the best of what she had. In any case, how was she to know what his plans for her were? That last attempt to assert herself might have been why she had to die – because Dougal knew that she wasn't completely under his control.

The contract was signed on the 19th of January 1899. On the 26th of January, the couple moved to furnished rooms in Saffron Walden, where they stayed for three months while the sale was finalised and the house made ready for them. Miss Holland brought her little dog, Jacko, to whom she was devoted.

Their landlady, Mrs Wiskens, later said that when she was dressed for the day, Miss Holland looked ten or fifteen years younger than she really was. But Mrs Wiskens noted signs of strain in her lodgers' relationship, even then. 'Mrs Dougal' made it quite clear that the money that had bought the farm was hers. And she disliked the way that Dougal had a habit of making trips to London, wiring at the last moment to say that he was 'detained by business' and obliged to spend the night. 'I don't believe he needed to stay up at all,' she confided to Mrs Wiskens. 'He could have come back if he'd wanted to.'

On the 27th of April, Samuel Dougal and Miss Holland moved to Moat Farm. As the crow flies, it is not much more than thirty miles from the centre of London, but even now it's an isolated place surrounded by farmland between the village of Clavering and the hamlet of Rickling. In those days the nearest house was Rickling Vicarage, nearly half a mile away.

F. Tennyson Jesse must have seen the place in the 1920s, 'The house itself is a building that even on a sunny day holds something sinister and dreary, a look as of a house in some wild Brontë tale, and that on a wet, grey day might stand for the epitome of everything that is lonely and grim.' Indeed, she goes on to describe it in language reminiscent of the scarier sort of fairytale, which is perhaps appropriate in view of poor Miss Holland's fate, 'Surrounded by dark fir trees and gnarled apple trees in a very ecstasy of contortion, it is a small, neat, almost prim house ...'

Even the names of the farm workers and servants had an otherworldly quality that might have come from Bunyan. The trap that took Miss Holland and Dougal to the farm on that first day was driven by a man called Henry Pilgrim. One of the maidservants, who came and went at Moat Farm with bewildering speed, was called Lydia Faithful.

Everything conspired to make the fairytale darker. The countryside was blighted by an agricultural depression. The heavy clay soil clung to the feet. The few inhabitants of the area, with 'their slouching walk and heaviness of mien', were both physically and morally depressed. F. Tennyson Jesse dropped dark hints of widespread sexual depravity. 'Life was at a very low ebb ... and the habits of the beasts of the field, so blameless in them and so degrading in human beings, were the rule rather than the exception in the small, overcrowded cottages.'

Miss Holland had three miserable weeks to live. The farm was at the end of a long, muddy cart track; the house was accessible only by a single footbridge over the moat. The post was left in a box on the lane, at the far end of the cart track; every morning Dougal would walk down to collect it. No tradesmen ever called – everything was fetched in the trap. On the couple's first morning at the farm, the maid complained that her master had tried to kiss her.

At about 6.30 p.m. on Friday the 19th of May, Miss Holland told the maid that Mr Dougal was taking her shopping in the trap. That was the last time anyone, apart from her murderer, saw her alive. We now know that, a few minutes after this, when she was waiting in the trap by the bridge over the moat, Dougal shot her with his revolver. Soon afterwards he buried her in a disused ditch between the farmyard and the moat.

Later that evening Dougal returned to the house alone. He told the servant that 'Mrs Dougal' had decided to go to London. The following morning, he claimed to have had a letter from his 'wife' (though the post had not arrived), and that she had gone away to stay with a friend. On the same day he sent a telegram to his real wife (who is believed to have been his third) inviting her down to the farm. He introduced her to the local clergyman as his daughter. The real Mrs Dougal was soon wearing some of Miss Holland's clothes and jewellery, and generously gave the clergyman's wife a shawl and some sheet music that had once belonged to her.

A few months later, Jacko, Miss Holland's dearly loved dog, ran away from Moat Farm and turned up at the home of Mrs Wiskens, the Saffron Walden landlady. Mrs Wiskens, who had been surprised and rather hurt that Miss Holland hadn't said goodbye to her, wrote to Moat Farm. Dougal eventually collected the dog. He avoided questions about where his wife was.

The years passed. It was easy for Dougal to forge Miss Holland's signature. Gradually he sold her shares and withdrew her money. He transferred the ownership of the farm to himself.

At first he was a popular addition to the neighbourhood – genial, talkative, an excellent shot; he was always ready to stand a drink or contribute to a good cause. He was noteworthy too for having one of the few bicycles in the neighbourhood, and also the very first car (which he referred to as his 'locomobile').

The only problem was sex, and in particular the fact that (in F. Tennyson Jesse's discreetly convoluted prose) Dougal was unable 'to restrain his amours within the not at all narrow limits of the not very exiguous circle in which he lived.' He had a succession of affairs close to home, and barely bothered to conceal them. It 'was unwise of him to seduce one sister in front of the other, and to deny paternity when confronted with affiliation orders, both of which things he did.' In one case he 'had relations with three sisters and with their mother.' No doubt this was 'the conduct of a man in whom sex was a disease, who was so mad with lust that he did not know ordinary prudence.'

People began to talk about Moat Farm. Stories circulated about Dougal giving bicycling lessons to naked girls in the gently sloping meadow to the north of the house. 'What a picture,' wrote F. Tennyson Jesse in some excitement, '– in that clayey, lumpy field, the clayey, lumpy girls, naked, astride that unromantic object, a bicycle, and Dougal, gross and vital, cheering on these bucolic improprieties …!'

People also began to remember the past – and to ask questions about what had happened to Miss Holland. Among them was the real Mrs Dougal, who was no doubt anxious about her own future. (She later ran off with another man, and Dougal tried to divorce her.) Doubts accumulated, hardened into suspicions, and at last, in March 1903, led to a full-blown police investigation into Miss Holland's disappearance. Dougal concocted a story to explain her departure, but it was soon shown to be false. The trail of forgeries was exposed after a close examination of financial transactions in Miss Holland's name since May 1899.

> 'a man in whom sex was a disease, who was so mad with lust that he did not know ordinary prudence.'

Even before the body was found, the case aroused widespread interest. The police took up residence in the house, drained the moat and dug up many parts of the surrounding land. According to *The Times*, 6,000 'excursionists' swooped on the farm during the Easter Bank Holiday of 1903. Many were souvenir hunters. Some were armed with 'Kodaks' – enterprising photographers printed postcards of the scene and sold them to the tourists. Others sold snacks.

At last they found the body of a woman. The corpse was much decayed. A foot broke off when they moved it. The hair had gone, and so had most of the face. There was a bullet hole in the skull. But enough remained of the body and its clothing for the police to establish that it was Miss Camille Holland. Dougal would have been better advised to conceal the body in the farm's midden, where the workings of the acid it contained would have left nothing identifiable after four years.

The Coroner's inquest was held in the barn at Moat Farm, which the police had hastily converted into a courtroom. The jury withdrew for only five minutes before delivering a verdict of wilful murder against Samuel Herbert Dougal. Miss Holland's killer protested his innocence but the evidence mounted steadily against him. Much of it depended on railway timetables and postal deliveries, on bank clerks' statements and landladies' gossip – reinforcing the sense that this real-life murder case eventually had a misty afterlife in the imaginations of so many authors and readers of inter-war golden age detective stories.

Dougal was tried and convicted. While awaiting execution, he sold his story to the *Sun*. His presumably ghosted account claimed implausibly that Miss Holland's death was a dreadful accident. He was hanged at Chelmsford Gaol on the 14th of July 1903. His grave is unmarked, though his initials and number are carved on a nearby wall.

His victim lies in Saffron Walden cemetery. F. Tennyson Jesse remarks that Miss Holland would have approved of the delicate phrasing of the inscription on the cross above the grave, 'In sympathetic memory of Camille Cecile Holland, of Maida Vale, London, who died at Clavering under distressing circumstances on the 19th May, 1899, aged 56 years.'

As for Jacko, Miss Holland's little dog, he was given a home by Mrs Wiskens, the Saffron Walden landlady, who had been an important witness for the prosecution at Dougal's trial. F. Tennyson Jesse records that, in later life, Jacko became 'the object of admiring curiosity'. Death itself did not bring an end to this, 'And now he stands, stuffed and in a glass case, on a side table, in the parlour where Miss Holland used to listen for the sound of Dougal's bicycle bell.'

The Moat Farm Murder is in essence a very simple story of a lonely woman who was looking for love and a conman who was looking for easy money. The victim had to die almost certainly because in the end she refused to be entirely a victim: she became a potential danger instead. Hence the distressing circumstances, hence the deaths of both parties – and hence one of the classic templates for murder in both fact and fiction.

MARSALI TAYLOR

Marsali grew up near Edinburgh and came to Shetland over thirty years ago as a newly qualified teacher. She lives with her husband, five cats and two Shetland ponies on Shetland's scenic west side. Marsali is a qualified STGA tourist guide who is fascinated by history, and has published plays in Shetland's distinctive dialect, as well as a history of women's suffrage in Shetland. She's also a keen sailor who enjoys exploring in her own 8-metre yacht, and an active member of her local drama group. She has now written three Shetland-set crime novels starring liveaboard skipper and reluctant sleuth, Cass Lynch.

www.marsalitaylor.co.uk

A BABY HIDDEN IN A KAILYARD

MARSALI TAYLOR

I was told the basis of this story by the old man who cast my peats, at the time of the discovery of buried babies in an Orkney cottage.

'There was a case like that in Walls,' he told me. 'It was an older sister and a younger sister living together, and the younger sister had a bairn, and the older one killed it, and buried it in the kailyard. My midder remembered seeing the policeman coming for the sister in his gig, and she watched him driving away with the sister sitting up beside him.'

It was a vivid picture which stayed in my mind, and I asked a couple of Walls folk if they'd ever heard of the story. 'Why,' one older lady answered, 'that's our house, Bardister! When we bought it, we were told there'd been a baby buried there – it gave us the shivers.'

The story goes back to the 1870s. Walls is a sizeable township on the west side of Shetland, made up of clusters of houses spreading over several miles. In 1871, there were seven houses at Bardister, just above the loch at Walls, with thirty-seven people crowded into them.

Among them, at numbers 2 and 3 Bardister, were the Twatt and Thomson families. Magnus Twatt, shoemaker, lived with his sister Isabella and their mother. The Thomson family was headed by Janet, sister to Magnus and Isabella. Her husband John had died in 1850, leaving her with five children aged between twelve and two. Her oldest daughter, Mary, was married, and her son Robert had gone to sea, leaving only Janet and her three single daughters, Janet, Margaret and Joan, in the household. All three gave their occupations as 'croft labourer' on the 1871 census.

This small community was to be broken up when the houses were cleared to create the current Bardister House. Magnus and Isabella Twatt stayed close by, at Dykes, Bardister, but the Thomson family split up. Robert married their neighbour, Lilias Hughson, and they went north to Stennestwatt. Janet and her daughters went westwards to a crofthouse at Song, one of three houses there. The residents of the house were Peter and Margaret Williamson, both in their eighties. The Williamsons lived in the 'but' room, and the Thomson family lived 'ben', with a door going into the byre, where there was an extra bed, and a kiln for drying corn. One or other of the Thomson women regularly slept there. In 1877, Janet was sixty; the younger Janet was thirty-six, Margaret was thirty and Joan was twenty-nine.

Thanks to the prison records, still in the Shetland Archives, we have a description of Margaret. She was five feet four inches tall, and weighed ten stone. Her eyes were blue, her hair brown. She could read 'a little', but she could not write. Her occupations were knitting and spinning. She was not a church member.

The precognition statements are also preserved, two thick packets of yellowed foolscap paper filled with copperplate writing in black ink. Fourteen witnesses gave their testimony.

Around Christmas of 1876, Margaret had a cold and 'a fright', and she blamed those for 'the cessation of her menses'. When she complained of wind and pains in the stomach, her older sister Janet went to Dr Murison in Walls, described her symptoms and was given some medicine for flatulence. She returned in April, and the doctor gave her tincture of iron.

Peter Williamson died on the 7th of May, leaving his widow to be cared for by the Thomson family. She was now almost blind – 'I cannot see your face just now,' she told the clerk taking down her statement – and grateful to them, 'They have been very kind to me, they are in my room nearly every hour of the day.'

In May, Janet returned to Dr Murison, saying her sister was no better. The doctor asked if she was with child. When Janet replied, 'No,' Dr Murison refused to prescribe for Margaret without seeing her.

By this time the village was starting to talk. Margaret Williamson heard the rumour that Margaret was in the family way in the month of May, and 'As soon as I heard it I spoke to her about it and asked her if it was true. She said to me, "You need not be frightened for that," and made me think it was not true.'

Margaret's mother and sisters also challenged her over the rumours, and again she denied the story, holding up her hand and offering to swear she was not in the family way. When she and Janet were alone in the fields together, Janet said to her, 'Now, if you are with child tell me, and it will make no difference on my part with you.'

In reply, Margaret sat down and loosened her petticoats, and putting her hand upon her stomach said, 'It is there where any trouble is.' After that she caught her abdomen in her hands, and taking hold of it and squeezing it said, 'See, there is no child there.'

Her younger sister, Joan, and her friend, Christina Fraser, from Quam, Setter, also questioned her about the rumours, and felt she was telling the truth when she said she was not with child. Margaret stopped going to church, saying that she could not suppress the wind for any length of time, although she still did her share of the work around the house and croft.

All her family noticed she had put on weight, but took this as caused by her lack of periods. Her mother said she had not 'grown up' like a woman in child; her sister Joan, who shared a bed with her, said she had got bigger around the abdomen, but her breasts had not enlarged. Mrs Williamson said that she still wore her usual clothes, a jacket and petticoat.

The rumours continued throughout the summer. Margaret was feeling increasingly unwell, and spent a lot of time in bed. In August, she and Janet went to see the doctor in Scalloway, Dr Charles Macpherson – a journey of twenty miles on foot, or three hours around the coast by boat. By this time Margaret was seven and a half months pregnant.

'She called on me on 15th August last complaining of dyspepsia and cessation of the menses,' Macpherson told the investigating officer. 'I examined her and satisfied myself that there was no need of medical interference with the uterine complaint and asked her if she was married. She said no. I told her that I would treat her for her stomach complaint and that the enlargement of which she complained would cure itself in a few months. I did not directly ask if she was with child and she did not tell me she was.'

He gave Margaret a phial of medicine and two boxes of Holloway's pills, a popular Victorian 'cure-all'.

In mid-September, Margaret's aunt, Isabella Twatt, herself the mother of two illegitimate children, came to talk to her, urging her to confide in her, and offering to break the news to her mother. Isabella said she believed Margaret was telling the truth when she said she was not pregnant.

The constant questioning suggests the family weren't convinced. In the third week of September, a local woman lost a child because she had delayed too long in calling for help. Mrs Williamson recalled, 'We commenced to talk of this woman's case and said it would be a warning to others in similar situations. The conversation was pointed at Margaret but she said we need not be frightened for her. That was all she said.'

On the 5th of October, the Thomsons killed a sheep in the yard, and the head was put in the byre, hanging from a hook on the opposite side from the drying kiln. On the 6th October, Margaret did the housework as usual while the other women were outside shearing sheep. They had their dinner between two and three, then the others went back out, and Mrs Williamson went to a neighbour for some milk. While she was out, Margaret went to bed in the byre. When the other women came in, her mother asked what ailed her, and she said her menstruation had come on.

Margaret's friend, Christina, called in about nine o'clock and stayed the night, sharing her bed. 'We did not speak much after I went to bed and she never spoke about herself except to say that she thought she was getting better.'

The next day Margaret stayed in bed, but she rose on Monday, and worked as usual. She did not say to anyone that she had had a child.

The Inspector of the Poor for the parish was William Thomson, aged only twenty in 1877. On the 5th, 6th and 7th of October, there were rumours that Margaret was very ill, and on Monday the 8th he heard the rumour that Margaret had been confined, and that the child was not to be seen. He went to consult Dr Murison, who visited the household:

Some believed this report and others said it was untrue … I thought it right to ascertain if possible the truth of the matter and accordingly on the forenoon of 13th October I called on Margaret at her house. When I entered she was sitting at the fireside with her mother and the other members of the family came in with me. Both the sisters and mothers said they were glad I had come to satisfy myself about the reports as they did not think there was any truth in them. The younger sister said she thought there was something weighing on her sister's mind. Margaret was looking very pale and weakly and had the appearance of a woman recently confined. After some remarks about the weather I asked her if the reports current in the neighbourhood were true or not. She replied 'No.' I then asked her to go to bed that I might examine her and ascertain the truth of the report or clear her. Without saying a word she undressed and went to bed.

The doctor's examination left him in no doubt: Margaret had given birth to a child some days previously. 'I told her so and asked her where the child was.'

The doctor's account is the only one we have of Margaret's own explanation:

She then told me that on the Friday night (5th October) she began to feel curious. She got up feeling pains in the inside, but after a short time she lay down again, the pains having gone away. On Saturday she lay in bed till 9 a.m. when she had a cup of tea and rose about 11 a.m. Then her mothers and sisters were out shearing. She went about the house for some time when she again felt curious. She then took a tub into the barn with a little hot water in it to ease the pains and sat over it, and the pains came on more violently and the child was born into the bucket or tub. She said the child did not cry, that she did not look at it and did not know there was a child till the Monday. I asked her if there was a cord and how she had separated it. She said she did not know but took her hand and broke it. She said she then rose and pushed the bucket to the side close to the kiln and covered it and went to bed. She said the child lay there till Monday about noon when she rose and looked into the bucket when she first knew it was a child. She then got a bit of linen, wrapped the child in it and took it through the back window and hid it between the corner of the haystack and the yard dyke and covered it with some bundles of heather. She said her people knew nothing about it.

Dr Murison took Margaret's older sister, Janet, with him to look for the body. 'She came to the side of the haystack with me and saw me lift the heather bundles but would not look at the child. The child was lying on its back but inclining to the left side wrapped in a linen rag. I did not lift the body there but went for the Inspector of the Poor. I covered it as I found it and on the Inspector coming I showed the body to him and asked him to take possession of it.'

Margaret was then visited by Peter Urquhart, the Criminal Investigator, on the 15th of October, and the precognition statements were taken from all the household. She was admitted to Lerwick Prison on the 16th of October. Lawrence Robertson, the Sheriff's Officer, took charge of the child's body. It was taken to the burial ground in Lerwick, where a post-mortem was performed by Drs Skae and Murison. It was a female child. It had two wounds on its head, and a fractured skull. Both doctors were agreed that the wounds could not have been caused by the child falling on the edge of the tub as it was born, nor by it falling on the floor, 'unless it fell upon some hard projectory edge with several projecting points such as a rugged stone or projecting nails or some such similar substance,' Dr Skae said, although he agreed that the fracture could have been caused by it falling.

Peter Urquhart returned to search the house on the 19th of October, along with J. Kirkland Galloway, the Procurator Fiscal. In their search of the byre, they found a number of pieces of wood on top of the kiln, for laying the corn on to dry. Some of them were black with smoke, others not. It was too dark to see them properly, so Galloway opened one shutter, and they saw what appeared to be blood on one piece of wood, 'about two feet long from 1¼ to 1½ inches broad and from 1 to 1¼ inches thick and of a ragged and uneven surface. There were a great many pieces of wood at the kiln – over 20 pieces – and none of them were stained but the one before referred to.'

They also took possession of the tub that Margaret said she had sat over. Wood and tub were shown to the doctors who had performed the post-morten. Dr Skae said, 'Blows with this piece of wood would have caused the wounds which we found on the child's head,' and Dr Murison agreed, 'Blows with that piece of wood would have caused the wounds on the child's head referred to in my report. I have seen two buckets taken possession of by the Police Officer. If accused was sitting over either of these when the child was born and it fell from her into the bucket that could not have caused all the wounds.'

Dr Skae did add, 'I would however have expected the wood to be more stained with blood than it is.'

Concealment of pregnancy was then a crime. Margaret's hearing was on the 20th of November 1877 at 12 noon, in the presence of Andrew Mure, Esquire, Advocate, Sheriff Substitute of Caithness, Orkney and Zetland at Lerwick, sitting in judgement. The Sheriff Court records give the Procurator Fiscal's long, formal speech. The *Shetland Times* of 24th November 1877 reported:

> On Tuesday at the Sheriff Court, before Sheriff Mure, the first pleading diet was held in the case of the woman Margaret Thomson, Walls, who was suspected of having murdered her infant. The panel was charged with concealment of pregnancy merely, and having pleaded guilty as libelled was sentenced to 15 months imprisonment in the general prison at Perth.

We can't know now why the Procurator Fiscal didn't try for the murder charge. But was Margaret Thomson guilty of murder?

The Case for the Defence

From the statements of others, Margaret's denial seems genuine. The poor girl convinced those closest to her that she was telling what she believed (or desperately hoped) to be the truth, that a cold and 'fright' had stopped her periods, and she put on weight because of that, and because of the wind in her abdomen. It's interesting that one person who's not mentioned in any deposition is the child's father. Her family knew she had no regular boyfriend; who, then, was the father, and what was the 'fright' she'd had around Christmas? Had she been assaulted during the Christmas festivities, or perhaps at her brother's wedding, in January? If the child was the result of rape, that could make her more determined not to believe she was pregnant. Local tradition even names the man: Robert Law, remembered by my informant's mother as a 'nasty old man'.

Her sister was convinced enough of her illness to go three times to the local doctor for treatment for her, and to accompany her to Scalloway – an arduous journey to permit to a woman so advanced in pregnancy.

On the day of the birth, Margaret thought her periods were beginning again, and although she felt herself passing something, thought it to be blood. The darkness of the byre was emphasised by the Fiscal. She covered the tub and pushed it away to be emptied later before falling back into bed. When she discovered the dead baby, two days later, she was terrified and hid it. At the doctor's visit, she owned up readily, and told him where the baby was hidden.

This case has a terrified country girl sticking to her denial until she was forced to confront the truth. A good defence lawyer would have emphasised the recent killing of the sheep to explain the blood on the wood, and Dr Skae's comment that the skull fracture could have been caused by the baby falling on something sharp as it was born. The byre would have contained all sorts of implements. There was no proof that the baby had been born alive, so Margaret had to be given the benefit of the doubt.

The Case for the Prosecution

The scenario above fits a young girl, but Margaret was a thirty-year-old woman in 1877 and there's no suggestion anywhere in the statements that she was 'simple'. She, and the mature women around her, had spent their lives in the child-filled township of Bardister. That her family should believe in her story of 'wind', or periods stopped by a cold, is hard to credit; even if she herself was in denial, her family would have seen the truth – as it seems they did, by the number of people who questioned her.

The baby could have been born as she said, but it seems a particular piece of luck that it should have arrived at the only two hours that weekend while the other women were shearing, and Margaret was alone in the house.

The wounds on the baby's head are hard to explain away. Both doctors agreed that the bloodstained wood was likely to have caused them, and the conclusion is hard to resist: the poor mite was hit hard on the head, twice, with enough force to fracture its skull. The blood was only on that one piece of wood, the sheep had been killed outside, and the head was hung on the other side of the byre, making it unlikely that the blood came from there.

The women insisted there was no truth in the rumour that Margaret had just had a child, yet the doctor said she looked like a women who'd just given birth. He saw her a week later; her mother and sisters saw her within an hour of the birth. It's hard to believe that not one of her family noticed she looked ill, or tried to investigate. The byre, where she'd been lying, would have been the first place to search.

Perhaps the Procurator Fiscal changed the charge because there was no evidence that the baby had been born living; or perhaps he gave Margaret the benefit of the doubt because he'd heard other, more sinister, rumours about how the baby had died. The first version of the story that I'd heard blamed the older sister for the death, and another local version agreed.

'She was very proud,' I was told by a friend whose mother came from the house next door to Song, 'and she wasn't having her little sister having an illegitimate baby, so she killed it. But it was the baby's mother who got the prison sentence. When they kept her in jail in Lerwick, the dead baby was kept with her, in a box, and she was never the same again.'

Was the story of ignorance agreed between the women to protect the actual murderer, Janet, who 'would not look at the child', and who, when confronted with the bloodstained wood, said first, 'I never saw that piece of wood to my knowledge before,' before changing to, 'It and a number of other pieces of wood were in the barn of our house when we came to it four years ago.' The sentence for concealment of pregnancy was a maximum of two years; the sentence for murder was death by hanging, but while Margaret maintained that her family knew nothing of the birth, Janet was safe.

'she was never the same again.'

I was puzzled, too, why the baby's death was associated with Bardister, the house they'd left, but my friend had an answer for that too: 'It wasn't the first baby she'd killed. The other one was at Bardister, and buried in the kailyard.' If that's true, the body was never discovered.

The Thomson family remained at Song after the death of Mrs Williamson a year later. Margaret returned there after her time in prison. Soon after, the youngest sister, Joan, now in her mid-thirties, had a baby boy; it died of 'teething' aged only six months. Janet, the mother, died there in 1890; Joan followed her in 1895, dead of a brain tumour. Janet and Margaret, the two sisters implicated in the baby's death, both lived until the 1930s.

A couple of interesting things came out when I mentioned the story to other people. The first was rather horrifying: everyone I spoke to knew of another case, a different case each time. If infanticide wasn't exactly rife in Shetland, it was certainly not uncommon. One woman even told me that her mother had told her that in the case of an unwanted baby, there were men who would come along and made sure the baby didn't live after it was born. That sent a shiver down my spine.

The other surprising thing was the way this story from 1877 was told to me as an eyewitness event. My peat caster's mother had 'seen the woman in the policeman's gig', and 'My mother knew it was a murder,' claimed the friend whose mother grew up at Song, 'because she and my aunt were playing in the garden next door, and they heard the baby screaming as it was hit.' The horror felt by the community had lived on so vividly that people born fifty years later had adopted the story as their own memories.

STEPHEN WADE

Stephen has written extensively on regional crime, mostly in relation to Yorkshire and Lincolnshire. He has worked for several years as a writer in residence in prisons (though not actually residing in a cell) and 'The Bite of Truth' was conceived after seeing the court cells in Dublin's Green Street court. He has a special interest in prison history and in the development of the police. He has recently turned to crime fiction also, and his book 'A Thief in the Night', was published by The Mystery Press in 2014.

www.stephen-wade.com/truecrime

THE BITE OF TRUTH

STEPHEN WADE

It was a cold day in January in the heart of Dublin when I walked towards Green Street. I had an old map and I was looking for Newgate Prison, as I was researching a crime story from the city's Georgian period. Georgian Dublin was dark and murky, with long years of violent crime and brutal retribution from the authorities. Now all that was vestigial, and I sensed a strange, undefined appeal from the distant past as I turned a corner from a street of old cafés and sweetshops to see a police cordon a hundred yards ahead. Whatever the trouble was, it was happening where Newgate either was or where it used to be.

I asked the Garda officer standing by the white tape what was going on. He explained that there was to be a trial; a degree of isolation was required for the court area because the men being tried were hard men with hard friends and trouble was a possibility. I explained that I was looking for Newgate, and that I was a crime historian. He must have thought I was a harmless, academic-looking soul with one foot in the past and he called his sergeant: fortunately, he relished giving visitors a tour of the gruesome past. In minutes we were walking into the imposing Georgian façade of the court.

In the vestibule two lawyers were deep in conversation and an officer carrying a gun gave me a piercing look. The sergeant explained who I was and that he had offered to take me into the court and down into the ancient cells beneath the floors. It was at that moment, as my eyes scanned the place for telling detail, that I saw a gold plaque. There was a simple text on this, noting that William Kirwan had been tried there in 1852 for the murder of his wife, on the island of Ireland's Eye, across the bay from the village of Howth, north of Dublin. The name lodged in my imagination after the sergeant said, 'Oh yes, the artist … not many painter murderers I guess?' The name, William Burke Kirwan: it was easy to imagine that spoken in court as he stood in the dock. 'William Burke Kirwan, you are hereby charged …' Later on it seemed that everyone had heard of this death at a beauty spot where the promise was an idyllic few hours with nature, not an appointment with a violent death. Naturally, the name stuck with me.

What was so special about this mysterious death? The body of his wife had been found with a bite on her face and on her chest, well away from her husband. How she died was riddled with ambiguity, yet Kirwan had been found guilty of murder. That was left to be sorted out later. First, I had the tour of the cells. The sergeant led me to the huge, imposing courtroom, an intimidating assemblage of wooden panels, polished mahogany and oak with great shiny seats and benches, way above the dock and the steps from the holding cells beneath. It was an arena. There might as well have been blood and sand and galleries of crowds ready with the thumbs down. Law was always a department of theatre, but this was exactly the kind of dominating seat of ritual one would expect from the place where an imperial power dealt out justice and punishment.

'Robert Emmet stood right there when sentenced to die,' the sergeant said, pointing to the dock. 'They all would have stood there – big names and little ones too, my friend!'

I thought of Robert Emmet, the United Irishman who was hanged in the city in 1803. When sentenced to death, his speech from the dock became iconic: 'When my country takes her place among the nations of the earth … then write my epitaph.'

There had been thousands of nameless transgressors in that dock, their textless histories transient as the breeze whipping around the stones outside.

We walked down into the shadows, sticks of amber sunlight poking through cracks into the dank half-light. William Kirwan would have walked down there, no doubt registering that light, maybe constructing some kind of Dante-esque image, or a still life. I found out later that he used to frame pictures when he was not earning fees drawing skeletons and muscles. I imagined him alone in one of these cells: we walked past several of them, each one more separately tight and despairing than the first, and he must have found ways to keep his mind from despair. He probably lost the battle.

'I reckon they were a noisy lot. Sometimes I fancy I can hear their screams … maybe that's because I spend too much time with today's criminals down the bridewell …' The sergeant smiled. 'Seen enough?'

I nodded. 'Yes, let's get some twenty-first century back in our heads,' I said.

I bought the sergeant a coffee at a little place around the corner. This was a café squeezed between the court and an old prison known as the Black Dog back in the days when the debtors and vagrants were banged up with the flotsam and jetsam of urban excess. It was as if a tide of smelly amorality flowed in and left a putrid water among all the classes that would have walked Dublin. Somehow I could sense that depravity.

Men were talking in undertones in the café, looking sideways at me. After all, there was a chance that some desperate gang would turn up to liberate their man. But the lawyers, police officers and journalists in there decided I was no threat and went back to their coffee and muffins. The sergeant said he had to get back to work and I shook his hand. The men on their way to trial were dangerous, a threat to our moments of reflection on the past.

If some of those hard cases were not the scum of the street, men of shadows, knives and threats, but respectable public men who were in the chattering classes, then what could a decent citizen believe in? A respected artist up for murder, and there were rumours that he carried a sword-stick too.

I came to the spot where Newgate should have been. It was a little park for kids, with a small memorial to register the fact that unlucky members of the criminal class once rotted there, but not Kirwan: he was not one of the everyday fingersmiths and robbers whose names were in the lists of those sentenced. No, he was big news, guaranteed to set them talking in the pubs. He was destined for Spike Island, off Cork harbour, a holding pen before transportation to the colonies. I said to myself, 'cocktail parties to stone-breaking parties ...' There was an irony, and a transmutation: his modern, acceptable middle-class suit had been stripped from his back and he was made into a non-person, a convict, a person beyond all civilised contemplation, and a wife-killer as well. That's what the gossip would have been. A century and a half later the sergeant still had no more than the accepted story: that of the wife-killer who chose a lover's picnic as a place to take Maria's life. But was it true? If I could find it, the truth would be lurking under heaps of paper, stacks of archives and sad, lonely years in cells.

A few streets away from the gift shops and the sightseeing buses, I had stumbled upon the brutal heart of a Dublin which was long gone, where felons lost everything and stepped into a shadow world or onto a scaffold on Stephen's Green. I resolved to look for William Kirwan, his family and his truth, in those dusty files of history. He had grabbed my imagination when I saw for the first time that he was condemned for his ambivalence: he lived in a time when men were expected to be known to wear their hearts on their sleeves. He had protected a private life and mysteries had grown like cancers over his reputation.

I couldn't accept that this man was a monster who would kill; it was when I read the lawyer, Isaac Butt's account of why he failed to win the case for Kirwan that I saw the ambivalence in the artist in the dock. I sensed that he was seen as a Lothario, and that reputation condemned him.

What I never expected was a series of puzzles. I started to look for the origins of the stories about him. Where was the private man, the human being beneath the media frenzy? *The Times* reported in May 1853:

The convict Kirwan. Yesterday intelligence was received at Lloyd's, that the *Robert Small*, hired convict ship, had sailed from Queenstown, with 300 male convicts, for Freemantle, Western Australia. Among the convicts is the artist Kirwan, condemned to death for the murder of his wife, at Ireland's Eye, whose sentence has been commuted to transportation for life.

This was yet another fragment of misinformation about him.

He was transported, but not to Australia. He was sent to Bermuda and then returned to Millbank Penitentiary in London, and from there to Spike Island in 1863, as I learned from the archives. The hard facts of official documents contradicted the newspaper stories. In 1850, the government in Bermuda had decided that convict labour was needed on public works. William was to be a bridge-builder in the Caribbean before he came home again. Some said he was the last Spike Island convict when he was relocated in 1883, going to that island prison in the Cork harbour where felons died in their dozens, of disease and floggings.

After his conviction, out came the shreds of memories and anecdotes. Kirwan became the dark celebrity, a popular villain like Punch at the seaside, beating his wife. Letters to the press increased the mystery about him. The condemnation of him at his trial percolated through the bedrock of the community like a poison, tainting every fragment of biography.

'felons died in their dozens, of disease and floggings.'

The man was elusive, moving from one woman to the other. Residing in Sandymount, a place of writers, poets and artists, he worked in the centre of Dublin, with the clubmen and the professionals. Artists on the fringe in 1850s Dublin lived by desperate free-lance suggestions, facile friendships and the breathless pursuit of potential patrons. They loved the new rich and their desire for self-portraits.

There were many men like Kirwan in Victorian Dublin: young men who were thought to have great futures in the arts, but obscurity was their destiny. Yet Kirwan had been saved for history, reclaimed for posterity by a homicide. Thirty years ago, Alma Brooke-Tyrell wrote about her search for a 'Mr Howis, the artist of Jervis Street' in Dublin, saying that her grandfather had once written of Howis, 'He is considered a good painter by his fellow artists at this time … he has been an exhibitor of his own works at the Royal Dublin Society, also Abbey Street … and in many public exhibitions of the Fine Arts in Dublin.' That could be an account of Kirwan.

But I found that he did have fame: he had the kind of accidental, tainted fame that he surely would have hated. His own truths went with him on the long journey across the world and the myths and reappraisals continued, as they do now. He was given the obverse of fame, like some Roman coin on which the Emperor's face is preserved but the other, erased side has had its meaning rubbed away by time.

Then, as the research began, there was a paragraph that arrested my attention:

> It is my opinion, as the result of 20 years' experience in the investigation of those cases, that the resistance which a healthy and vigorous person can offer to the assault of a murderer intent on drowning him or her is in general such as to lead to the infliction of greater violence than is necessary to insure the death of the victim. The absence of any marks of violence or wounds on the body of Mrs Kirwan ... may be taken in support of the only view which it appears to me can be drawn, that death was not the result of homicidal drowning or suffocation, but most probably from a fit resulting from natural causes.

This was written by a Dr Taylor in 1853, an accepted authority on medical jurisprudence at the time. He was not alone: his opinion was shared by eight other contemporary professors and doctors.

The court in Green Street was still in my mind that night, and I recalled the words, so often repeated down the centuries: 'You shall be taken to a place of execution and there you shall be hanged by the neck until you are dead ...'

The story towering over this, demanding my attention, was that of William and Maria. One Michael Nagle, there on the fateful day, had said, 'Mr Kirwan went over ... and threw himself down upon the body and began to moan and cry.' No one dwelt too long on that reaction. They were more concerned with the fact that his 'real' partner was a few miles down the road with their bastard brood. In the little house in Sandymount not only were there seven children, but, in his garden at the house, at Harold's Cross, police had found a coffin with the bones of a small child inside. That was in January 1853. There was another missing page in this story.

At the time, the boatmen knew that sensible matters had to come first. They did not bother with awkward questions. The lady's body must be covered and then she must be brought in, as they had brought in the corpses of those lost at sea, over their long lives as mariners. By God this was going to be a tale to tell that night in the inn. Murders, yes, in the streets of the city and in the dark, by villains in their cups – but surely not at a picnic-place? Surely not by an artist chap?

Yet the world beyond Howth was a terrible place indeed. People were still talking of the great hunger, still needing to explain why so many had gone forever and why so many were down in the earth.

I had been in Dublin twenty years earlier: I had walked around Kilmainham Jail and stared in wonder and revulsion at the flogging yard where John Connolly, one of the leaders of the violent 1916 Easter Rising against Britain, had been dragged out to be shot. Then, driving back to the city, I had witnessed a police chase: officers running after a man who turned and fired a revolver at them. I sat in the Abbey Theatre the night after that and there was a drug-related killing in the next street. This was not the Dublin of the Book of Kells, Trinity College, folksongs and Guinness: it was the other one: the shadow land where the bad-tempered, cold-hearted brother of the foot-tapping, smiling city resided.

Had William Kirwan stepped into both those cities and known how to change his face to meet the different societies and their ways? Or had he never been more than he seemed to those who supped with him and discussed Turner or Goya at dinner parties? Was he a victim or was he Dublin's Mr Hyde? His complex story had come down to this golden plaque and a myth.

William Kirwan had been married to Maria for twelve years in 1852 when they set foot on Ireland's Eye for the day. But he had also had his mistress, Teresa Kenny, in the village of Sandymount, just a little way south of Dublin. It appears that the two women knew that they had to share their man almost from the marriage in 1840. At the trial, the prosecution tried unconvincingly to show that neither woman had known of the other until six months before the day of the tragedy.

William lived by his trade: when he was not earning from art directly, he was an anatomical draughtsman. He lived among medical men in Merrion Square, close to the centre of Dublin and just a few streets from the Dáil, the parliament house. They must have needed his skills. The example of George Stubbs, the famous painter of horses who studied anatomy in depth, shows this: Stubbs' friend Dr Atkinson at York found him work in drawing for anatomical studies. Artists had traditionally been assistants to surgeons, as was the case with the great surgeon, John Hunter, who had an artist called Bell as his assistant; Hunter had issued a ten-year contract with Bell for him to draw the contents of the surgeon's special collection of medical items. He even paid Bell to write a catalogue of specimens a little later. An anatomical draughtsman was paradoxically a talented dogsbody in some places: though he had exceptional skill, he was not seen as a 'proper' painter.

Kirwan was a man trying to keep his business alive in one of the smarter areas of the city, while spending time with two women. A double life emerges – something common in the middle-class Victorian world in which a mistress was often an acquisition little different from a horse or a servant. Here was a man struggling to keep his head above water, an ironic metaphor, given his destiny. He was clearly increasingly desperate once his family with Teresa grew apace: by 1852 he had seven children by her.

In the years immediately after Kirwan's residence there, Dr Wilde, father of Oscar, settled there, and again, the good doctor's life and nature brought a legal scandal to the august façades of that Georgian gentrified haven. Oscar's father, Sir William, had been accused of raping a patient while she was under anaesthetic. It was only through Lady Wilde's determined prosecution of the young woman for libel that Wilde senior preserved his reputation. Again, I sensed we had another whiff of scandal, of something sinister under the cultivated lives of the glitterati.

We have a man living with a 'front' of respectability, yet with a family tucked away just down the road. He is a man in need of finance, a man with a false face shown to the world. His landlord in suburban Sandymount was a Mr Bridgeford, who testified that, 'Mr Kirwan lived in one of the four houses in Spafield of which I am the landlord. He resided there for about four years. I saw a woman there whom I always supposed to be his wife. I saw children in the house. I have notes from the woman and I think she signed herself Theresa ...' This was Teresa Kenny – her full name being Teresa Mary Frances Kelly. Though the family lived in a poor part of Dublin, the Kirwans were not so badly off that they could not afford a servant. Catherine Byrne lived in the house as a maid, and she told the court that there were seven children, that Kirwan was often there for long periods in the day, and often he stayed the night.

Spafield, where Kirwan chose to settle with his family, was yet another focus of a murderous tale. Just over twenty years before this story the Revd George Wogan was murdered in his own home at Spafield Place, just off Sandymount Avenue. He was much liked, and the killing was sensational. The killers were caught and hanged. Spafield was not a secure place in the decades around the Eye mystery: there was an old inn known as the 'Bird House' and this was on the Kingstown road. It was used often as a place for travellers to stay on their way into Dublin – rather than chance nocturnal travel and be attacked and robbed. As one writer on the area has said, 'The inhabitants of ... Sandymount seldom ventured out of doors at night time, without being fully armed, as they were almost entirely dependant upon their own arrangements for the protection of themselves ...'

William Kirwan, then, was a man with one foot in respectable and bohemian Dublin, a man found being sociable at parties or alone in the early hours being melancholic; the other foot was in the dangerous, more vulnerable world of uncertainty and fear along the bay by the South Wall. Was he a man who longed for the thrill, the challenge, the pump of adrenaline?

One writer in 1853 gave us a picture of William: 'Mr Kirwan is a little above forty, a native of Mayo ... He is tall and well-looking, strongly built, and the expression of his countenance, firmness, corresponds with his strong limbs, broad chest and duly-proportioned body.' The writer knew him and commented that he was admired as an anatomical artist 'from which he realised a handsome income.' Yet he would have had to have been very wealthy to pay the rent on two houses and maintain two families.

An artist who was reasonably well off, then, but who had an obstacle to further success which he had to remove? It makes no sense; he and Maria had taken a lodger for the summer at Howth and they often went out to Ireland's Eye. I could still see no reason for him to kill her. That was lost in the supposition and legal bungling.

'Yet, he still would have been richer and happier without her?' The writer to *The New York Times* in 1853, who knew William, wrote. 'I shall not notice any of the reports current as to the unfortunate gentleman's previous wrong-doings ... When a man is knocked down, he is *down.*'

But no, this was an artist, a sensitive man. He created, he did not destroy. That day on Ireland's Eye he was surely joyful, celebrating his time alone, fulfilled with sketchbook and a day of possibilities in mood and colour where Nature brooded. Then there was Maria, surely happy in her own time doing what she loved – immersing herself in the welcoming seawater and loving the privacy and peace of the Long Hole. In any case, one doctor had said the cause of death was most likely an epileptic fit. If the arranged death was Kirwan's manufacture, then it was one of his most seamless products.

It is a large rock of fifty-three acres, in the bay opposite the fishing port of Howth. In Irish it is *Inis Mac Neasain*, referring to St Nessan, whose ruined chapel lies there. No one lives there; it is a place to visit with a relaxed state of mind and a picnic basket. The little boats shuttle visitors across all day and there is little evidence that in 1805 Howth was selected as the best place to have a storm-protection harbour, and also for a steam packet for the Dublin to Holyhead run. By 1822, that trip from Wales took just six hours and the future must have looked bright for the locals. But the harbour was always silted and there was no reliable docking for ships, so by 1834 Dun Laoghaire, on the other side of Dublin Bay, took over the steam packet trade.

When the Vikings sailed there in 837 with sixty-five ships they saw a sheltered haven, protected by Howth Head, and with an island in the bay; they saw Howth Head as a cat mousing, and the Eye a spot waiting for the creature to pounce on. It has been a place of good fortune but also dark foreboding. Only a few years after the Kirwan story, a ship was wrecked there. The cat had put a hex on the place it was said – or was it the killer artist?

Images of Ireland's Eye from around 1900 show the landmarks of Howth: the Church of the Assumption and a Martello Tower. There were still thatched cottages in Howth main street into the 1920s and it was a place held dear to Dubliners, comparing it to the sleepy seaside town of Bray to the south of the city. Yeats' sweetheart, Maud Gonne, lived there as a little girl after her mother had died of TB, and her memories of the village go to around 1870, not so long after the Kirwan affair. She recalls in her memoir, 'No place has ever seemed so lovely … Sometimes the sea was as blue as Mama's turquoises, more strikingly blue even than the Mediterranean because so often grey mists made it invisible and mysterious.' These were mists which, in fact, could have seeped into the rocks that day in 1852 when a day's leisure brought death on the Eye. Kirwan was drawn there by that blueness and no doubt to the grey mists.

A day out to Ireland's Eye back in the Victorian years was ideal for William and Maria Kirwan. He could sketch, or at least take in, the perfectly framed picturesque vista, while she let the breeze play on her features and dream of the old days when ships came with rovers and chancers to make a new Ireland; maybe she heard the shrieks of the gulls, skrying danger, perhaps presaging a child's grief at her loss? She might have passed dreamily into sleep, the elements around her closing in, or the sea encroaching with its hidden terrors from beneath that benign seaside ease.

For the artist, it was perfect for taking his sketchbook, for monitoring the changing moods and colours. He was doing what locals had seen him do many times before: take a picnic and his sketchbook out to a tranquil place, somewhere that city people were drawn to for their repose and their recreations. Maria and William took lodgings in Howth, at the home of Mrs Power. Maria went bathing and William sketched. On Monday, the 6th September, they set off for the Eye at ten in the morning, taking Maria's clothes in a carpetbag, some food, two bottles of water and his art materials. When they landed, the boatman was told to pick them up at eight o'clock that evening. It was early September, so it would have been almost dusk at eight. Kirwan may have wanted that late, sinking residue of light for the colours, following Turner, the artist who had taught the Victorians about the colours in the skies above them. Yet in 1852, that darkness of advancing night seemed to some to be a cloak to hide a killer's intent.

Maria was thirty-five years old; the couple had been married for twelve years, and had been living at 11 Merrion Square. At No. 60 Merrion Square, Daniel O'Connell, the great politician and lawyer, had lived a few decades before, and the square was, in 1859, according to one Dubliner, 'closed off from the common mob'. The writer, Sheridan Le Fanu, also lived there, and it is well documented, as Peter Somerville-Large has written, that 'A number of doctors were reputed to keep mistresses round Sandymount or Park Avenue, a pleasant gallop away from Merrion Square.' Kirwan was making enough money to join the medical men in that habit; what he lacked was a reputation to match his lifestyle. That is, he was entirely typical of his age and class. But that lifestyle was to play a part in condemning him, something to sway the jury, along with his religion and the scandal that he had a kept woman and a brood of bastards.

Maria was a very strong swimmer and loved to bathe in the sea. A witness later described her as 'a well-made and extremely good-looking woman'. She was confident to trust her skills in the sea, and she was very fit and well. At around four o'clock, she could have come back to Howth on her own, as a couple called Brue offered her a seat in their boat. She turned that down and stayed on. That has to be important: Maria wanted to stay out on the Eye until dusk. Why? Are we to believe he still sketched in semi-light and that she still bathed in darkening waters?

As the boat going to collect them set off, a man called Hugh Campbell heard a cry from the island. He was leaning against the harbour wall. Close to the area where ladies bathed at Howth, two women, Alice Abernethy and Catherine Flood, heard some cries as well. John Barrett was in a boat passing the island after a day's fishing; he heard cries coming from a place on the Eye called Long Hole.

Four men were in the boat going out to bring home the artist and his wife: Patrick and Michael Nagle, Thomas Styles and Edward Campbell. William Kirwan was alone on a high rock above the landing-place, and said that after a shower of rain, his wife had walked from him and he had not seen her since. Everyone started searching for her, and eventually one of the sailors saw a white shape below. Light was failing by then, but they climbed down to have a closer look, and there on a rock they found Maria's body, dry and with the water well below her. She was on her back and her bathing dress was pulled upwards. Her movement could have caused that, as nothing else suggested an attack at the time.

William dashed to her in a frenzy and lunged over her body, shouting, 'Maria! Maria!' But her clothes, from the bag, were nowhere to be seen so William asked the men to find them. Why did he want her clothes? Why was that his first thought? Those questions would haunt me later as I tried to piece together these events. Patrick Nagle later found the clothes. The next step was very bold: in the dusk, the men rowed their boat around the island to the Long Hole, and there they took Maria's body, wrapped around in some sailcloth. The party then returned to Howth.

For William, his own private hell was just beginning. He had taken one short step to his ruin, and every word he uttered, every move he made, was then to be observed, and in that scrutiny, many could not forget his other woman, living nicely in Sandymount, while his wife lay stone-cold dead.

Questions were asked like rifle enfilades, but some obvious ones were left out, such as what was an artist doing wanting to sketch in the dusk? Was he looking for those Turner-esque skies? Many thought he was looking, like Macbeth, for the 'cloak of darkest night', in which to kill his wife. The story was destined to be as two-faced as the accused and his life in the artistic colony around the clubs and dance parties.

Kirwan was found guilty of murder, and then reprieved, the sentence commuted to life. Recently discovered forensic notes appear to confirm his guilt. But there is a hint of unease over the mystery yet – like a shadow passing over a sun-lit lawn.

MARK MOWER

Mark's work focuses on true crime and social history. His books include 'Bloody British History: Norwich' and 'Suffolk Murders' (both for The History Press). His first book, 'Suffolk Tales of Mystery & Murder' (Countryside Books), contained a potent blend of tales from the seamier side of country life — described by the East Anglian Daily Times Suffolk magazine as 'a good serving of grisliness, a strong flavour of the unusual, a seasoning of ghoulishness and just a hint of the unexpected.' Alongside his writing, Mark lectures on crime history and runs a murder mystery business.

www.markmower.co.uk

MARGARET CATCHPOLE: THE WOMAN, THE LEGEND

MARK MOWER

The tale of Margaret Catchpole – an infamous and enigmatic late-eighteenth-century felon – has all the hallmarks of a later Victorian melodrama: her love for a roguish smuggler and descent into crime; a daring ride to London; a prison break and transportation to Australia; and her eventual rehabilitation and reprieve. That her colourful story has passed into folklore is no surprise, but it does obscure the fact that her real life was indeed truly remarkable. So where did the reality end and the tall tales begin?

Margaret was born to parents Jonathan and Elizabeth Catchpole in Nacton on the 14th of March 1762. While little is known of her childhood, it is believed that she had no formal education and only learnt to read and write while working later as a domestic servant. Her early employment saw her working for a number of prominent Suffolk families and by May 1793, she had secured the position of under-nurse and under-cook to the affluent and well-connected Cobbold family.

It is clear that her employer, Mrs John Cobbold, regarded Margaret highly and saw her as an integral part of the household. On more than one occasion, Margaret was instrumental in saving the lives of the children in her care and also achieved local acclaim after riding bareback from Nacton to Ipswich in order to fetch a doctor to attend to her critically ill mistress. The affection Margaret had for the family would remain with her throughout her turbulent life.

Well before taking up her position with the Cobbold family, Margaret had met and fallen in love with William Laud, a sailor who became immersed in the nefarious activities of a local smuggling gang. He was eventually outlawed after shooting another smuggler during a fight and went on the run to evade capture. Margaret's infatuation with the roguish Laud would also lead her into a period of criminality and infamy.

In 1795, she left her job and her health began to decline. Without work and pining for her lover, Margaret received word that Laud was believed to be in London. With her heart overruling her head, she set out on the night of 23rd May 1797 to steal John Cobbold's distinctive 'strawberry roan' gelding from the family stable. Dressed as a young man to avoid attention and reduce the chances of being caught for the theft, she then rode the horse to London – a remarkable journey of 70 miles in under ten hours.

Margaret's reckless action resulted in stiff retribution. Arrested on her arrival in the capital, the hapless prisoner was taken back to Suffolk to stand trial at the Bury Assizes in August 1797. Found guilty of the theft, she received a death sentence, although this was later commuted to transportation for seven years, following an unexpected and heart-felt appeal by the Cobbold family, who vouched for her previously unblemished record of service.

> '**Margaret's reckless action resulted in stiff retribution'.**

As it transpired, Margaret was detained for the next three years within the confines of Ipswich Gaol where her conduct was, for the most part, exemplary. But in April 1800, she absconded from the prison in spectacular fashion, hoping to escape to Holland with William Laud on board a smuggling vessel. Pulling a ruse at locking up time, she managed to pass unseen down the stairs from her cell and into the main yard of the gaol, where – with the ingenious use of a gardening frame, wooden prop and length of linen line – she succeeded in scaling the 22-foot outer wall.

It was clear that Margaret had planned the escape for some time, for she had also equipped herself with a suitable disguise. After her arrest near the coast a few days later, the *Ipswich Journal* reported on 5th April that, 'The pantaloons and smock frock she had made herself, while in prison, with the sheets of her bed; and on pulling off her frock, when brought back, she appeared the complete sailor, with a pig tail and round hat, and might be taken for a smart young man …'

When tried at the Bury Assizes, Margaret received a second death sentence, once again commuted to transportation, this time for life. Along with two other female prisoners, she was transported to Australia – arriving in Sydney on 15th December 1801.

Life down under evidently suited the hardworking and resourceful Margaret Catchpole. Working first as a domestic servant to the wealthy John Palmer, a former ship's purser, she eventually went on to become a midwife, nurse and farmer. Crucially, she also sent frequent letters home to both her kinfolk and the Cobbold family. These not only chronicled her life but provided an invaluable – and often unique – insight into many of the dramas being played out in colonial Australia.

And it seems that her conscientious endeavours brought her a somewhat unexpected reprieve. On 31st January 1814, she was pardoned for her earlier crimes and given the opportunity to return to England. In the event, she never made the passage home and passed away on 13th May 1819. She had succumbed to influenza, caught from a shepherd she was nursing at the time. Her final resting place was the graveyard of St Peter's church in Richmond, New South Wales.

Much of what is often recounted about the Catchpole legend stems from a novel published in 1845. *The History of Margaret Catchpole: A Suffolk Girl* was written by the Reverend Richard Cobbold, son of Margaret's former mistress. He asserted that much of his tale was based on Margaret's own letters home and described the text as a '… romantic but perfectly true narrative.'

Writing of the newly released book in February 1845, the *Norfolk Chronicle* was inclined to agree. It observed that: 'Truth is stranger than fiction. We have here a veritable history, with incidents more startling and extraordinary than are to be found in any romance with which we are acquainted …'

While popular and entertaining, Cobbold's book was, in reality, a highly sentimentalised account containing discrepancies and factual distortions. His story includes inaccurate dates for his heroine's birth and death and suggests that Margaret married in 1812, before going on to have three children – one of her own letters suggests that she remained unmarried and had no intention to wed.

Viewed from a modern perspective, the book can be seen as a cautionary tale, with the central character being led astray and suffering at the hands of the malevolent men in her life before experiencing a form of moral redemption. While crafted to suit the salacious taste for feminine 'victims' in Victorian art and literature, the portrayal of Margaret Catchpole is at odds with her real life exploits as a resourceful, self-reliant, caring and tenacious woman living on the frontiers of society at home and abroad. She was a true heroine we can all admire.